Azure Fundamentals (AZ-900) Study Guide
In-Depth Guidance & Practice for Aspiring Cloud Engineers

Jack Lee

Azure Fundamentals (AZ-900) Study Guide

by Jack Lee

Copyright © 2026 ReadyConcept Inc. All rights reserved.

Published by O'Reilly Media, Inc., 141 Stony Circle, Suite 195, Santa Rosa, CA 95401.

O'Reilly books may be purchased for educational, business, or sales promotional use. Online editions are also available for most titles (*http://oreilly.com*). For more information, contact our corporate/institutional sales department: 800-998-9938 or *corporate@oreilly.com*.

Acquisitions Editor: Megan Laddusaw
Development Editor: Sara Hunter
Production Editor: Ashley Stussy
Copyeditor: Paula L. Fleming
Proofreader: Dave Awl

Indexer: BIM Creatives, LLC
Cover Designer: Karen Montgomery
Cover Illustrator: José Marzan Jr.
Interior Designer: David Futato
Interior Illustrator: Kate Dullea

February 2026:   First Edition

Revision History for the First Edition
2026-02-13:   First Release

See *http://oreilly.com/catalog/errata.csp?isbn=9781098167820* for release details.

The O'Reilly logo is a registered trademark of O'Reilly Media, Inc. *Azure Fundamentals (AZ-900) Study Guide*, the cover image, and related trade dress are trademarks of O'Reilly Media, Inc.

The views expressed in this work are those of the author and do not represent the publisher's views. While the publisher and the author have used good faith efforts to ensure that the information and instructions contained in this work are accurate, the publisher and the author disclaim all responsibility for errors or omissions, including without limitation responsibility for damages resulting from the use of or reliance on this work. Use of the information and instructions contained in this work is at your own risk. If any code samples or other technology this work contains or describes is subject to open source licenses or the intellectual property rights of others, it is your responsibility to ensure that your use thereof complies with such licenses and/or rights.

978-1-098-16782-0

[LSI]

Table of Contents

Foreword.. xv

Preface... xvii

Part I. Cloud Concepts

1. **Introduction to Cloud Computing**... 3
   What Is Cloud Computing?   3
   Understanding Compute Power   4
   Storage Capabilities Explained   4
   Advantages of Cloud Computing Over Traditional On-Premises
     Infrastructure   5
   Understanding Cloud Service Models   6
   Overview of Common Azure Services   7
   How Cloud Pricing Works   8
   Summary   8
   Chapter 1 Quiz   9

2. **Benefits of Using Cloud Services**.. 11
   High Availability   12
     Redundant Infrastructure   12
     Automated Failover and Recovery   13
     Service Level Agreements   13
     Business Continuity and Disaster Recovery   14
     Key Takeaways for High Availability   14
   Scalability   14
     Elastic Infrastructure   15

Vertical and Horizontal Scaling	15
Pay-per-Use Pricing Model	18
Global Reach and Accessibility	18
Key Takeaways for Scalability	18
Reliability	18
Designing for Reliability	19
Key Takeaways for Reliability	20
Predictability	20
Performance Predictability	20
Cost Predictability	21
Key Takeaways for Predictability	21
Security	21
Data Encryption	22
Identity and Access Management	22
Threat Detection and Prevention	22
Compliance and Governance	23
Key Takeaways for Security	23
Governance	24
Centralized Policy Enforcement	24
Role-Based Access Control	25
Cost Management and Optimization	25
Audit Logging and Compliance Reporting	25
Key Takeaways for Governance	25
Manageability	26
Management of the Cloud	26
Management in the Cloud	27
Key Takeaways for Manageability	28
Summary	28
Chapter 2 Quiz	29
3. Cloud Service Types.	**31**
Demystifying Cloud Service Types Using Everyday Examples	31
IaaS: Owning a Car	31
PaaS: Renting a Car	32
SaaS: Using a Rideshare Service	32
Infrastructure as a Service	33
Key Benefits of IaaS	33
The Benefits of IaaS Services: A Real-Life Example	34
Platform as a Service	34
Key Benefits of PaaS	35
The Benefits of PaaS Services: Real-Life Examples	35
Software as a Service	36

    Key Benefits of SaaS   36
    The Benefits of SaaS: Real-Life Examples   37
  Choosing the Right Azure Service Type for the Job   38
    When to Use IaaS   38
    When to Use PaaS   38
    When to Use SaaS   39
  Summary   39
  Chapter 3 Quiz   40

4. The Shared Responsibility Model..41
  Shared Responsibility: From On Premises to the Cloud   41
  Responsibilities Are Closely Tied to Cloud Service Types   42
  Shared Responsibility for IaaS   42
  Shared Responsibility for PaaS   43
  Shared Responsibility for SaaS   44
  Comparison of Responsibility Areas Across Cloud Service Types   45
  Examples of Varying Responsibilities by Cloud Service Type   46
  More Real-World Examples of Responsibility Shifts   46
    Example 1: Operating System Patching   47
    Example 2: Identity Management and Security   47
    Example 3: Data Security and Compliance   47
  Bringing It All Together   48
  Summary   48
  Chapter 4 Quiz   49

5. Cloud Models..51
  What Are Cloud Models?   51
  Public Cloud   51
  Private Cloud   53
  Hybrid Cloud   55
  Multi-Cloud   56
  Comparison of Cloud Models   58
  Key Microsoft Azure Offerings   59
    Azure VMware Solution   59
    Azure Arc   60
    Azure Local   60
  Summary   61
  Chapter 5 Quiz   61

Part II. Azure Architecture and Services

6. Introduction to Microsoft Azure... 65
    A Brief History of Microsoft Azure (Optional Reading)   66
        2008: The Announcement of Windows Azure   66
        2010: General Availability of Windows Azure   66
        2014: Rebranding to Microsoft Azure   67
        2015–2018: Expansion and Innovation   67
        2019–2021: Microsoft Entra, Azure Synapse Analytics, and Azure Arc   67
        2022–Present: AI Leadership and Sustainability   68
    Benefits of Microsoft Azure   68
        Cost Savings and Efficiency   68
        Scalability, Elasticity, and Flexibility   68
        Agility and Innovation   69
        Reliability and Performance   69
        Security and Compliance   70
        Ecosystem, Integration, and Interoperability   70
        Global Presence and Hybrid Capabilities   70
        AI, Machine Learning, and IoT   70
    Getting Started with Azure   70
        What Is an Azure Account?   71
        What Is an Azure Subscription?   71
        What Is the Relationship Between an Azure Account and a Subscription?   72
        Azure Subscription Types   72
    How to Create a Free Azure Account: A Step-by-Step Guide   74
        Creating a Free Account if You're Not a Student   74
        Creating a Free Azure for Students Account   77
    Explore the Azure Portal   77
    How to View Your Subscription Details   78
    How to View the Azure Product Catalog   79
    Summary   80
    Chapter 6 Quiz   81

7. Core Architectural Components of Azure.................................. 83
    The Physical Infrastructure of Microsoft Azure   83
    What Are Azure Regions?   84
        Service Availability   85
        Data Residency and Regulatory Compliance   85
        Proximity and Latency   85
    What Are Azure Availability Zones?   86
        Key Features of Availability Zones   86
        How to Use Availability Zones   87

Key Considerations About Availability Zones	87
What Are Azure Region Pairs?	89
Advantages of Region Pairs	90
How Region Pairs Work	91
Key Considerations About Region Pairs	91
Typical Use Cases for Region Pairs	92
What Are Azure Sovereign Regions?	92
Types of Azure Sovereign Regions	92
Why Use Sovereign Regions?	93
Key Considerations About Sovereign Regions	94
Use Cases for Sovereign Regions	94
Summary	94
Chapter 7 Quiz	95

8. The Azure Management Infrastructure 97

What Is the Azure Management Infrastructure?	97
The Core Layer: Azure Resources	98
The Second Layer: Azure Resource Groups	99
Structural Layers: Azure Subscriptions	99
The Outer Layer: Azure Management Groups	100
Benefits of a Well-Designed Azure Management Infrastructure	101
Best Practices for Planning Your Azure Management Infrastructure	102
Real-World Example: Hierarchical Integration of Management Groups,	
Subscriptions, and Resource Groups	102
Breaking Down the Azure Management Structure	103
How the Structure Works	104
Summary	105
Chapter 8 Quiz	106

9. Azure Compute Services 107

Infrastructure as a Service	108
Azure Virtual Machines	109
Resources Required for Azure VMs	111
Virtual Machine Deployment	113
Azure Virtual Machine Scale Sets	113
Azure availability sets	115
Azure Virtual Desktop	117
Platform as a Service	119
Azure App Service	119
PaaS: Serverless Computing	121
Containers and Azure Kubernetes Services	123
Azure Container Instances	126

PaaS: Managed Container Services and Azure Container Apps	129
Choosing the Right Compute Service	131
Bonus Material: Azure Application and Integration Services (Optional)	133
Azure API Management	134
Azure Logic Apps	135
Azure Event Grid	135
Azure Service Bus	136
Summary	137
Chapter 9 Quiz	137

10. Azure Networking Services 139

The OSI Model	139
Azure Networking	141
Why Is Azure Networking Important?	141
Key Services in Azure Networking	142
Core Infrastructure: Azure VNet and Subnets	142
What Is a VNet?	143
What Is a Subnet?	143
Key Features of Azure VNet	143
Best Practices for Using Azure VNet	144
Use Cases for Azure VNet	144
How to Create an Azure VNet	144
Virtual Network Peering	148
Key Features of Virtual Network Peering	149
Best Practices for Using Virtual Network Peering	149
Use Cases for Virtual Network Peering	149
Securing Azure Networking	150
Network Security Groups	150
Key Features of NSGs	150
Best Practices for Using NSGs	151
Use Cases for NSG	151
Azure Firewall	151
Key Features of Azure Firewall	152
Best Practices for Using Azure Firewall	152
Use Cases for Azure Firewall	153
Azure Bastion	153
Key Features of Azure Bastion	153
Best Practices for Using Azure Bastion	154
Use Cases for Azure Bastion	154
Public Endpoints Versus Private Endpoints	154
When to Use Public Endpoints Versus Private Endpoints	155
Comparison of Public and Private Endpoints	155

Controlling Traffic: Load Balancing	156
Azure Load Balancer	156
Key Features of Azure Load Balancer	156
Types of Azure Load Balancers	157
Best Practices for Using Azure Load Balancer	157
Use Cases for Azure Load Balancer	157
Azure Application Gateway	157
Key Features of Azure Application Gateway	158
Best Practices for Using Azure Application Gateway	158
Use Cases for Azure Application Gateway	159
Azure Traffic Manager	159
Key Features of Azure Traffic Manager	159
Best Practices for Using Azure Traffic Manager	160
Use Cases for Azure Traffic Manager	160
Azure Front Door	160
Key Features of Azure Front Door	161
Best Practices for Using Azure Front Door	161
Use Cases for Azure Front Door	161
Comparison of the Load-Balancing Services	162
Hybrid Connectivity	162
Azure VPN Gateway	162
Azure ExpressRoute	163
Azure Domain Name System	165
Key Features of Azure DNS	165
Best Practices for Using Azure DNS	166
Use Cases for Azure DNS	166
Azure Content Delivery Network	166
Key Features of Azure CDN	167
Best Practices for Using Azure CDN	167
Use Cases for Azure CDN	167
Azure Network Watcher	168
Key Features of Azure Network Watcher	168
Best Practices for Using Azure Network Watcher	169
Use Cases for Azure Network Watcher	169
Summary	169
Chapter 10 Quiz	171
11. Azure Storage Services..	**173**
Introduction to Azure Storage Account	174
Benefits of Azure Storage Versus On-Premises Storage	175
Cost-Efficiency	175
Scalability and Elasticity	176

High Availability and Disaster Recovery Capacity	176
Security and Compliance	177
Performance and Accessibility	178
Backup and Retention Policies	178
Comparison of Azure Storage Versus On-Premises Storage	178
Supported Data Types	179
Azure Storage Services	180
Azure Storage Services and Data Types	180
Globally Unique Namespace for Azure Storage Account	180
Storage Service Endpoints	181
Azure Managed Disks: A Separate Storage Service	181
Comparing Azure Storage Services	181
Choosing the Right Storage Account Types and Options	182
Types of Azure Storage Accounts	183
Choosing the Right Storage Account Type	184
Azure Redundancy Options	185
Types of Redundancy Options	186
Choosing a Redundancy Option	188
Options for Transferring Files to Azure Storage	189
Different Tools for File Transfer	189
Comparison of File Transfer Options	192
Migration Options to Azure Storage	193
Types of Migration Solutions	193
Comparison of Azure Migration Options	195
Summary	195
Chapter 11 Quiz	196

12. Azure Identity, Access, and Security 197

Understanding the Zero Trust Security Model	198
Why Do We Need Zero Trust?	198
The Core Principles of Zero Trust	199
Comparing Traditional Security and the Zero Trust Model	199
Real-World Scenario	199
Defense-in-Depth Model	200
Microsoft Entra ID	202
What Does Microsoft Entra ID Offer?	202
Why Use Microsoft Entra ID?	202
Microsoft Entra Connect Sync: Connecting On-Premises Active Directory to Azure	203
Microsoft Entra Domain Services	203
Comparing Microsoft Entra ID and Microsoft Entra Domain Services	204
Authentication in Azure	204

Single Sign-On	205
Multifactor Authentication	205
Passwordless Authentication	206
Comparison of Authentication Methods at a Glance	207
Microsoft Entra External ID	207
Key Benefits of Microsoft Entra External ID	208
A Real-World Scenario	209
Microsoft Entra Conditional Access	209
How It Works	210
A Real-World Example	210
Common Use Cases for Conditional Access	211
Why Conditional Access Matters	211
Azure Role-Based Access Control	211
Why Use RBAC?	212
How Does RBAC Work?	213
Real-World RBAC Scenarios	213
How Is RBAC Applied?	214
Key Points to Remember	214
Azure Key Vault	215
What Does Azure Key Vault Do?	215
Why Use Azure Key Vault?	215
How Applications Access Secrets	216
Real-World Scenario	216
Microsoft Defender for Cloud	217
Why Use Microsoft Defender for Cloud?	217
Key Components of Microsoft Defender for Cloud	218
How Microsoft Defender for Cloud Protects Different Environments	218
Summary	218
Chapter 12 Quiz	219

Part III. Azure Management and Governance

13. Cost Management in Azure... 223

Cost Management in Azure	224
From CapEx to OpEx: A Shift in Cost Models	224
Factors That Influence Azure Costs	225
Tools to Help Estimate and Manage Azure Costs	227
Azure Migrate: Assessment & Business Case	228
Azure Pricing Calculator	229
Azure Advisor	231
Cost Management + Billing	231

Bringing It All Together	234
Organizing Resources with Azure Tags	235
What Are Tags?	236
Managing Tags in Azure	236
Top 10 Tips for Saving Money with Azure	237
Summary	239
Chapter 13 Quiz	240

14. Azure Governance and Compliance 241

Microsoft Purview: Unified Data Governance	241
The Microsoft Purview Portal	242
What Microsoft Purview Enables	243
Key Functional Areas of Microsoft Purview	243
Deep Integration with Microsoft 365 Compliance	243
Common Use Cases of Microsoft Purview	244
A Real-World Example: Healthcare	244
Integration with the Microsoft Data Ecosystem	245
Azure Policy: Enforce Organizational Standards	245
What Is Azure Policy?	245
Why Azure Policy Matters	246
Common Use Cases of Azure Policy	246
Key Components of Azure Policy	246
Built-In Policies	247
Custom Policies	247
Monitoring and Remediation	247
Policy Effects: What Happens When a Rule Is Triggered?	248
Resource Locks: Protecting Critical Resources	248
What Are Resource Locks?	248
Two Types of Resource Locks	249
Where to Use Resource Locks	249
Real-Life Example: Protecting a Production VM	249
How to Apply a Resource Lock	250
Comparing Resource Locks and Azure Policy	250
Best Practices and Limitations	251
Service Trust Portal: Compliance Transparency	251
What Is the Service Trust Portal?	251
Key Features of the Service Trust Portal	252
Real-World Example: Preparing for a GDPR Audit	253
How Do These Azure Governance Tools Work Together?	253
Summary	254
Chapter 14 Quiz	255

15. Managing and Deploying Azure Resources 257
Azure Portal 258
   Key Features of the Azure Portal 259
   What Are the Best Uses of the Azure Portal? 259
   Key Benefits of Azure Portal 259
   Common Tasks in the Azure Portal 260
   When to Use the Azure Portal (and When Not To) 260
Azure Cloud Shell 261
   Why Use Cloud Shell? 262
   Key Features of Cloud Shell 262
Azure CLI 263
   Why Use Azure CLI? 263
   Example: Creating a Resource Group Using Azure CLI 264
   Where You Can Run Azure CLI 264
   Azure CLI Versus Azure Portal 264
Azure PowerShell 265
   Example: Creating a Resource Group Using Azure PowerShell 265
   Why Use Azure PowerShell? 266
   Where Can You Use Azure PowerShell? 266
   Azure CLI Versus Azure PowerShell 266
   Which Tool Should You Use? 267
Infrastructure as Code 267
   Why IaC Matters 268
   IaC Approaches: Declarative Versus Imperative 268
   Azure Resource Manager 269
   Bicep 270
   Terraform 271
   IaC Tool Comparison 272
Managing Hybrid and Multi-Cloud Environments Using Azure Arc 273
Best Practices for Managing and Deploying Azure Resources 274
Summary 276
Chapter 15 Quiz 276

16. Azure Monitoring Tools 277
What Is Azure Advisor? 278
What Is Azure Service Health? 279
What Is Azure Monitor? 281
   Azure Log Analytics 282
   Azure Monitor Alerts 282
   Application Insights 282
Summary 283
Chapter 16 Quiz 284

Wrap-Up... 285

A. Practice Exam... 289

B. Answer Keys.. 299

Index... 317

Foreword

Over the past decade working in cloud and developer technologies, I've learned that success in this space depends not just on mastering tools but on understanding the principles that connect them. Whether it's Linux, software development, Kubernetes, or AI-assisted tools like GitHub Copilot, the foundational concepts of cloud computing remain the bedrock of everything we do. That's why I believe books like this—clear, approachable, and rooted in real-world experience—are invaluable for anyone starting their Azure journey.

I've had the privilege of working alongside Jack for over 10 years, collaborating across customer engagements, technical workshops, and community events. We've tag-teamed on countless training sessions for joint customers, and I've had the pleasure of speaking at several of the Toronto-based meetup groups that Jack has tirelessly organized. What's always stood out to me is his ability to make complex topics accessible—blending technical precision with a teacher's instinct for clarity.

One of my favorite examples of this can be found in Chapter 3, where Jack explains the infrastructure, platform, and software as a service models (IaaS, PaaS, and SaaS) through a set of analogies that perfectly demystify the differences for anyone new to cloud. His approach helps readers visualize how the shared responsibility model works and maps those concepts to real-world equivalents in a way that's both intuitive and memorable. It's exactly the kind of teaching that transforms abstract theory into practical understanding—something every learner appreciates when approaching cloud computing for the first time.

Jack's long-standing recognition as a Microsoft MVP, awarded multiple times over the past decade, speaks to his consistent impact on the community. But titles alone don't tell the whole story. What sets Jack apart is his genuine passion for helping others learn. He meets people where they are and guides them forward with patience, humor, and a depth of knowledge that few in this field can match.

Azure Fundamentals (AZ-900) Study Guide reflects that same spirit. It's not just a certification aid—it's a roadmap to understanding the *why* behind the cloud. Whether you're taking your first step into Azure or building a foundation for a future in cloud architecture, this book will help you connect concepts, not just memorize them.

As someone who's spent years helping organizations modernize through Azure, DevOps, and AI developer tooling, I can confidently say that cloud fluency begins here. Jack's guide is the ideal starting point for anyone ready to begin that journey— or for experienced professionals looking to strengthen the fundamentals that everything else is built on.

I'm honored to introduce this work, and I'm confident it will serve as both a learning companion and an inspiration for your career ahead.

— Raymond Kao
Principal Solutions Engineer
Microsoft Toronto, Canada

Preface

When Microsoft first announced Azure, I remember being both excited and curious. Back then, "the cloud" was still a mysterious concept for many. The idea that you could spin up servers, store data, and build applications in someone else's data center instantly felt revolutionary. I dove in headfirst, exploring every service, learning and gaining hands-on experience with each and every feature.

Since then, I've watched Azure grow into one of the most powerful and trusted cloud platforms in the world. What fascinates me most isn't just the technology—it's the people. Over the years, I've met business leaders reinventing their operations, IT professionals retooling their careers for the digital era, and students discovering their passion for cloud computing. No matter their background, they all shared one thing: the inclination to take the first step.

For many, that starting point was the AZ-900 Microsoft Azure Fundamentals exam. It's more than just a certification—it's an introduction to a new way of thinking about technology. It helps you understand why the cloud matters, how Azure works, and what possibilities lie ahead.

When I first began mentoring others in Azure, I noticed how often learners would run into roadblocks trying to connect all the pieces. They'd jump straight into complex topics without first mastering the basics. That's what makes AZ-900 so valuable—it builds that essential foundation. Once you grasp the fundamentals, every advanced concept becomes easier to understand.

This guide is my way of helping you start strong. I want to make Azure approachable and practical, not overwhelming. We'll explore the same core ideas that underpin every cloud solution, and by the end, you'll not only be ready for the exam—you'll also see the bigger picture of how Azure fits into the modern world.

Whether you're here to kickstart your career, add a valuable credential to your name, or simply understand the cloud that's shaping our digital future, welcome. You've already taken the most important step: deciding to begin.

Thank you for reading this book. Let's start your journey into the world of Microsoft Azure—one concept, one service, and one success at a time.

Why Should You Take the AZ-900 Exam?

The AZ-900 exam is the perfect entry point into the world of cloud computing. It's designed to validate your understanding of basic cloud concepts and how Microsoft Azure delivers cloud services securely, efficiently, and at scale. Whether you're an IT professional, a business analyst, a project manager, or just someone who's curious about the cloud, this certification helps you build confidence and credibility. Passing the AZ-900 exam demonstrates that you understand the fundamentals of Azure's core services, pricing, governance, and compliance—a skill set in high demand across industries.

Who Should Take the AZ-900 Exam?

You don't need a technical background to succeed in this exam. The AZ-900 is ideal for:

- Beginners exploring cloud technologies for the first time
- Business or sales professionals working with Azure-based solutions
- Students looking to strengthen their résumés with an industry-recognized credential
- IT professionals who want to solidify their foundational knowledge before pursuing role-based certifications

What Should I Know About the AZ-900 Exam?

To prepare for the exam, it's important to understand what it covers and its structure and timing.

Topics Covered on the AZ-900 Exam

The exam covers a broad range of foundational topics, including:

Cloud concepts
    The benefits of cloud computing and the different types of cloud models

Core Azure services
    Virtual machines, storage, databases, networking, and more

Azure management and governance
  Subscriptions, resource groups, and management tools like the Azure portal and Azure Resource Manager

Security, privacy, and compliance
  Microsoft Defender for Cloud, network security groups, and Microsoft's compliance offerings

Azure pricing and support
  Cost management, service-level agreements, and support plans

These topics provide a strong foundation for anyone planning to work with Azure or simply looking to understand how the cloud fits into modern IT strategies.

For more information about the AZ-900 Azure Fundamentals exam, please visit the official Microsoft certification site (*https://oreil.ly/9LPGh*).

Exam Structure and Duration

The AZ-900 exam typically includes 40–60 questions and lasts about 45 minutes. You can expect a mix of multiple-choice, drag-and-drop, and scenario-based questions.

There are no prerequisites for the AZ-900 Azure Fundamentals exam, and the exam is available in multiple languages.

The passing score is 700 out of 1000. You can take the exam online from home or at an authorized testing center.

To learn more about the exam experience and duration, please visit the official Microsoft Learn site (*https://oreil.ly/l2X7n*).

Does the AZ-900 Serve as a Stepping Stone to Advanced Certifications?

Think of AZ-900 as a strong foundation for your cloud certification journey. While it isn't a mandatory prerequisite for advanced certifications, earning it will better prepare you with essential Azure concepts, making the transition to more specialized and role-based exams smoother. Here are some role-based certifications that you can consider taking:

- Microsoft Certified: Azure Administrator Associate (*https://oreil.ly/MBci3*)
- Microsoft Certified: Azure Developer Associate (*https://oreil.ly/6Ctxy*)
- Microsoft Certified: DevOps Engineer Expert (*https://oreil.ly/o8S6y*)
- Microsoft Certified: Azure Solutions Architect Expert (*https://oreil.ly/5zW29*)

Each of these builds on the foundational knowledge you'll gain through AZ-900.

What Other Foundational Certifications Are Available?

Depending on your interests, you might explore other foundational paths alongside or after AZ-900, such as:

AI-900: Microsoft Azure AI Fundamentals (https://oreil.ly/qAMSp)
    Ideal for those curious about artificial intelligence and machine learning

DP-900: Microsoft Azure Data Fundamentals (https://oreil.ly/1cuTF)
    Great for aspiring data professionals exploring Azure data services

SC-900: Microsoft Security, Compliance, and Identity Fundamentals (https://oreil.ly/rXIw6)
    Essential for anyone focused on security and governance in the cloud

What's Covered in This Book?

This book is organized into six easy-to-follow parts, with the first three aligned to the AZ-900 exam structure. The final parts provide a high-level recap, followed by a comprehensive Practice Exam in Appendix A. Appendix B contains the answer keys for the chapter quizzes and the practice exam.

Here's a brief overview of the book's structure and each chapter.

Part I, "Cloud Concepts"

- Chapter 1, "Introduction to Cloud Computing"
- Chapter 2, "Benefits of Using Cloud Services"
- Chapter 3, "Cloud Service Types"
- Chapter 4, "The Shared Responsibility Model"
- Chapter 5, "Cloud Models"

Part II, "Azure Architecture and Services"

- Chapter 6, "Introduction to Microsoft Azure"
- Chapter 7, "Core Architectural Components of Azure"
- Chapter 8, "The Azure Management Infrastructure"
- Chapter 9, "Azure Compute Services"
- Chapter 10, "Azure Networking Services"

- Chapter 11, "Azure Storage Services"
- Chapter 12, "Azure Identity, Access, and Security"

Part III, "Azure Management and Governance"

- Chapter 13, "Cost Management in Azure"
- Chapter 14, "Azure Governance and Compliance"
- Chapter 15, "Managing and Deploying Azure Resources"
- Chapter 16, "Azure Monitoring Tools"

Wrap-Up

Appendix A, "Practice Exam"

Appendix B, "Answer Keys"

Conventions Used in This Book

The following typographical conventions are used in this book:

Italic
: Indicates new terms, URLs, email addresses, filenames, and file extensions.

`Constant width`
: Used for program listings, as well as within paragraphs to refer to program elements such as variable or function names, databases, data types, environment variables, statements, and keywords.

`Constant width bold`
: Shows commands or other text that should be typed literally by the user.

This element signifies a tip or suggestion.

This element signifies a general note.

 This element indicates a warning or caution.

O'Reilly Online Learning

For more than 40 years, O'Reilly Media has provided technology and business training, knowledge, and insight to help companies succeed.

Our unique network of experts and innovators share their knowledge and expertise through books, articles, and our online learning platform. O'Reilly's online learning platform gives you on-demand access to live training courses, in-depth learning paths, interactive coding environments, and a vast collection of text and video from O'Reilly and 200+ other publishers. For more information, visit *https://oreilly.com*.

How to Contact Us

Please address comments and questions concerning this book to the publisher:

> O'Reilly Media, Inc.
> 141 Stony Circle, Suite 195
> Santa Rosa, CA 95401
> 800-889-8969 (in the United States or Canada)
> 707-827-7019 (international or local)
> 707-829-0104 (fax)
> *support@oreilly.com*
> *https://oreilly.com/about/contact.html*

We have a web page for this book, where we list errata and any additional information. You can access this page at *https://oreil.ly/azure-fundamentals-AZ900-SG-1e*.

For news and information about our books and courses, visit *https://oreilly.com*.

Find us on LinkedIn: *https://linkedin.com/company/oreilly*.

Watch us on YouTube: *https://youtube.com/oreillymedia*.

Acknowledgments

I would like to express my gratitude and appreciation to the entire O'Reilly team for their exceptional collaboration throughout this project.

I am grateful to Raymond Kao, a longtime friend and colleague, for generously contributing his time to write the foreword.

My sincere thanks go to the technical reviewers, whose thoughtful feedback has greatly enhanced the quality of this book.

Above all, I am profoundly appreciative of my family, friends, and colleagues for their unwavering support throughout my journey of writing this book.

To my readers, I hope this book will help you achieve your goals and bring you success.

PART I
Cloud Concepts

In the first part of this study guide, you'll explore the foundational cloud concepts that lay the groundwork for the AZ-900 Azure Fundamentals exam. Mastering these concepts will help you understand what the cloud is, why it matters, and how it transforms the way technology is delivered and managed.

- Chapter 1, "Introduction to Cloud Computing"
- Chapter 2, "Benefits of Using Cloud Services"
- Chapter 3, "Cloud Service Types"
- Chapter 4, "The Shared Responsibility Model"
- Chapter 5, "Cloud Models"

CHAPTER 1
Introduction to Cloud Computing

Welcome to the first chapter of the *Azure Fundamentals (AZ-900) Study Guide*!

In this chapter, you'll be introduced to the foundational ideas behind cloud computing—what it is, why it matters, and how it transforms traditional IT.

If you're already familiar with these basics, feel free to skip ahead to Part II, beginning with Chapter 6.

The objective of this chapter is to help you build a strong base for everything that follows.

What Is Cloud Computing?

At its core, *cloud computing* is the delivery of computing services, including servers, storage, databases, networking, security, monitoring, and analytics. These services are hosted in secure, enterprise-grade datacenters managed by cloud providers such as Microsoft Azure (the focus of this study guide). Other popular cloud service providers include Amazon Web Services (AWS) and Google Cloud Platform (GCP).

One of the greatest advantages of the cloud is its enterprise-level security. Cloud providers, such as Microsoft Azure, invest billions of dollars into multilayered defenses, global threat intelligence, compliance frameworks, and continuous monitoring. This is far beyond what most organizations could implement on their own. For many businesses, this level of protection would be prohibitively expensive to build or maintain in a traditional on-premises setup.

You'll learn more about security in Chapter 12.

Let's start our journey into cloud computing with the two foundational building blocks of any cloud environment: compute and storage.

Understanding Compute Power

The first foundational building block of any cloud environment is compute.

Compute power refers to the processing capability of a system (provided by elements such as its CPU cores, memory [RAM], GPU options, and network throughput) which together determine how efficiently workloads run.

Suppose you're working in an on-premises environment and your server has 8 GB of RAM. You discover that it's not enough to handle a new workload, so you must purchase and install additional physical memory. This upgrade process often involves downtime, shipping delays, and capital expense—a familiar pain point for anyone who's managed physical infrastructure.

By contrast, cloud computing lets you adjust compute power on demand. If your application needs more resources, you can scale up within minutes. When demand drops, you scale down to save costs. You only pay for what you actually use. In many cases, scaling can even be automated through *autoscaling*.

There are two main types of scaling:

Vertical scaling (scale up/down)
    Increasing or decreasing the size of an existing resource, such as by upgrading a 2-core virtual machine (VM) to 4 cores

Horizontal scaling (scale out/in)
    Adding or removing instances, such as by deploying additional VMs behind a load balancer to handle more web traffic

Together, these capabilities ensure high availability and resilience so your applications remain responsive even as workloads fluctuate.

You'll explore this concept further in Chapter 2.

Storage Capabilities Explained

Storage is another foundational building block of any cloud environment. Instead of relying on physical hard drives, cloud storage lets you store, access, and manage data through distributed, highly available systems.

In a traditional on-premises setup, if your server has a 500 GB hard drive and it becomes full, you must buy additional hardware, install it, and ensure that it's backed up and protected.

Cloud storage removes these limitations. For example, Azure provides virtually unlimited capacity, durability, and built-in redundancy without requiring you to manage physical devices.

Table 1-1 introduces several Azure storage types you may encounter on the AZ-900 exam. As you can see, each storage type supports different kinds of data and different use case requirements.

Table 1-1. Different Azure storage types to serve different needs

Type	Description	Example use case
Blob Storage	Stores unstructured data such as images, videos, and backups.	To store large data objects or host web application assets
Files	Shared file systems are accessible by multiple machines.	To migrate legacy applications that require shared file system access
Queue Storage	Stores messages that applications can send to each other to communicate asynchronously.	To enable a web application to add tasks to a queue, where a background service will process them
Table	A key-value store holds large amounts of structured, nonrelational data.	To store user profiles and application metadata at scale

Azure also offers multiple *storage access tiers* (such as Hot, Cool, Cold, and Archive) to help balance cost and performance based on how often data is accessed. Additionally, Azure automatically replicates your data to protect against hardware failures and ensure high availability.

You'll learn more about Azure storage services (including Blob, Files, Queue, and Table storage) in Chapter 11.

Advantages of Cloud Computing Over Traditional On-Premises Infrastructure

You may have heard the cloud described as "renting instead of buying," but that only scratches the surface.

In a traditional on-premises IT environment, organizations purchase and maintain their own servers, storage, and networking gear—much as you probably own and maintain your own equipment.

Cloud computing goes far beyond this idea by introducing *virtualization, resource pooling*, and *multi-tenancy*, enabling a globally scalable infrastructure that's shared securely across customers.

Thus, a more accurate way to picture cloud computing is as a virtual datacenter that you can access instantly through a web portal, command-line interface (CLI), or application programming interface (API).

The cloud provider manages the physical infrastructure—power, cooling, and hardware—while you deploy and configure virtualized resources such as virtual machines, databases, or web apps.

Table 1-2 provides a comprehensive comparison between cloud and traditional on-premises infrastructure.

Table 1-2. A comparison of cloud computing and traditional on-premises infrastructure

Factor	Cloud computing	Traditional on-premises infrastructure
Infrastructure cost	No up-front hardware; flexible pay-as-you-go or reserved billing	High up-front capital and maintenance costs
Deployment	Resources deployed securely over the internet	Deployed locally on owned hardware
Scalability	Autoscaling that enables rapid adjustment to demand	Scalability that depends on physical infrastructure limitations
Maintenance	Managed by the cloud service provider	Requires in-house IT staff for maintenance
Accessibility	Securely accessible from anywhere with internet access	Typically limited to local networks, with any remote access enabled and configured by IT staff
Security	Shared responsibility wherein cloud provider secures infrastructure and customer secures data and access	Managed internally by IT staff
Disaster recovery	Built-in redundancy and geo-replication	Must be self-designed and maintained
Flexibility	Highly flexible in resource allocation and deployment	Limited flexibility due to physical infrastructure constraints
Updates & upgrades	Managed automatically by cloud service provider	Performed manually by IT staff

You'll learn how these management responsibilities are divided between the provider and the customer in Chapter 4.

Understanding Cloud Service Models

So far, you've been introduced to compute and storage. But that's only the beginning. The cloud offers a rich portfolio of services, including AI, networking, databases, and monitoring. These services are grouped into three *core service models*, each defining a different level of control and responsibility as shown in Table 1-3.

Table 1-3. The three core service models

Service model	Description	Examples
Infrastructure as a service (IaaS)	Provides virtualized computing resources such as servers, storage, and networking; you manage the OS, apps, and data	Azure Virtual Machines
Platform as a service (PaaS)	Offers a managed environment for developing and deploying applications without managing the underlying infrastructure	Azure App Service, Azure SQL Database
Software as a service (SaaS)	Delivers ready-to-use applications hosted and maintained by the provider	Microsoft 365, Dynamics 365

We'll explore these models in detail in Chapter 5, where you'll see how each approach aligns with different business and technical goals.

Overview of Common Azure Services

Here's a quick preview of popular Azure services:

Azure Virtual Machines
    Deploy and manage scalable Windows or Linux VMs.

Azure App Service
    Build and host web and mobile apps without server management.

Azure Functions
    Executive serverless code triggered by events.

Azure Kubernetes Service (AKS)
    Use managed Kubernetes for containerized applications.

Azure Blob Storage
    Use scalable object storage for unstructured data.

Azure SQL Database
    Leverage a fully managed relational database service.

Microsoft Entra ID (formerly Azure AD)
    Rely on cloud-based identity and access management.

Azure Migrate
    Assess and migrate on-premises workloads to Azure.

Foundry Tools
    Harness prebuilt AI APIs for vision, speech, and language.

Azure Monitor
    Gain real-time insights into resource health and performance.

Don't worry if some of these names are unfamiliar—you'll get to know more about them in Part II.

How Cloud Pricing Works

One of the most powerful features of cloud computing is its consumption-based (pay-as-you-go) model: you pay only for what you use.

This allows organizations to avoid the waste of idle hardware and align spending with actual usage. However, not all resources are free when idle. For instance, provisioned storage and reserved instances continue to incur charges.

Azure provides several pricing options—consumption based, reserved, and spot pricing—to help you optimize costs for your workloads.

Because prices vary by region and service type, understanding cost management is key. You'll learn more about this in Chapter 13.

Summary

In this chapter, you learned:

- What cloud computing is and why enterprise-grade security is one of its key benefits
- How cloud computing differs from traditional on-premises infrastructure
- The three core cloud service models: IaaS, PaaS, and SaaS
- The basics of compute, scaling, and storage in the cloud
- A preview of Azure's most common services and what to expect in upcoming chapters

Up next is Chapter 2, where you'll learn more about the advantages of cloud computing and the services that it offers.

Chapter 1 Quiz

To check your answers, please refer to the "Chapter 1 Answer Key" on page 299.

1. How does cloud computing differ from traditional on-premises infrastructure in terms of scaling compute power?

    A. Traditional on-premises infrastructure allows effortless scaling.

    B. Cloud computing requires physical upgrades.

    C. Cloud computing allows effortless scaling.

    D. Traditional on-premises infrastructure offers flexibility.

2. In terms of storage flexibility, what advantage does cloud computing offer over traditional on-premises infrastructure?

    A. Fixed storage limits

    B. Scalable storage capacity

    C. Limited storage options

    D. Inability to expand storage

3. In terms of infrastructure cost, what is a significant advantage of cloud computing over traditional on-premises infrastructure?

    A. Up-front hardware costs

    B. Lower cost due to limited scalability

    C. In-house maintenance

    D. Pay-as-you-go model

CHAPTER 2
Benefits of Using Cloud Services

Cloud computing has revolutionized the way businesses operate by offering on-demand access to essential computing resources like virtual machines (VMs), storage, databases, networking, and software over the internet. This approach eliminates the need for significant investments in physical infrastructure, offering businesses greater flexibility, scalability, and cost-efficiency.

As you are preparing for your AZ-900 Microsoft Azure Fundamentals exam, be mindful of the key benefits of cloud services, shown in Figure 2-1.

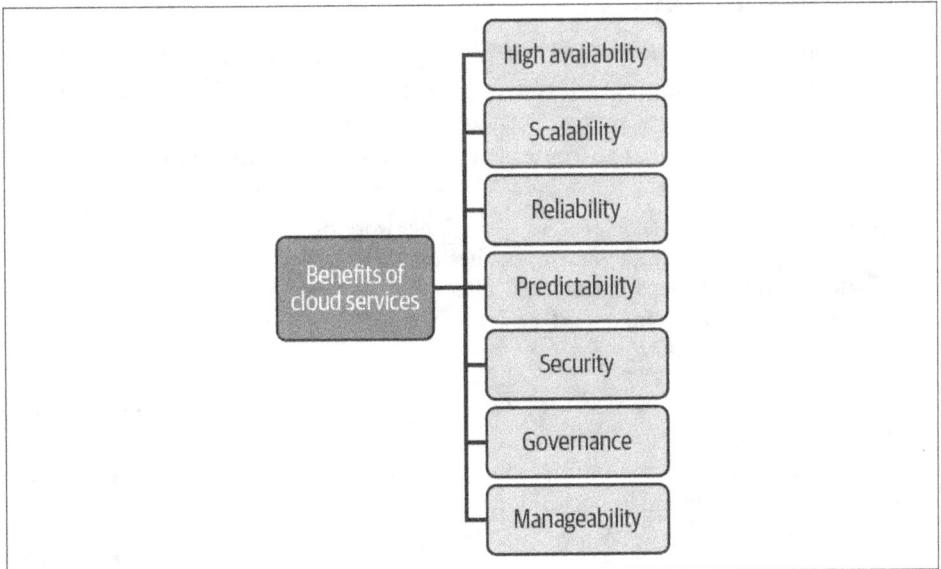

Figure 2-1. Key benefits of cloud services

11

In this chapter, I'll focus on each of these benefits as they relate to Microsoft Azure to keep you focused on your upcoming exam.

Let's begin with high availability.

High Availability

One of the major benefits of using cloud services like Azure is that they ensure *high availability*, or the continuous availability and reliability of applications, data, and infrastructure. Backed by a global network of datacenters across multiple regions, Azure provides unparalleled levels of redundancy and fault tolerance, allowing organizations to reduce downtime and maintain seamless operations, even during unexpected outages or disasters.

Azure's resilient infrastructure, combined with industry-leading service level agreements (SLAs), supports and defines expectations for high availability and reliability, enabling businesses to deliver reliable and uninterrupted services to their customers. This capability makes Azure ideal for mission-critical applications and services, where uninterrupted performance is vital.

In this section, you'll gain an understanding of how high availability works in general cloud computing. Later, in Chapter 7, you'll learn how these principles are implemented within Azure.

Redundant Infrastructure

Azure's global network of datacenters is designed with high availability in mind. Datacenters are interconnected through high-speed networks. This ensures that if one experiences a failure, services can quickly failover to redundant systems in another location, minimizing disruption and maintaining continuous availability.

Failover is the process of shifting workloads from a failed or unavailable component to a healthy standby resource. This transition happens quickly and often without user impact, helping to maintain continuous service availability.

To further enhance resilience, Azure also uses advanced technologies such as load balancers, DNS-based traffic routing, and content delivery networks (CDNs). These tools distribute traffic across multiple endpoints, reduce the pressure on any single resource, and minimize the impact of localized failures.

Automated Failover and Recovery

Azure offers built-in mechanisms for automated failover and recovery, helping organizations promptly respond to issues and minimize downtime. Features like health checks, load balancing, and multizone deployments, combined with autoscaling, enable organizations to automatically adjust resource allocation and redirect traffic away from faulty systems to healthy ones.

Azure Monitor is a robust monitoring and alerting system that continuously checks the health and performance of cloud resources, detecting anomalies and performance degradation in real time and triggering when issues arise. Organizations can configure automated responses and remediation workflows using services such as Automation or Azure Logic Apps to maintain smooth operations by applying predefined corrective actions to resolve issues that are identified by Azure Monitor. Don't worry if you don't know what these Azure services are quite yet. I'll talk about these in Chapter 16.

Service Level Agreements

Azure provides SLAs that define uptime and performance commitments for its cloud services. These SLAs outline the percentage of guaranteed availability within a billing period—typically starting at 99.9% for standard services and increasing to 99.99% or 99.999% for mission-critical or zone-redundant offerings.

SLA guarantees vary depending on the service tier or SKU selected. For example:

- Basic tiers (such as Basic Load Balancer or Basic App Service plans) often have lower or no financially backed SLA, making them suitable for development or noncritical workloads.

- Standard or Premium tiers typically offer higher availability guarantees, such as 99.95% or 99.99%, because they include more resilient infrastructure features like zone redundancy and improved fault tolerance.

Some services can achieve even higher levels of availability when deployed across availability zones or multiple regions, often increasing the SLA from 99.9% to 99.99% or higher.

If Azure fails to meet the stated SLA for a given service tier, customers may be eligible for service credits; such provisions incentivize Azure's commitment to maintaining reliable and enterprise-grade performance.

Business Continuity and Disaster Recovery

Azure goes beyond ensuring high availability within datacenters by offering business continuity and disaster recovery (BCDR) solutions. Organizations can replicate their critical data and workloads across multiple geographic regions to ensure resilience in the event of unexpected outages, natural disasters, or large-scale regional disruptions.

Managed services like Azure Site Recovery and Azure Backup provide backup, replication, and failover capabilities. These services enable organizations to establish effective disaster recovery strategies without significant capital expenditure or specialized expertise.

Table 2-1. Comparing Azure Site Recovery and Azure Backup

Azure Site Recovery	• Allows for the replication of VMs and other essential workloads, enabling automatic failover to the replicated environment in the event of a regional outage or disaster. • Minimizes data loss and reduces recovery times, ensuring minimal disruption to business operations.
Azure Backup	• Provides comprehensive data protection by supporting backups for a range of data types. • Integrates seamlessly into disaster recovery strategies by enabling data restoration, ensuring that data remains available and recoverable even during catastrophic events. • Plays a key role in broader disaster recovery strategies by ensuring data availability and recoverability.

Together, these services help organizations implement strong BCDR plans without large up-front investments or specialized infrastructure, making enterprise-grade resilience accessible to businesses of all sizes.

Key Takeaways for High Availability

High availability is a core capability of cloud services that helps ensure applications remain accessible even when components fail. Cloud platforms use features such as redundancy, fault isolation, automated failover, and defined SLAs to minimize downtime and maintain service continuity.

However, high availability and disaster recovery are not automatic by default. In Azure, customers must plan, configure, and enable the appropriate services (such as Availability Zones, load balancers, backup, geo-replication, or Azure Site Recovery) to achieve the level of resiliency their workload requires. Understanding which features to implement and how they align with your business requirements is a key part of managing cloud architecture and a common focus area on the AZ-900 exam. You'll learn more about this in upcoming chapters.

Scalability

Another core benefit of cloud computing is *scalability*, which allows businesses to adjust computing resources (such as processing power, storage, and network bandwidth) based on demand. Such flexibility is essential for managing fluctuating workloads, and it prevents issues related to the over- or underprovisioning of resources.

Azure's elastic infrastructure supports dynamic scaling of computing resources, optimizing both performance and cost-efficiency. Whether handling sudden traffic spikes or gradual growth, Azure enables seamless adjustments in resource allocation. Features like autoscaling and VM scale sets empower businesses to scale their applications effortlessly, ensuring consistent performance and an optimal user experience.

Elastic Infrastructure

Azure offers elastic infrastructure that allows organizations to scale resources up or down on demand, in near real time. You'll learn more about this in the next section on vertical and horizontal scaling.

Whether facing sudden spikes in traffic during peak periods, seasonal fluctuations in demand, or unpredictable growth trajectories, cloud services enable businesses to allocate additional resources dynamically to meet increased demand and ensure uninterrupted service delivery. With features such as autoscaling and serverless computing, organizations can automate resource provisioning and deprovisioning based on predefined metrics or triggers, optimizing resource utilization and minimizing costs.

Vertical and Horizontal Scaling

Azure provides both vertical and horizontal scaling strategies to adapt to varying workload patterns and resource needs. Compared to on-premises environments, these cloud scaling options offer more flexibility and cost-efficiency.

Let's talk about these two scaling strategies in detail.

Vertical scaling

Vertical scaling, also known as "scaling up" or "scaling down," involves increasing or decreasing the capacity of an existing resource by upgrading its CPU, memory, or storage. Cloud platforms simplify this process with on-demand resource adjustments and minimal downtime.

To illustrate, if your VM needs more processing power, you can quickly scale it up by adding more CPU or RAM (see Figure 2-2). Conversely, if resources are overprovisioned, you can scale down to optimize costs.

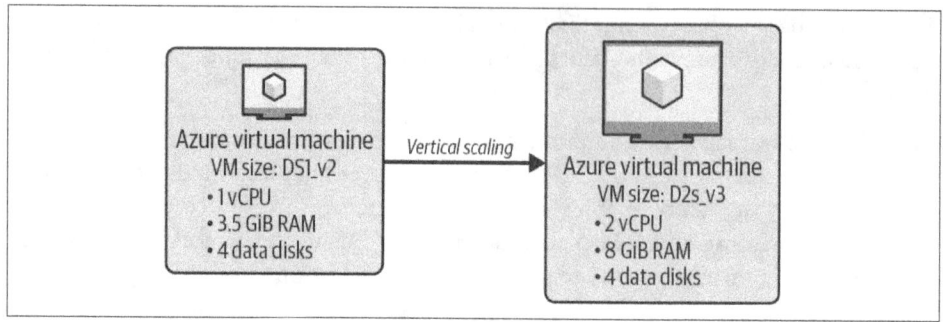

Figure 2-2. Vertical scaling of an Azure virtual machine by increasing its vCPU and RAM

Horizontal scaling

Horizontal scaling, or "scaling out" and "scaling in," involves adding or removing resources, such as VMs or containers, to handle changing demands. This method spreads the workload across multiple instances, enhancing performance and scalability.

To illustrate, suppose you deploy a web application using an Azure Virtual Machine Scale Set configured with a minimum of 1 VM instance. Under normal traffic conditions, this single VM is sufficient to handle all incoming requests. However, as user demand increases (such as during a new product launch or peak usage period), the Azure Virtual Machine Scale Set can automatically scale out by adding two additional VM instances, increasing the total from 1 VM to 3 VMs (see Figure 2-3). Conversely, once the peak usage period is over, you can "scale in" to a single VM instance again to optimize cost.

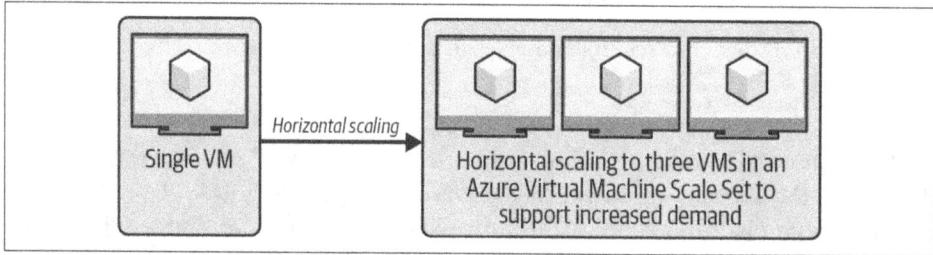

Figure 2-3. Horizontal scaling from a single VM to 3 VMs in an Azure Virtual Machine Scale Set to support increased demand

Comparing vertical and horizontal scaling

Consider the following comparison between vertical and horizontal scaling in cloud and on-premises environments:

Cloud
- *Vertical scaling*: Vertical scaling can be performed with ease and flexibility. Cloud providers offer a variety of instance types and configurations that can be adjusted without significant operational impact.
- *Horizontal scaling*: With features like load balancers and container orchestration tools, cloud platforms make horizontal scaling efficient and seamless. When demand increases, you can scale out by adding more instances, and when it decreases, you can scale in to minimize costs. This elasticity allows for dynamic adjustment to varying workloads with minimal overhead.

On-premises
- *Vertical scaling*: Vertical scaling involves physical hardware changes, which can be cumbersome and expensive. Upgrading a server's CPU or RAM often requires purchasing new hardware and performing complex installations, potentially causing downtime. The process can be slow and costly, with additional expenses related to hardware procurement, installation, and disruption to ongoing operations.
- *Horizontal scaling*: Horizontal scaling is often complex and costly. Adding more servers involves significant capital investment and putting capacity toward installation, configuration, and integration. Scaling also requires substantial planning and resources to ensure that new instances are properly networked and integrated with existing systems. Additionally, managing and maintaining additional hardware can increase operational complexity and costs.

Here's how vertical and horizontal scaling work with Azure:

- Azure allows vertical scaling of VMs by upgrading their size for increased CPU or memory capacity. A company running a critical database on Azure SQL can easily scale vertically by moving to a higher tier to handle increased query loads, without the need for physical hardware adjustments.
- Azure's Virtual Machine Scale Sets and AKS support horizontal scaling. For instance, an ecommerce platform can use Azure's autoscaling to manage high traffic during a holiday sale by scaling out its web servers. When traffic subsides, resources can be scaled back in, optimizing costs without manual intervention.

As you can see, vertical and horizontal scaling in a cloud environment offers a more agile and cost-effective solution than is possible in a traditional on-premises environment. Cloud services enable dynamic resource adjustments with minimal impact, whereas on-premises scaling involves more complex, costly, and time-consuming processes.

Pay-per-Use Pricing Model

One of the key benefits of cloud scalability is its alignment with a pay-per-use pricing model, which helps organizations optimize costs and maximize return on investment (ROI). Azure offers flexible pricing plans based on actual resource consumption. By allowing businesses to pay only for what they use, this pricing model eliminates the need for up-front capital investment or long-term commitments. Consumption-based pricing ensures that organizations can scale their infrastructure and applications in a cost-effective manner, provisioning additional resources as needed to accommodate demand spikes or scaling down during periods of low activity to minimize costs.

Global Reach and Accessibility

Cloud scalability also encompasses global infrastructure. Platforms like Azure operate datacenters worldwide, enabling businesses to deploy applications closer to users for improved performance. This geographic diversity ensures low-latency access and enhances the user experience, especially for globally distributed workloads. With cloud scalability, businesses can broaden their reach, tap into new markets, and deliver seamless experiences to users around the world.

Key Takeaways for Scalability

Scalability is a core characteristic of cloud services, empowering organizations to adapt, innovate, and grow in today's fast-paced business landscape. Cloud platforms provide elastic infrastructure, supporting both vertical and horizontal scaling, pay-per-use pricing models, and global accessibility. Using the cloud enables businesses to scale their operations seamlessly, respond to changing demands, and capitalize on new opportunities for success.

In an era characterized by rapid technological advancement and digital disruption, scalability is not just a competitive advantage but a strategic imperative for organizations seeking to thrive and differentiate themselves in the digital economy.

Reliability

Reliability refers to a system's ability to recover from failures and continue functioning smoothly, ensuring that applications remain operational even when disruptions occur. As one of the core pillars of the Azure Well-Architected Framework (*https://oreil.ly/ppqgX*), reliability emphasizes the need to design resilient cloud infrastructures to ensure continuous services.

Cloud platforms, with their decentralized architecture, are inherently built to support reliable and resilient systems. Azure enables organizations to deploy resources across multiple regions globally, ensuring that applications remain accessible even if one region experiences a failure or catastrophic event.

Thanks to Azure's global scale, organizations can replicate resources across geographically dispersed regions, providing both high availability and fault tolerance. This architecture helps protect against regional failures, such as natural disasters or large-scale outages, by automatically rerouting traffic to healthy regions, ensuring uninterrupted service delivery. For example, if a datacenter in one Azure region fails, your workload can be automatically routed to another region, maintaining continuous availability without manual intervention.

Services like Azure Traffic Manager and Azure Front Door offer automatic failover. By redirecting users to backup regions or instances during an outage, they improve overall system reliability.

It is important to note that while Azure provides the capabilities for cross-region redundancy, it is the customer's responsibility to configure, enable, and pay for the additional services and resources required to achieve multiregion resilience. This includes costs for secondary instances, replicated data, and global routing services.

Designing for Reliability

Designing cloud applications for reliability means intentionally building systems that can continue functioning even when individual components fail. As a foundation, organizations must establish *service level objectives* (SLOs), which are measurable targets for availability and performance. SLOs help teams determine the level of resilience required and guide architectural decisions such as redundancy, failover design, and recovery expectations.

To meet these reliability goals, organizations can deploy applications across multiple availability zones or even multiple Azure regions, ensuring that failures at one level (whether a single datacenter or an entire region) don't disrupt the service. Multiregion deployments are especially important for mission-critical workloads that can't tolerate extended downtime.

While some Azure services provide built-in resiliency within a region or offer automated failover when configured, achieving end-to-end reliability is ultimately the customer's design responsibility. Azure supplies the global infrastructure and redundancy features, but organizations must decide how to use them to meet their SLOs.

By aligning architectural choices with well-defined SLOs and leveraging Azure's global capabilities, organizations can build systems that remain available and performant even during unexpected failures.

Key Takeaways for Reliability

By leveraging the reliability features built into Azure, organizations can design systems that can recover quickly from failures, ensuring business continuity and improving customer satisfaction.

Predictability

Another key benefit of cloud computing is *predictability*, which gives businesses confidence in their operations by offering clarity about both performance and cost. Predictability ensures a reliable understanding of how applications will perform (*performance predictability*) and how cloud expenses will unfold (*cost predictability*) over time.

Performance Predictability

Ensuring consistent performance is essential for delivering a seamless user experience, even as demand fluctuates. Azure provides several features that enhance performance predictability:

Autoscaling
　　Allows resources to scale automatically based on demand. For example, during a surge in traffic, autoscaling can deploy additional VMs or containers to handle the increased load. Once demand drops, these resources can automatically scale back to reduce costs.

Load balancing
　　Distributes incoming traffic evenly across multiple instances, preventing any single instance from being overwhelmed. This helps maintain consistent performance, even during periods of high traffic.

High availability
　　Ensures that applications remain operational during hardware failures or outages. Although high availability is often discussed as a standalone cloud benefit, it also directly contributes to performance predictability by reducing unplanned downtime.

Azure Advisor
　　Provides proactive, data-driven recommendations to help maintain consistent performance. It analyzes resource configurations and usage patterns, then offers guidance and recommendations to help improve responsiveness, optimizing workloads, and resolving performance bottlenecks before they impact users.

Azure's built-in tools help businesses predict resource needs, ensuring that systems perform optimally, even under varying conditions.

Cost Predictability

Cost predictability is another significant benefit of cloud computing. In traditional on-premises setups, costs can be enormously high due to large up-front investments in hardware and infrastructure. With cloud computing, costs are usage based and much more transparent. Azure provides tools and services that allow businesses to monitor resource usage and costs in real time, making it easier to plan and forecast cloud spending.

With Azure, organizations can:

- Track real-time resource usage to pay only for what's actually consumed.
- Monitor usage trends and apply analytics to predict future costs more accurately.
- Use tools like the Azure pricing calculator and Azure Migrate to estimate cloud expenses and compare them to those of on-premises solutions. You'll learn more about this in Chapter 13.
- Leverage Azure Reservations (*https://oreil.ly/A6WpS*) (reserved instances and reserved capacity) to improve long-term cost predictability and reduce costs by committing to one-year or three-year terms for eligible services (such as VMs, Azure SQL Database, Cosmos DB, and more).

These tools allow organizations to better manage their costs and adjust resource usage to align with budget goals.

Key Takeaways for Predictability

By designing for predictability in both performance and cost, organizations can manage their cloud environments more effectively and plan for future growth with confidence. Predictable behavior (whether it involves maintaining consistent application responsiveness or anticipating cloud spending) gives businesses greater control of and visibility into their operations. This level of transparency and stability is a major reason why organizations worldwide continue to adopt cloud services.

Security

While some organizations initially worry that moving to the cloud might introduce new security risks, cloud platforms like Azure actually strengthen an organization's security posture. This is because cloud providers invest in advanced, enterprise-grade protections that most organizations would find difficult or cost-prohibitive to implement on-premises. Azure benefits from continuous monitoring, global threat intelligence, and large-scale security investments that help safeguard customer environments when properly configured by the customer.

A key concept behind Azure's security approach is the *shared responsibility model*.

Microsoft is responsible for securing the underlying cloud infrastructure, such as physical datacenters, networking, host hardware, and core platform services.

Customers are responsible for securing what they put in the cloud, such as identities, data, configurations, network controls, and application settings.

You'll learn more about the shared responsibility model in Chapter 4.

Adhering to top compliance standards like ISO 27001 and SOC 2, Azure helps businesses meet regulatory requirements while ensuring data privacy and security. By utilizing Azure's security features, organizations can enhance their defenses, reduce the risk of breaches, and maintain customer trust.

Data Encryption

Data encryption is a fundamental part of cloud security, protecting sensitive information both in transit (as it moves across networks) and at rest (while stored). Azure uses strong, industry-standard encryption methods by default, and most Azure services (including Azure SQL Database, Cosmos DB, storage accounts, and Azure managed disks) automatically enable encryption at rest without requiring any configuration.

Azure also encrypts data in transit using Transport Layer Security (TLS) to ensure that information cannot be intercepted or tampered with as it travels between services, users, or applications. By relying on these built-in encryption capabilities, organizations can safeguard their data against unauthorized access and meet many security and compliance requirements with minimal setup.

Identity and Access Management

Identity and access management (IAM) is vital for controlling who has access to cloud resources. Microsoft Entra ID (formerly Azure Active Directory) provides centralized authentication and authorization, allowing organizations to define granular permissions and enforce multifactor authentication (MFA) for verifying user identities. These features, coupled with detailed activity monitoring, help organizations reduce the risk of unauthorized access, data breaches, and insider threats.

For example, a financial services company using Azure can use Microsoft Entra ID to restrict access to sensitive customer data, ensuring that only authorized personnel in specific roles can view or modify information.

Threat Detection and Prevention

Microsoft Defender for Cloud offers real-time threat detection and prevention services, continuously monitoring cloud environments for abnormal activity and known security threats. It uses machine learning and threat intelligence to identify potential incidents and provides immediate alerts to help organizations take action.

In addition, Azure provides services like Azure Firewall, Microsoft Sentinel, and distributed denial-of-service (DDoS) protection to defend against a wide array of cyberthreats. These capabilities allow organizations to proactively manage and mitigate risks before they escalate into breaches.

Compliance and Governance

Ensuring compliance with industry standards and regulatory requirements is essential for businesses in sectors such as healthcare, finance, and government. Azure simplifies compliance management through tools like Microsoft Purview Compliance Manager, which provides documentation, reports, and assessments to meet various requirements. For example:

SOC 2 (System and Organization Controls 2)
　　Focuses on security, availability, processing integrity, confidentiality, and privacy of customer data in cloud and service environments.

HIPAA (Health Insurance Portability and Accountability Act)
　　Protects the privacy and security of sensitive healthcare data in the United States.

GDPR (General Data Protection Regulation)
　　Protects the personal data of individuals in the European Economic Area by regulating what data is collected and how it's handled.

ISO 27001 (International Organization for Standardization 27001)
　　Defines a framework for establishing, implementing, maintaining, and continually improving an information security management system (ISMS).

Azure's compliance certifications are regularly validated through independent audits, enabling businesses to demonstrate their commitment to security and regulatory adherence. These tools also reduce the complexity of audits and regulatory reporting, allowing organizations to focus more on innovation and growth.

Key Takeaways for Security

Security forms the backbone of modern cloud services, enabling organizations to operate safely in an increasingly interconnected world. Azure's comprehensive security features—ranging from encryption and identity management to advanced threat detection and compliance tools—help businesses fortify their cloud environments. As cyberthreats evolve and regulatory demands grow, leveraging cloud security tools like those offered by Azure empowers organizations to protect their data, maintain customer trust, and continue to deliver innovative solutions securely and efficiently.

It's important to note that security of your own applications is always your responsibility. Azure can provide tools to help you, but a wrong configuration or bugs in your code will still leave you vulnerable.

Governance

In the rapidly evolving world of cloud computing, effective *governance* is essential for managing, controlling, and optimizing cloud resources while ensuring compliance with internal policies and external regulations. Strong governance helps organizations maximize cloud investments; enhance operational efficiency; and reduce risks such as unauthorized access, data breaches, and compliance violations.

Azure provides a wide range of tools and services to help businesses establish solid governance frameworks.

Azure management groups
: Enable organizations to organize subscriptions into hierarchical structures, allowing policies and access controls to be applied consistently across multiple subscriptions. This simplifies large-scale management and ensures governance at every level of the organization.

Azure Policy
: Enforces compliance with internal standards and regulatory requirements, ensuring that resources across cloud environments adhere to best practices. For example, an organization might use Azure Policy to ensure that resources meet security standards, such as by enforcing encryption on all new storage accounts.

Role-based access control (RBAC)
: Allows fine-grained access management, restricting sensitive data and resources based on user roles and responsibilities.

Monitoring and auditing tools
: Provide real-time visibility into resource usage, enabling organizations to detect anomalies, track consumption, and ensure regulatory compliance.

Responsible AI and Azure AI governance
: Enable organizations to establish policies and controls for the ethical, secure, and compliant use of AI services. This includes managing access, monitoring usage, and enforcing governance for tools such as Microsoft Copilot and other Azure AI capabilities.

Centralized Policy Enforcement

Cloud platforms like Azure offer mechanisms for centralized policy enforcement, ensuring that compliance and security standards are consistently applied across all resources. Tools such as Azure Policy allow organizations to define resource configurations and enforce compliance with both internal security policies and external regulatory requirements. Policies can be applied at multiple scopes (such as management groups, subscriptions, resource groups, or individual resources), allowing organizations to tailor enforcement to the level of granularity needed. This centralized control reduces the risk of misconfigurations, unauthorized access, and security breaches, as policies are applied uniformly across cloud environments.

Role-Based Access Control

RBAC is essential for managing user access based on roles and responsibilities. The RBAC framework allows organizations to assign specific roles to users, groups, or applications and define detailed permissions to control access to cloud resources. By implementing the *principle of least privilege*, businesses ensure that users have only the access necessary for their tasks. This approach minimizes the risk of privilege escalation and strengthens security by limiting access to sensitive resources.

Cost Management and Optimization

Cost management is a key aspect of cloud governance. Azure provides tools such as Microsoft Cost Management, which help organizations gain insights into cloud spending, analyze cost trends, and identify opportunities for optimization. Features like cost allocation tags, autoscaling policies, and reserved instances enable businesses to reduce unnecessary expenses and use resources more efficiently. Governance frameworks can also enforce budget controls and spending limits, preventing overruns and ensuring financial transparency. You'll learn more about these capabilities in Chapter 13.

Audit Logging and Compliance Reporting

Effective governance also involves monitoring cloud activity and ensuring compliance with regulatory standards. Azure's audit-logging and monitoring tools, such as Azure Monitor, capture detailed logs of resource activities, configuration changes, and user actions. These logs can be retained for audit purposes, analyzed to identify security incidents, and used to demonstrate compliance. Azure also offers Microsoft Purview Compliance Manager, which provides documentation and reports to support organizations in meeting regulatory requirements and simplifying audit processes.

Key Takeaways for Governance

Governance is a critical element of cloud operations, enabling organizations to manage risk, ensure compliance, and optimize performance. By implementing centralized policy enforcement, role-based access control, cost management, and audit logging, businesses can establish control, transparency, and accountability within their cloud environments. In today's digital era, where regulatory compliance and security are more important than ever, strong cloud governance helps organizations unlock the full potential of cloud services while maintaining trust with customers, partners, and other stakeholders.

Manageability

One of the major benefits of cloud computing is the broad range of manageability options that it offers. *Manageability* refers to the simplification of deployment and maintenance of cloud infrastructure while operational efficiency and control over resources are enhanced.

Cloud manageability can be divided into two primary categories:

- Management *of* the cloud
- Management *in* the cloud

Though these look nearly identical, they address different concerns.

Management of the Cloud

Management of the cloud refers to the various tools and services that cloud providers offer to help you efficiently manage cloud resources. These management tools simplify the operational aspects of cloud resource deployment and maintenance, offering automation, monitoring, and scaling features that minimize the need for manual intervention.

Let's explore the capabilities of a handful of these management tools and services, some of which I've already discussed in the previous sections.

Automatically scale resource deployment
    Azure's autoscaling dynamically adjusts resources based on real-time demand, ensuring that systems can handle workload fluctuations without manual intervention.

Deploy resources using preconfigured templates
    With tools like Azure Resource Manager (ARM) templates and Bicep, you can deploy resources based on predefined configurations, reducing the need for manual setup and reducing the risk of errors. This automation ensures consistency across deployments and saves time.

Monitor health and replace failing resources
    Cloud services provide real-time monitoring and alerts to track the health of your resources. For example, if a VM or container fails, it can automatically be

replaced, ensuring minimal downtime. Azure's monitoring and diagnostic tools help identify potential issues before they affect performance.

Receive real-time alerts
Azure Monitor can be configured to send notifications based on specific performance metrics, keeping you informed about the health and performance of your applications and infrastructure in real time.

These management capabilities enhance the operational efficiency of cloud deployments, making it easier for organizations to scale, monitor, and address issues quickly.

Management in the Cloud

Management in the cloud refers to how users interact with and manage their cloud environment and resources. Cloud platforms like Azure offer a variety of interfaces to control and manage cloud resources, allowing users to choose the method that works best for their specific needs.

Following are examples of the capabilities that various interfaces have to manage Azure cloud resources.

Azure portal
This user-friendly graphical user interface for quickly deploying, configuring, and monitoring resources is ideal for users who prefer a visual management approach.

Azure command-line interfaces (CLI)
For more automation and scripting, Azure CLI provides a CLI to manage cloud resources. This is particularly useful for developers and system administrators who want to automate deployment and management tasks.

Azure PowerShell
Azure also supports Azure PowerShell, which enables users to manage cloud resources through a set of cmdlets. Azure PowerShell is particularly useful for automating complex administrative tasks and is favored by system administrators who are familiar with scripting.

APIs
For deeper integration with applications or other systems, Azure provides robust APIs that enable programmatic management of cloud resources. These allow businesses to integrate cloud resource management directly into their workflows or custom applications.

These manageability options give organizations flexibility in how they control and interact with their cloud environment, allowing them to choose the management approach that best fits their operational and technical requirements. You'll learn more about the Azure portal, Azure CLI, and Azure PowerShell in Chapter 15.

Key Takeaways for Manageability

By using the manageability features offered by Azure, businesses can effectively manage their cloud infrastructure, ensuring optimized performance, streamlined operations, and rapid responses to evolving business needs. This flexibility allows organizations to scale and manage resources in a way that best aligns with their goals, enhancing overall operational control and efficiency.

Summary

Cloud services offer transformative benefits that drive growth, efficiency, and resilience for organizations. Key advantages include exceptional scalability, which allows businesses to adjust resources dynamically based on demand, enhancing both performance and cost-efficiency. Platforms like Azure ensure high availability and global reach, keeping applications and data accessible and reliable even during disruptions.

Additionally, the flexible, pay-per-use pricing models of cloud services help organizations manage costs effectively while maintaining high performance. Azure's robust infrastructure and comprehensive suite of tools provide unmatched agility, efficiency, and security, supporting mission-critical applications and dynamic workloads.

Embracing cloud technology enables businesses to utilize advanced disaster recovery solutions, leverage global infrastructure for improved user experiences, and scale operations seamlessly. As the digital landscape evolves, cloud services offer a strategic advantage that supports operational excellence, drives innovation, and fosters competitive differentiation. In today's fast-paced environment, the ability to adapt, scale, and recover with agility is crucial, making cloud services a central element of modern business strategy.

Up next: You'll continue your journey through Azure foundations by learning about the various cloud service types.

Chapter 2 Quiz

To check your answers, please refer to the "Chapter 2 Answer Key" on page 300.

1. Your ecommerce platform experiences a surge in traffic during seasonal sales.

    Which Azure feature allows you to meet this requirement without manual intervention?

    A. Governance

    B. Manageability

    C. Predictability

    D. Scalability

2. Which of the following best describes the benefit of high availability in cloud computing?

    A. It ensures that services are accessible even during failures or high demand.

    B. It reduces the need for data encryption.

    C. It enables the automation of software patch deployment.

    D. It guarantees lower operational costs.

3. Which of the following best describes how Azure cloud services benefit organizations' IT governance?

    A. They automatically back up sensitive data.

    B. They help organizations enforce policies, compliance, and security requirements.

    C. They ensure that cloud services remain affordable for businesses.

    D. They allow for the unlimited scaling of resources.

CHAPTER 3
Cloud Service Types

As you prepare for the AZ-900 Azure Fundamentals exam, be mindful of the three primary cloud service types:

- IaaS, or infrastructure as a service
- PaaS, or platform as a service
- SaaS, or software as a service

In this chapter, I'll take a microscopic view of each of these cloud service types. First, I'll explain them using everyday examples, and then we'll explore what Microsoft Azure offers for each cloud service type. This approach will provide a comprehensive understanding of this topic that can be applied in practical scenarios.

Demystifying Cloud Service Types Using Everyday Examples

These cloud service types (and their acronyms) can be confusing at first. Let's talk about them using the analogy of owning a car, renting a car, or using a rideshare service. In this analogy, the division of responsibilities shifts depending on the level of service you opt for (IaaS, PaaS, or SaaS).

IaaS: Owning a Car

With IaaS, you have full control over the infrastructure—just like when you own a car. When you own a car, you decide what car to buy, maintain it, fill it with fuel, and handle repairs. I'll dig more into how this directly translates to IaaS in a later section. For now, you can start to let this analogy sink in.

IaaS
: Like owning a car. You purchase a car when you want total control as well as all the responsibilities that come with ownership. You will:

- Enjoy maximum control and usage of the car
- Be the driver of the car
- Be responsible for (and in control of) everything, including maintenance, repairs, insurance, and fuel

PaaS: Renting a Car

When you rent a car, you can drive it wherever you want, but the car rental company handles routine maintenance, and if the car breaks down, you can call the rental company for a tow and a replacement vehicle.

PaaS
: Like renting a car. You rent a car when you want the convenience of using the vehicle but are willing to rely on the rental company to ensure that the car is well maintained. You will:

- Have complete access to use the car
- Be the driver of the car
- Have no responsibility for (or control over) the maintenance of the car

SaaS: Using a Rideshare Service

When you use a service like Uber or Lyft, you simply hop in, tell the driver where to go (or tell the car where to go, if it's driverless), and relax. Everything (including maintenance, fuel, driving, and repairs) is managed for you.

SaaS
: Like using a rideshare. You rely on a rideshare app when you want your only relationship with the vehicle to be the fact that you get taken from point A to point B in it. You will:

- Be able to use the car on demand
- Have no responsibility (or access) to drive the car
- Have no responsibility for (or control over) the maintenance of the car

With this foundational understanding in mind, let's use real-world examples to explore how this analogy relates to the cloud service types available in Microsoft Azure. By connecting these concepts to familiar situations, you'll better grasp how IaaS, PaaS, and SaaS operate within the Azure ecosystem.

Infrastructure as a Service

Let's now dive into IaaS, keeping the analogy in mind. As a reminder, with IaaS, you gain full control over the infrastructure, much like owning a car.

Just as you decide which car to buy and handle all aspects of owning it (e.g., maintenance, fuel, and repairs), you're responsible for managing VMs, operating systems, and security configurations in IaaS.

In the Azure IaaS model, Microsoft provides the underlying infrastructure. However, the day-to-day management and maintenance of the IaaS resources is your responsibility. Additionally, you may be responsible for software licenses.

IaaS offers the essential building blocks for compute, storage, and networking, empowering organizations to customize their cloud environment according to their needs.

Key Benefits of IaaS

Here are the main benefits of IaaS:

Flexibility and control
Customize your environment with full control over VMs, storage, and networking.

Scalability
Scale resources up or down dynamically, enabling your organization to meet changing demand without overprovisioning or underutilizing infrastructure.

Cost-effectiveness
Eliminate the up-front costs of purchasing and maintaining physical hardware, instead paying only for the resources consumed on a pay-as-you-go basis. This flexibility allows for better cost management and optimization, especially for fluctuating workloads.

Faster infrastructure provisioning
Provision new VMs and resources within minutes.

Reliability and security
Take advantage of the robust security features and compliance certifications offered by platforms like Azure, ensuring the confidentiality, integrity, and availability of data and applications when properly configured by the customers. With built-in encryption, identity management, and threat detection capabilities, organizations can mitigate risks and maintain regulatory compliance.

The Benefits of IaaS Services: A Real-Life Example

Table 3-1 outlines an IaaS service offered by Azure. Let's take a look to learn more about how IaaS can be used and the benefits it provides.

Table 3-1. An IaaS service offered by Azure

IaaS Service	Description	Use cases	Benefits
Azure VMs	On-demand virtual servers where you control the operating system, software, and security	• Hosting enterprise applications and databases • Running development environments	You have full administrative control over the VM, gaining the flexibility and customization to meet specific workload requirements.

IaaS offers a robust, flexible foundation for organizations that need scalable infrastructure but want to avoid the complexities and costs of managing physical hardware. It empowers businesses to deploy and manage VMs, storage, and networks without worrying about infrastructure upkeep, providing the agility to scale on demand. IaaS is often a first step for businesses with legacy/monolith applications. They move the app to a VM that everyone can access from anywhere, and now they're in the cloud. However, the true benefit of the cloud and a cloud-native application lies in the other models, such as PaaS.

Platform as a Service

Going back to our analogy, PaaS is like renting a car. You focus on the driving, while the car rental company handles routine maintenance such as oil changes, inspections, and car insurance.

In the Azure PaaS model, Microsoft takes care of the underlying infrastructure, operating system, and platform updates, empowering you to focus on developing and managing your applications and data.

In the Azure PaaS model, the customer does not have direct access to the underlying operating system (OS). The OS management is handled by Microsoft.

PaaS reduces your workload by taking care of the infrastructure and platform management, giving developers the tools to build, deploy, and scale applications without having to worry about servers or patching.

Key Benefits of PaaS

Let's review some key benefits of PaaS:

Faster time to market
Streamline your application development and deployment lifecycle, enabling developers to focus on writing code and delivering value to customers without the overhead of infrastructure management. Leverage features such as preconfigured environments, built-in services, and automated workflows to accelerate time to market for new applications and updates.

Scalability and elasticity
Built-in scalability and elasticity features allow applications to automatically scale resources up or down based on demand. Azure App Service, for example, automatically adjusts the number of application instances based on workload metrics, ensuring optimal performance and cost-efficiency without manual intervention.

Reduced management
The complexities of infrastructure provisioning, configuration, and maintenance are abstracted away, allowing developers to leverage prebuilt services and components for common tasks such as authentication, authorization, caching, and logging. This reduces development time, minimizes operational overhead, and improves overall productivity.

Cost-efficiency
With a consumption-based pricing model, you pay only for the resources and services you use, without any investment in up-front infrastructure or licenses. This pay-as-you-go pricing model, coupled with built-in cost management tools and optimizations, helps optimize costs and achieve better ROI on your cloud investments.

Built-in security and compliance
Leverage the built-in compliance tools and security updates.

Integration with DevOps
Enjoy seamless integration with CI/CD pipelines, allowing developers to automate the build, test, and deployment of their applications.

The Benefits of PaaS Services: Real-Life Examples

Let's take a look at some real-life examples, use cases, and benefits of PaaS services in Table 3-2.

Table 3-2. PaaS services offered by Azure

PaaS service	Description	Use cases	Benefits
Azure App Service	A managed platform to build, host, and scale web apps and APIs without worrying about the underlying infrastructure	• Deploying websites, REST APIs, or mobile backends quickly	You get simplified deployment with built-in scalability and security options.
Azure Functions	A serverless compute service that allows you to run event-driven code without managing infrastructure	• Automating workflows • Building microservices that respond to events like HTTP triggers or IoT messages	You pay only for the time your code runs, making this highly cost-efficient.
Azure SQL Database	A fully managed relational database service where Microsoft handles updates, backups, and patching	• Storing structured business data • Running analytics workloads	Eliminate the need to manage SQL servers so you can focus on database operations.

The PaaS model allows developers to focus on innovation rather than infrastructure. PaaS reduces operational overhead and accelerates the development process by providing preconfigured environments and platform services. It's the perfect solution for organizations looking to build and deploy applications faster while offloading platform management to Microsoft.

Software as a Service

Recall that using SaaS is like hailing a cab or using a rideshare service such as Uber or Lyft. You simply hop in, tell the driver where to go, and relax. Everything (including car maintenance, fuel, repairs, and even the driving) is managed for you. With SaaS, the cloud service provider handles the infrastructure, platform, and application, while you just use the service.

Key Benefits of SaaS

Let's look at some key benefits of SaaS:

No infrastructure management
    Microsoft handles all infrastructure, platform, and application maintenance.

Automatic updates
    Applications are always up-to-date, with patches and new features automatically rolled out.

Accessibility
    Access your tools from anywhere with an internet connection, ensuring business continuity.

Cost-effective
   No need to invest in hardware or maintain software—just pay through subscription-based licensing, typically per user or per service tier.

Scalability
   Easily scale your subscription as your business grows or your needs change.

Built-in security and compliance
   Services like Microsoft 365 come with security features, including data encryption and compliance tools.

Rapid deployment
   Your applications can be deployed and provisioned quickly, often within minutes or hours, compared to traditional software installations that may take days or weeks. This agility allows organizations to respond rapidly to changing business needs, launch new initiatives quickly, and bring products and services to market faster.

The Benefits of SaaS: Real-Life Examples

Let's look at some real-life examples, use cases, and benefits of SaaS in Table 3-3.

Table 3-3. SaaS services offered by Microsoft

SaaS service	Description	Use cases	Benefits
Microsoft 365	A suite of productivity tools, including Word, Excel, Outlook, and Teams, available as a subscription	• Managing email and documents • Enabling collaboration	You can access tools from anywhere with automatic updates and built-in security.
Dynamics 365	A set of business applications for customer relationship management (CRM) and enterprise resource planning (ERP)	• Managing customer interactions, financials, and supply chains	The modular, cloud-based tools integrate easily with other services.
Azure DevOps Services	A cloud-based platform for collaboration, CI/CD pipelines, and project management	• Conducting Agile planning • Managing code repositories • Automating builds	Robust tools for tracking, version control, and delivery pipelines streamline your software development.

The SaaS model is ideal for organizations looking to offload IT management entirely and focus solely on using software to drive business outcomes. SaaS offers a high level of convenience and efficiency, helping businesses remain agile and responsive with minimal overhead.

Azure customers also frequently develop their own SaaS or PaaS on Azure and offer it to customers of their own, taking advantage of the fact that people are free to build whatever they come up with. Microsoft offers plenty of SaaS solutions, but you can absolutely host your own on top of all the things discussed here, depending on your needs.

Choosing the Right Azure Service Type for the Job

In this section, let's explore how to identify the right cloud service type (whether it's IaaS, PaaS, or SaaS) based on specific use cases.

Each cloud service type serves different needs, and the trick is to match the workload to the right platform. In the following sections, I'll walk you through practical scenarios, showing when and why to use each service type, along with some real-life examples.

When to Use IaaS

IaaS provides maximum control over VMs, operating systems, and security configurations, making it perfect for lift-and-shift migrations. A *lift-and-shift migration* is when you move existing on-premises workloads (such as domain controllers, file servers, or line-of-business applications) to the cloud with minimal changes. In this scenario, IaaS is the right fit. Let's look at a specific use case scenario and solution:

Requirement
   Migration of on-premises servers with minimal changes

Solution
   Azure Virtual Machines

Reason
   Full access and control over the operating system and application configuration

Benefit
   Flexibility to run custom software and maintain control over the environment without the burden of maintaining hardware

When to Use PaaS

PaaS is ideal for web services and applications that don't need OS-level control but would benefit from managed infrastructure. If you're running web apps on IIS and want to minimize the time spent on maintenance, PaaS services like Azure App Service are a good fit. PaaS takes care of patching, scaling, and availability, so you can focus on developing applications. Let's look at a specific use case scenario and solution:

Requirement
   Hosting a web service with minimal management overhead

Solution
    Azure App Service

Reason
    Handles platform management automatically while providing scalability and high availability

Benefit
    Reduces maintenance efforts and allows developers to focus on code

When to Use SaaS

SaaS offers complete business solutions without the need to manage infrastructure, platform, or applications. Think of it like using Microsoft 365 where everything is preconfigured and ready to go. If your organization needs email, collaboration tools, or cloud-based office applications, SaaS is the easiest option. There's no need to set up Exchange Servers, SharePoint, or other software manually. It's all managed by Microsoft. Let's look at a specific use case scenario and solution:

Requirement
    Email and collaboration tools

Solution
    Microsoft 365

Reason
    Zero infrastructure to manage, allowing you to just focus on using the tools

Benefit
    Faster setup and lower maintenance

In summary, by aligning workloads with the appropriate service type, you ensure efficiency, scalability, and ease of management. Choosing SaaS means minimal effort with a focus on outcomes. IaaS provides maximum flexibility, while PaaS strikes a balance between control and convenience. The key is to match the workload to the best service type for your needs.

Summary

This chapter offered a practical overview of IaaS, PaaS, and SaaS, demonstrating how these cloud service models differ in terms of control, management, and convenience. You also gained insights into selecting the right Azure service type to align with your specific needs and business goals, helping you make informed decisions when building your cloud strategy.

Up next is Chapter 4, where you'll learn how security, compliance, and operational duties are shared between you and your cloud provider. This is an important concept for working safely and effectively in the cloud.

Chapter 3 Quiz

To check your answers, please refer to the "Chapter 3 Answer Key" on page 300.

1. Which of the following is the best example of IaaS in Microsoft Azure?

    A. Microsoft 365

    B. Azure Virtual Machines

    C. Azure App Service

    D. Azure Functions

2. You are deploying a web application using Azure App Service so you can take advantage of platform as a service. In PaaS, which aspect of the platform do you NOT have direct control over?

    A. The operating system

    B. Automatic scaling configuration

    C. Custom domain and SSL configuration

    D. Continuous deployment configuration

3. Which cloud service type is the best choice for a ready-to-use team collaboration tool that you will not need to develop yourself?

    A. IaaS

    B. PaaS

    C. SaaS

    D. No cloud service type is well suited for this use case.

CHAPTER 4
The Shared Responsibility Model

In the previous chapter, you learned about the three primary cloud service types (IaaS, PaaS, and SaaS). In this chapter, you'll build on that knowledge by exploring the shared responsibility model and how responsibilities differ across each cloud service type.

If you're already familiar with this topic, you can skip to the next chapter or to Part II.

Understanding the shared responsibility model is important when navigating Azure's ecosystem. The shared responsibility model delineates the responsibilities between Microsoft and its customer.

Shared Responsibility: From On Premises to the Cloud

In a traditional on-premises infrastructure setting, the customer bears the sole responsibility of managing the physical infrastructure, implementing security measures, and addressing server maintenance or replacement needs. Essentially, the customer is tasked with overseeing all aspects of the hardware and software required to ensure the smooth operation of the infrastructure.

In cloud computing, responsibilities are shared between the cloud service provider (CSP) and the customer. How these responsibilities are divided depends on the cloud service types (which you should be quite familiar with after reading Chapter 3).

Responsibilities Are Closely Tied to Cloud Service Types

Unlike traditional on-premises environments, where the organization is responsible for every layer of the technology stack, cloud computing uses a shared responsibility model that divides security and operational duties between the CSP and the customer.

In this AZ-900 study guide, the CSP refers to Microsoft.

The following sections describe how these shared responsibilities differ across each cloud service type: IaaS, PaaS, and SaaS.

Shared Responsibility for IaaS

With IaaS, the customer assumes the greatest share of responsibility. The CSP manages only the foundational components, such as the physical datacenters, networking hardware, and compute hosts. IaaS provides customers with virtualized resources like VMs, storage, and networks, but everything above the virtualization layer is customer-managed. This includes operating system maintenance, patching, application installation, network configuration (such as subnets, IP addresses, and security groups), identity management, and data protection. While IaaS offers maximum flexibility and control, it also requires the customer to handle most operational and security tasks.

In the shared responsibility model for IaaS (see Table 4-1), Microsoft takes care of the physical infrastructure (e.g., datacenters, physical hosts, and networking hardware). However, the customer is responsible for managing, securing, and maintaining everything above the virtualization layer.

Table 4-1. Responsibility for each layer with IaaS

Responsibility	Who is responsible?
Information and data	Customer
Devices (mobile and PCs)	Customer
Accounts and identities	Customer
Identity and directory infrastructure	Customer
Applications	Customer
Network controls	Customer
Operating system	Customer
Virtualization layer (hypervisor)	Microsoft
Physical hosts	Microsoft
Physical network	Microsoft
Physical datacenter	Microsoft

With the IaaS model, Microsoft ensures that the underlying infrastructure is secure, stable, and well maintained, while you retain complete control over everything within your cloud environment. This level of control allows you to tailor and optimize resources to align with your specific business needs.

Shared Responsibility for PaaS

PaaS, residing between IaaS and SaaS, shares responsibility more evenly between the cloud service provider and the customer. With PaaS, the CSP manages the infrastructure, operating systems, runtime environments, and platform updates. Customers can focus on building and running applications without managing the underlying platform. However, customers remain responsible for application code, data, identity and access management, and application-level security configuration. For example, with services like Azure App Service or Azure SQL Database, Microsoft manages the platform itself, while the customer controls the application logic, database schema, and user permissions. PaaS reduces operational overhead and enables faster development by abstracting much of the infrastructure complexity.

In the shared responsibility model for IaaS (see Table 4-2), Microsoft takes on more responsibilities than with IaaS. It manages infrastructure, operating systems, and platform updates, while the customer remains responsible for application management, data, and access controls.

Table 4-2. Responsibility for each layer with PaaS

Responsibility	PaaS
Information and data	Customer
Devices (mobile and PCs)	Customer
Accounts and identities	Customer
Identity and directory infrastructure	Microsoft + Customer
Applications	Microsoft + Customer
Network controls	Microsoft + Customer
Operating system	Microsoft
Virtualization layer (hypervisor)	Microsoft
Physical hosts	Microsoft
Physical network	Microsoft
Physical datacenter	Microsoft

The PaaS model allows developers to focus on innovation rather than infrastructure. PaaS reduces operational overhead and accelerates the development process by providing preconfigured environments and platform services. It's the perfect solution for organizations looking to build and deploy applications faster while offloading platform management to Microsoft.

Shared Responsibility for SaaS

At the other end of the spectrum, SaaS shifts most technical responsibilities to the CSP. SaaS delivers fully managed applications such as Microsoft 365 or Dynamics 365, with the provider handling infrastructure, platform components, operating systems, and application updates. Customers still retain responsibility for managing user access and identities, configuring data privacy and sharing settings, and ensuring compliance with organizational and regulatory requirements. Although SaaS minimizes operational effort, customers must still apply proper governance to control how data is accessed and used.

In the shared responsibility model for SaaS (see Table 4-3), Microsoft manages nearly everything (e.g., datacenters, physical infrastructure, networks, operating systems, and the applications themselves). However, users are still responsible for certain aspects, such as managing user access and identities and ensuring that data privacy settings are correctly configured.

Table 4-3. Responsibility for each layer with SaaS

Responsibility	SaaS
Information and data	Customer
Devices (mobile and PCs)	Customer
Accounts and identities	Customer
Identity and directory infrastructure	Microsoft + Customer
Applications	Microsoft
Network controls	Microsoft
Operating system	Microsoft
Virtualization layer (hypervisor)	Microsoft
Physical hosts	Microsoft
Physical network	Microsoft
Physical datacenter	Microsoft

The SaaS model is ideal for organizations looking to offload IT management entirely and focus solely on using software to drive business outcomes. SaaS offers a high level of convenience and efficiency, helping businesses remain agile and responsive with minimal overhead. It is important to note that even when the CSP takes on a major share of the duties, the customer retains control over the most critical areas: their data and who can access it.

As a rule of thumb, the more control you have, the more responsibilities you assume. Leveraging cloud services such as Microsoft Azure allows you to offload some responsibilities while retaining control over critical areas like data.

Across all cloud service types, the CSP is responsible for securing and maintaining the physical infrastructure, while customers always retain responsibility for their identities, devices, and data. As organizations move from IaaS to PaaS to SaaS, operational control decreases, but simplicity, efficiency, and speed of adoption increase. This progression allows organizations to choose the level of responsibility that best aligns with their technical capabilities and business goals. You will see a comparison of responsibility areas across cloud service types in the next section.

Comparison of Responsibility Areas Across Cloud Service Types

The *shared responsibility model* (see Table 4-4) outlines which tasks are managed by the CSP and which remain the customer's responsibility. As you move across different cloud service types (IaaS, PaaS, and SaaS), operational control decreases, but simplicity, efficiency, and speed of adoption increase.

Exam Tip

Table 4-4 how responsibilities shift between the CSP and the customer across the different cloud service types. As you move from IaaS to SaaS, the customer's area of responsibility decreases. This is an important rule of thumb to remember for the exam!

Table 4-4. Comparison of responsibility areas across IaaS, PaaS, and SaaS

Area of responsibility	Who takes responsibility for service			
	On-premises	IaaS	PaaS	SaaS
Information and data	Customer	Customer	Customer	Customer
Devices (mobile and PCs)	Customer	Customer	Customer	Customer
Accounts and identities	Customer	Customer	Customer	Customer
Identity and directory infrastructure	Customer	Customer	CSP + Customer	CSP + Customer
Applications	Customer	Customer	CSP + Customer	CSP
Network controls	Customer	Customer	CSP + Customer	CSP
Operating system	Customer	Customer	CSP	CSP
Virtualization layer (hypervisor)	Customer	CSP	CSP	CSP
Physical hosts	Customer	CSP	CSP	CSP

Area of responsibility	Who takes responsibility for service			
	On-premises	IaaS	PaaS	SaaS
Physical network	Customer	CSP	CSP	CSP
Physical datacenter	Customer	CSP	CSP	CSP

In the shared responsibility model, the CSP (e.g. Microsoft) assumes responsibility for the physical datacenter, network, and hosts since the customer isn't physically present at the datacenter. Consequently, these tasks will always remain the responsibility of the cloud service provider.

Customers, on the other hand, retain responsibility for the data and applications they store and manage in the cloud. This includes classifying sensitive information, controlling access, and ensuring compliance with internal policies and regulatory standards. To protect data, customers can implement measures such as encryption at rest and in transit. Furthermore, maintaining access security falls to the customer, who must ensure that only authorized individuals can gain access.

Examples of Varying Responsibilities by Cloud Service Type

Let's take a look at some examples of varying responsibilities based on cloud service type.

If you deploy a VM and install your own instance of SQL Server, you're responsible for database maintenance, updates, and data management. This is an example of IaaS.

Conversely, when using the cloud-based instance of Azure SQL Database, Microsoft takes care of maintaining the database engine and underlying platform, while the customer remains responsible for the data ingested into it. This is an example of PaaS.

Moreover, for services like Microsoft 365, Microsoft manages the application, platform, and infrastructure, but the customer is responsible for user access management, data input, and configuring application-specific settings. This is an example of SaaS.

These examples illustrate how the customer's responsibilities generally decrease as you move from IaaS to PaaS to SaaS, though some tasks (such as data protection and access control) remain with the customer across all models.

More Real-World Examples of Responsibility Shifts

The following examples illustrate how responsibility boundaries change across different Azure service models by examining common operational and security tasks. They show how duties shift between the customer and Microsoft as organizations move from IaaS to PaaS and SaaS.

Example 1: Operating System Patching

In an IaaS scenario, such as running SQL Server on an Azure VM, the customer is responsible for operating system patch management. This includes scheduling, testing, and applying security updates to the Windows or Linux operating system running on the VM.

In contrast, with a PaaS offering like Azure SQL Database, Microsoft automatically patches and maintains both the underlying operating system and the SQL engine, removing this responsibility from the customer.

Example 2: Identity Management and Security

In IaaS and PaaS deployments, customers are responsible for managing their identity infrastructure, such as maintaining domain controllers or integrating with a hybrid identity solution.

In a SaaS scenario using Microsoft Entra ID, identity becomes a shared responsibility. Microsoft operates the identity provider service, while the customer manages user accounts, licenses, and security controls such as conditional access policies.

Example 3: Data Security and Compliance

Even when using PaaS services like Azure App Service, customers remain responsible for securing their applications and data. For example, when configuring a custom domain, the customer is responsible for setting up and managing the TLS/SSL configuration, including choosing whether to upload a customer-managed certificate or use a Microsoft-managed certificate to secure communications. Customers are also responsible for monitoring regulatory compliance, such as ensuring data handling aligns with GDPR by defining policies, auditing access patterns, and responding to compliance issues. At the same time, Microsoft is responsible for protecting the underlying physical network infrastructure from physical threats.

> Being responsible for your data does not guarantee its confidentiality. You must actively implement security measures like data encryption, key management, and data access policies to meet internal and regulatory compliance requirements (like HIPAA or GDPR).

These examples reinforce a core principle of the shared responsibility model: moving from IaaS to PaaS or SaaS reduces operational overhead, but it never eliminates the customer's responsibility for protecting data and managing user access.

Bringing It All Together

Choosing the right cloud service type depends on your needs:

- Do you want full control over your infrastructure?
- Do you want a platform to build on without worrying about the infrastructure?
- Do you want a ready-made software service?

Understanding the shared responsibility model ensures that you know exactly where your responsibilities lie. This knowledge will help you avoid surprises, for example, by reminding you that securing a VM is your responsibility in the IaaS model. Table 4-5 summarizes where responsibilities lie for each of the three service categories.

Table 4-5. Summary of the shared responsibility model for IaaS, PaaS, and SaaS

Feature	IaaS	PaaS	SaaS
Analogy	Owning a car	Renting a car	Using a rideshare service
Use case	Azure Virtual Machines	App Service Azure SQL Azure Functions	Microsoft 365 Dynamics 365 Azure DevOps Services
Control	Full control over infrastructure	Focus on apps and data	Minimal control; focus on usage
Responsibility split	Customer assumes more responsibilities	Balanced	Microsoft assumes more responsibilities

Summary

This chapter explained the shared responsibility model, which defines how security and operational duties are divided between the CSP (e.g. Microsoft) and the customer.

The CSP is always responsible for securing the physical infrastructure and maintaining the underlying cloud platform. Customers are always responsible for protecting their data, including encryption and compliance, and for managing user identities and access permissions.

You also learned that responsibilities shift depending on the cloud service types:

- With IaaS, customers manage most components above the virtualization layer.
- With PaaS, the CSP manages the operating system and runtime, while customers manage their applications and data.
- With SaaS, the CSP handles most technical operations, and customers focus primarily on user access and data usage policies.

Up next is Chapter 5, which will introduce the fundamental ways in which cloud services can be structured: public, private, hybrid, and multi-cloud. You'll learn the characteristics, benefits, and trade-offs of each model, and this knowledge will provide useful context for understanding how organizations strategically adopt Microsoft Azure in their IT environments.

Chapter 4 Quiz

To check your answers, please refer to the "Chapter 4 Answer Key" on page 301.

1. Your team needs to deploy virtual machines and be responsible for managing the operating system, middleware, and network configurations for your applications.

   Which cloud service model is the most suitable for your requirement?

   A. IaaS

   B. PaaS

   C. SaaS

2. Your organization is considering moving its workloads to Azure. Management wants to know who is responsible for maintaining the physical servers, storage devices, and networking equipment on Azure.

   Who is responsible for maintaining those components?

   A. The customer

   B. The cloud service provider

   C. Both the customer and the cloud service provider

3. Your company wants to deploy an email solution where the provider manages the application, updates, infrastructure, and security. The objective is for the company to have the least possible operational responsibility.

   What should you use?

   A. IaaS

   B. PaaS

   C. SaaS

CHAPTER 5
Cloud Models

In this chapter, you'll learn about the foundational categories of cloud environments, often referred to as *cloud models*.

If you're already familiar with this topic, you can skip ahead to Part II.

What Are Cloud Models?

Cloud models define how computing resources, such as servers, storage, and applications, are deployed, managed, and delivered in the cloud. These models dictate the level of access, control, and ownership of the infrastructure and services provided.

The main types of cloud models are:

- Public
- Private
- Hybrid
- Multi-cloud

Each cloud model has unique characteristics and deployment scenarios. Let's look at each model in detail.

Public Cloud

Public cloud, as the name suggests, is a computing service that is made available to the general public over the internet. Typically, public cloud services and resources are built, managed, and controlled by a third-party cloud provider. With public cloud, anyone seeking cloud services can access and use these resources and services based on the access privileges granted to them. Table 5-1 compares the top three public cloud providers.

Microsoft Azure is a prime example of a public cloud provider. Azure owns and operates the underlying infrastructure, allowing individuals or organizations to easily subscribe and onboard to the service with a credit card transaction.

Table 5-1. Comparison of the top three public cloud providers

Feature / provider	Microsoft Azure	Amazon Web Services (AWS)	Google Cloud Platform (GCP)
Compute services	Virtual Machines, Azure App Service, Azure Kubernetes Service	EC2 (Elastic Compute Cloud), Elastic Beanstalk, EKS (Elastic Kubernetes Service)	Compute Engine, App Engine, GKE (Google Kubernetes Engine)
Storage services	Blob Storage, Disk Storage, Files	S3 (Simple Storage Service), EBS (Elastic Block Store), Glacier	Cloud Storage, Persistent Disk, Cloud Filestore
Database services	Azure SQL Database, Cosmos DB, Azure Database for PostgreSQL/ MySQL	RDS, DynamoDB, Aurora	Cloud SQL, Cloud Firestore, Bigtable
AI & machine learning	Foundry Tools, Azure Machine Learning	SageMaker, Rekognition, Comprehend	Vertex AI Platform, AutoML
Networking	Virtual Network, Load Balancer, VPN Gateway	VPC (Virtual Private Cloud), Elastic Load Balancing, Direct Connect	VPC (Virtual Private Cloud), Cloud Load Balancing, Cloud Interconnect
Global availability	70+ regions, multiple availability zones per region	30+ regions, multiple availability zones per region	30+ regions, multiple zones per region
Typical use cases	Enterprise applications, hybrid cloud, Microsoft ecosystem integration	Web apps, big data analytics, enterprise workloads, flexible APIs	Data analytics, AI/ML workloads, app hosting, multi-cloud integration
Strengths	Strong hybrid cloud support, deep enterprise integration, extensive compliance coverage	Broadest service portfolio, mature ecosystem, global reach	Advanced AI/ML tools, data analytics, high-performance networking

The advantages of public cloud include:

Scalability
Public cloud services offer elastic scalability, allowing users to easily scale up or down their resources based on demand without up-front investment cost in hardware.

Cost-effectiveness
Public cloud offers a pay-as-you-go model, where users only pay for the resources they consume, reducing up-front costs and enabling better budget management.

Accessibility
> Public cloud services are accessible over the internet from anywhere around the world, providing flexibility for users to access resources remotely.

Reduced staffing and maintenance burden
> The cloud provider manages hardware maintenance, software updates, and security patches, reducing the need for large IT teams and allowing staff to focus on business priorities.

Enterprise-level security
> Public cloud providers like Azure implement industry-standard security controls, certifications, and continuous monitoring, giving organizations access to advanced security features that may be difficult to achieve on-premises or with private cloud.

High availability and resiliency
> Azure provides availability zones and regions to ensure fault tolerance and minimize downtime. Businesses can deploy resources across multiple zones or regions to maintain continuous operations even during localized failures.

Global reach
> Public cloud providers typically operate data centers across multiple regions worldwide, offering users the ability to deploy resources closer to their target audience for improved performance and latency.

Innovation and agility
> Public cloud providers continuously innovate by introducing new services and features, allowing users to quickly adopt and leverage the latest technologies to drive innovation within their organizations.

Private Cloud

In many respects, a private cloud represents a natural progression from a traditional corporate data center. A traditional corporate data center is a facility owned and operated by a company to house its servers, storage, networking, and applications. It requires significant up-front investment, ongoing maintenance, and manual management of hardware and software.

Private clouds build on this concept but introduce virtualization, automation, and cloud management tools to improve resource utilization, scalability, and operational efficiency. The concept of a "private cloud" refers to IT services delivered exclusively for use by a single organization, typically over private networks or secure connections.

Typically, a private cloud is built on privately owned hardware and networking infrastructure. The infrastructure can be hosted on-premises or by a third-party provider, but it is dedicated solely to the organization that owns it. Examples include private cloud solutions built on OpenStack, VMware, or other enterprise cloud platforms.

While private clouds offer greater control, enhanced security, and customizable configurations, they also introduce higher up-front costs, operational complexity, and a need for specialized IT skills. Compared to public cloud services, private clouds can be less flexible for smaller organizations and often have limited scalability, as resource expansion requires additional hardware or capacity planning.

Microsoft Azure offers hybrid and private cloud solutions such as Azure Local, which enables customers to run cloud-like services on their own hardware and specialized clouds with restricted access like government networks. We'll discuss Azure Local in more detail later in this chapter.

The advantages of private cloud include:

Enhanced security
Private clouds allow organizations to implement customized security policies, access controls, and compliance measures tailored to their specific requirements. However, being on-premises or in a privately owned cloud does not automatically make a system more secure. In fact, public cloud providers like Azure typically maintain robust, industry-standard security certifications, managed protections, and automated monitoring that can surpass what many organizations can achieve on their own. Private clouds are best suited for organizations that need strict control over sensitive data or regulatory compliance, but achieving strong security requires significant expertise, resources, and ongoing management.

Customization and control
Private cloud environments provide organizations with complete control over their infrastructure, allowing for customized configurations, resource allocation, and management tailored to specific business needs.

Compliance requirements
Private clouds are ideal for industries with stringent compliance requirements, such as healthcare, finance, and government, as private clouds offer greater control over data residency, privacy, and regulatory compliance.

Predictable costs
Private clouds often involve higher up-front costs than public clouds but can provide predictable ongoing costs over time, as organizations have full visibility and control over resource usage and expenditures.

Isolation and privacy
> Private clouds offer isolation from other organizations, ensuring data privacy and minimizing the risk of unauthorized access or data breaches. This can be crucial for organizations handling sensitive or proprietary information.

Right now, you might be wondering if it's possible to blend public cloud and private cloud in one environment. The answer is a resounding "yes." In the next section, you'll learn about combining public and private clouds in the hybrid cloud model.

Hybrid Cloud

A *hybrid cloud* is a computing environment that combines elements of both public and private clouds, enabling the sharing of data and applications between them. This seamless integration offers flexibility and optimization of existing infrastructure, enhancing security and compliance. Various strategies can be employed to integrate public and private cloud resources. For instance, in a hybrid cloud environment, an organization can augment its current private cloud infrastructure to accommodate sudden spikes in computing demand by dynamically deploying additional resources to the public cloud as required.

Hybrid cloud can also enhance security by allowing organizations to selectively deploy services based on their security and compliance requirements. For example, organizations can choose to retain certain services within their private cloud environment while selectively deploying resources on their public cloud, thereby adding an extra layer of security and control.

> A hybrid cloud is a unified computing environment that connects public cloud (such as Azure) with on-premises infrastructure (including traditional data centers and private cloud platforms). In a hybrid cloud solution, organizations combine public and private cloud resources to meet their unique business and technical requirements.
>
> Azure plays a central role in enabling hybrid deployments by providing services and tools that seamlessly integrate these resources. Solutions such as Azure Arc, Azure Local, and Azure VPN/ExpressRoute allow businesses to extend Azure services, manage resources consistently, and run applications across both on-premises and cloud environments, creating a unified and flexible hybrid architecture.

The advantages of hybrid cloud include:

Flexibility
 Hybrid cloud offers the flexibility to leverage both public and private cloud environments, empowering organizations to choose the most suitable platform for each workload or application based on factors like performance, security, and compliance requirements.

Scalability
 With hybrid cloud, organizations can scale their infrastructure dynamically by seamlessly extending workloads between public and private clouds as needed, ensuring optimal resource utilization and cost-efficiency.

Data sovereignty
 Hybrid cloud enables organizations to maintain control over sensitive data by keeping it within their private cloud while still benefiting from the scalability and global reach of public cloud services for less sensitive workloads.

Disaster recovery and business continuity
 Hybrid cloud provides robust disaster recovery and business continuity solutions by replicating critical data and workloads across multiple cloud environments, ensuring resilience and minimizing downtime in the event of a disaster or outage.

Cost optimization
 Hybrid cloud allows organizations to optimize costs by leveraging public cloud resources for transient or seasonal workloads while retaining on-premises infrastructure for baseline or sensitive workloads, helping to balance performance and cost-effectiveness.

Innovation and agility
 Hybrid cloud enables organizations to take advantage of the latest innovations and services offered by public cloud providers while maintaining control over core business applications and data in their private cloud, fostering innovation and agility.

Up to this point, we've explored the three primary cloud models. However, there's a burgeoning fourth model on the rise: multi-cloud. We'll look at this next.

Multi-Cloud

The multi-cloud model involves using multiple cloud services from different providers to meet diverse organizational requirements. By adopting a multi-cloud approach, organizations can steer clear of vendor lock-in while optimizing performance and bolstering reliability.

Many organizations embrace the multi-cloud strategy to tap into a broader range of services from multiple cloud providers, streamline migrations between providers, and enhance redundancy and flexibility. However, proficient management of resources and security across multiple platforms is crucial to ensure peak performance and reliability.

In a multi-cloud solution, organizations use services from multiple cloud providers to avoid vendor lock-in, optimize performance, and improve reliability. Azure supports multi-cloud strategies through tools like Azure Arc, which enables centralized management and governance of resources across different cloud platforms, and Azure Lighthouse, which allows service providers to manage multiple customer environments securely. By integrating with other clouds, Azure helps organizations maintain flexibility, enforce consistent policies, and monitor workloads across a diverse cloud ecosystem.

The advantages of multi-cloud include:

Vendor flexibility
Multi-cloud allows organizations to select the best services from multiple cloud providers, avoiding vendor lock-in and ensuring they have access to the most suitable solutions for their specific needs.

Risk mitigation
Distributing workloads across multiple cloud providers can reduce the risk of service outages when applications are designed for portability and cross-cloud failover.

Performance optimization
Multi-cloud enables organizations to optimize performance by deploying workloads in cloud regions closest to their end users, reducing latency and improving overall user experience.

Cost optimization
Multi-cloud strategies can help organizations optimize costs by leveraging competitive pricing and discounts from multiple providers, as well as by matching workloads to the most cost-effective cloud services.

Compliance and data residency
Multi-cloud allows organizations to adhere to data residency requirements and compliance regulations by storing data in specific regions or with providers that meet regulatory standards.

Innovation and agility
Multi-cloud fosters innovation by allowing organizations to take advantage of unique services and features offered by different cloud providers, enabling them to stay at the forefront of technology and quickly adopt new tools and capabilities.

When determining the most suitable cloud model for your organization, it's valuable to have handy a quick overview of the pros and cons of each model. The following section provides a chart comparing the four cloud models that we've discussed so far.

Comparison of Cloud Models

Table 5-2 highlights a few key comparative aspects of the four primary cloud models.

Table 5-2. Comparison of cloud models

Feature	Public cloud	Private cloud	Hybrid cloud	Multi-cloud
Definition	Cloud resources provided by third-party providers and accessible to the general public	Cloud resources dedicated to a single organization, hosted either on-site or by a third-party provider	Combination of public and private clouds that allows data and applications to move between them	Use of multiple cloud services from different providers
Ownership	Third-party providers (e.g., Azure, AWS, GCP)	Single organization (can be hosted on-site or off-site by a third party)	Combination of third-party and single organization	Multiple third-party providers
Accessibility	Public, open to anyone with internet access	Restricted, only accessible by the specific organization	Mixed, with controlled access based on deployment and policy	Mixed, depending on each cloud's configuration and policy
Scalability	High scalability and flexibility; resources can be easily scaled up or down	High, but within the limits of the owned infrastructure	High, combining the scalability of public cloud with private control	Very high, leveraging the strengths of multiple providers
Cost	Pay-as-you-go model, which can be cost-effective for variable workloads	Higher initial and ongoing costs due to dedicated infrastructure and maintenance	Variable, depending on the mix of public and private resources	Variable and potentially higher due to multiple service agreements
Control	Limited control over infrastructure and policies but can be customized for specific needs	Complete control over infrastructure, security, and compliance	Balanced control, with some aspects managed privately and others publicly	Constrained by each provider's policies but can be customized for specific needs
Security	Standardized security measures, suitable for most needs	High security, customizable to meet specific requirements	High, combining public cloud flexibility with private cloud security	Varies, depending on individual cloud providers' security measures

Feature	Public cloud	Private cloud	Hybrid cloud	Multi-cloud
Use cases	Web hosting, application development and testing, big data analytics	Highly sensitive data processing such as in financial services, healthcare, government agencies	Disaster recovery, data integration, and application portability	Avoiding vendor lock-in, optimizing performance, enhancing reliability
Examples	Microsoft Azure, Amazon Web Services (AWS), Google Cloud Platform (GCP)	On-site data centers or dedicated third-party hosted clouds like OpenStack	Microsoft Azure Stack, AWS Outposts, Google Anthos	Using Azure for AI, AWS for serverless computing, and GCP for data storage

Before wrapping up this chapter, let's review three essential Azure services that exemplify the cloud models we've just explored.

Key Microsoft Azure Offerings

Let's have a look at each of these Azure offerings in more detail in light of an organization's chosen cloud model:

- Azure VMware Solution
- Azure Arc
- Azure Local

Azure VMware Solution

Azure VMware Solution offers a seamless pathway for organizations currently using VMware in a private cloud infrastructure to transition to a public or hybrid cloud environment. This solution enables organizations to run VMware workloads natively on Azure, seamlessly facilitating the extension or migration of their existing on-premises VMware environments to Azure without the need to refactor applications.

The key features of Azure VMware Solution (*https://oreil.ly/fiLAT*) include:

Seamless integration
    Extend or migrate on-premises VMware environments to Azure while maintaining consistent operations with existing VMware tools.

Scalability
    Scale VMware environments on-demand using Azure's global infrastructure.

Hybrid capabilities
    Integrate with Azure services like Microsoft Entra ID (formerly Azure Active Directory), Azure NetApp Files, and Azure Backup.

High availability
: Take advantage of Azure's infrastructure to ensure high availability and disaster recovery capabilities.

Enhanced security
: Utilize Azure's security and compliance features to protect VMware workloads.

Azure Arc

Azure Arc is a unified platform that extends Azure management, governance, and services to any infrastructure, including on premises datacenters, private clouds, edge environments, and other public clouds. You'll learn more about Azure Arc in Chapter 15's discussion of managing hybrid and multi-cloud environments. For now, know that Azure Arc provides a unified management platform to allow organizations to manage resources consistently across various cloud infrastructures.

The key features of Azure Arc (*https://oreil.ly/RdvC8*) include:

Unified management
: Take advantage of centralized management of resources across hybrid and multi-cloud environments.

Azure services anywhere
: Deploy and manage Azure services (such as Azure SQL Managed Instance and Azure Arc-enabled Kubernetes) on supported on premises, edge, or multi cloud infrastructure using Azure Arc.

Policy and governance
: Apply Azure policies and governance across all environments to ensure compliance and security.

Integration with Azure security
: Use Microsoft Defender for Cloud and Microsoft Sentinel for comprehensive security management.

Azure Local

Azure Local (*https://oreil.ly/vG7Pl*) is Microsoft's distributed infrastructure solution that extends Azure capabilities to customer-owned environments, creating a true hybrid cloud experience. It allows organizations to deploy and run Azure services (like VMs, AKS, and other Arc-enabled services) on their own validated hardware, on-premises or at the edge.

The key features of Azure Local include:

Hyper-converged infrastructure
   Combines storage, networking, and compute into a highly available and scalable cluster, eliminating the need for separate, siloed hardware setups.

Hybrid capabilities
   Enables seamless integration with Azure for backup, site recovery, and cloud-based monitoring.

Scalability
   Permits easy scaling by adding more nodes to the cluster.

Enhanced security
   Allows leveraging of Azure's security features and compliance certifications.

These offerings provide robust tools and services, empowering organizations to achieve flexible, scalable, and secure hybrid cloud solutions while maintaining control over their infrastructure and meeting regulatory requirements.

Summary

In this chapter, we explored the primary cloud models (public cloud, private cloud, and hybrid cloud) that organizations can adopt to fulfill their growing IT needs and infrastructure requirements.

Additionally, you learned about the emerging multi-cloud model, which is gaining prominence. I also presented a practical chart highlighting the distinct characteristics of each cloud model for easy comparison. Wrapping up this chapter, we examined three Azure offerings: Azure VMware Solution, Azure Arc, and Azure Local.

In the next chapter, you'll learn about the benefits of using cloud services.

Chapter 5 Quiz

To check your answers, please refer to the "Chapter 5 Answer Key" on page 301.

1. A hospital must store patient data on-premises to comply with regulatory requirements but wants to run analytics and AI workloads in Azure for research and operational efficiency.

   Which cloud model should the hospital use?

   A. Private cloud

   B. Public cloud

   C. Hybrid cloud

   D. Multi-cloud

2. A financial services company must comply with strict data privacy regulations. It wants full and exclusive control over its cloud environment, including security and compliance, even if this level of control is expensive.

   Which cloud model should the company use?

   A. Private cloud

   B. Public cloud

   C. Hybrid cloud

   D. Multi-cloud

3. A global ecommerce platform needs to rapidly scale resources during high-traffic periods, deploy new services quickly, and handle unpredictable workloads efficiently with minimal infrastructure management.

   Which cloud model should be used in this scenario?

   A. Private cloud

   B. Public cloud

   C. Hybrid cloud

   D. Multi-cloud

PART II
Azure Architecture and Services

In the second part of this study guide, you'll dive into the core architecture and services of Microsoft Azure, building directly on the foundational concepts to prepare you for the AZ-900 Azure Fundamentals exam. Mastering these elements will help you understand how Azure is structured, what services it offers, and how they work together to deliver secure, scalable cloud solutions.

- Chapter 6, "Introduction to Microsoft Azure"
- Chapter 7, "Core Architectural Components of Azure"
- Chapter 8, "The Azure Management Infrastructure"
- Chapter 9, "Azure Compute Services"
- Chapter 10, "Azure Networking Services"
- Chapter 11, "Azure Storage Services"
- Chapter 12, "Azure Identity, Access, and Security"

CHAPTER 6
Introduction to Microsoft Azure

Congratulations! After five chapters of building your foundational knowledge of cloud computing, you're now ready to dive into the main act: *Microsoft Azure*. All the concepts you've learned so far have set the stage for understanding Azure's capabilities and services. This groundwork will be crucial not only for mastering Azure itself but also for achieving success on the AZ-900 Azure Fundamentals exam.

Microsoft Azure is a comprehensive cloud computing platform that enables organizations to build, deploy, and manage applications and services across a global network of datacenters. It offers a full spectrum of solutions, including infrastructure as a service (IaaS), platform as a service (PaaS), and software as a service (SaaS), supporting needs ranging from computing, storage, and networking to databases, analytics, AI, IoT, and more.

Azure's ever-expanding catalog of services empowers developers, IT professionals, and businesses of all sizes to innovate and scale quickly. Its frequent updates and breadth of offerings ensure that Azure remains at the forefront of cloud technology, helping organizations achieve more with agility, reliability, and efficiency.

In this chapter, we'll explore:

- A brief history of Microsoft Azure
- The benefits of Microsoft Azure
- How to get started with Microsoft Azure
- Azure accounts versus Azure subscriptions
- The different types of Azure subscriptions
- How to create a free Azure account

- How to view your subscription details once your setup is complete
- How to explore the Azure product catalog

With your foundation in place, let's begin exploring Azure and see how all the pieces fit together in the cloud.

A Brief History of Microsoft Azure (Optional Reading)

Although you won't be tested on Azure's history on the AZ-900 exam, this section is included for context and interest to help you appreciate how Azure evolved into the robust platform it is today. Feel free to skip it if you're short on time!

Originally launched as Windows Azure, Microsoft Azure has undergone a remarkable evolution since its inception, keeping pace with the rapid growth of cloud computing.

Figure 6-1 shows a timeline of the key milestones in Azure's journey.

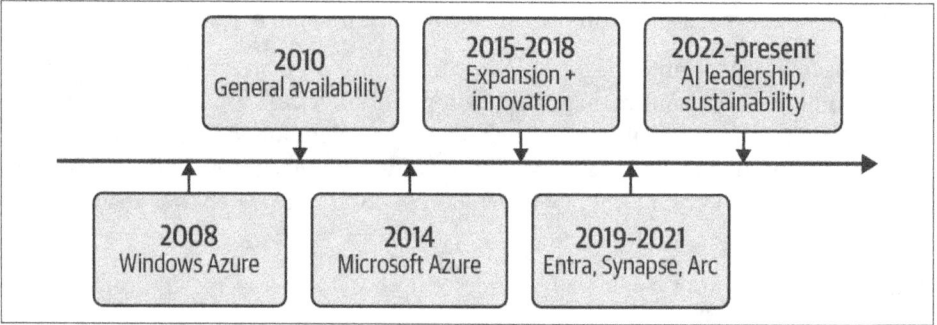

Figure 6-1. A timeline of the key milestones in Azure's journey

2008: The Announcement of Windows Azure

In October 2008, at the Professional Developers Conference (PDC), Microsoft unveiled Windows Azure. It was introduced as a platform for building and hosting applications in Microsoft's datacenters, marking Microsoft's entry into the burgeoning cloud market.

2010: General Availability of Windows Azure

On February 1, 2010, Windows Azure became generally available. Early offerings included PaaS, aimed at helping developers build and deploy applications without managing the underlying infrastructure.

Key initial features included:

- Azure App Service (formerly Web Roles and Worker Roles) for web applications and background processing
- Azure Storage, including blob storage, tables, and queues
- SQL Azure, a cloud-based relational database service

2014: Rebranding to Microsoft Azure

In 2014, Microsoft rebranded Windows Azure to *Microsoft Azure*, signaling its transition from a Windows-centric platform to a cloud service that embraced open source technologies, multiple programming languages, and cross-platform compatibility.

This shift aligned with the launch of an IaaS offering. This broadened Azure's appeal to enterprises needing to deploy virtual machines and other traditional infrastructure in the cloud.

2015–2018: Expansion and Innovation

This period saw explosive growth for Azure in the services it could provide and its global adoption. Here are some areas of focus during that period:

AI and machine learning
    Introduction of Azure Machine Learning and Cognitive Services for developers to build AI-powered applications

Hybrid cloud leadership
    Launch of Azure Stack, extending Azure's capabilities to on-premises environments

Container technology
    Support for Docker containers and Kubernetes through Azure Kubernetes Service (AKS)

Global datacenters
    Expansion to more than 50 regions worldwide, surpassing competitors in geographic coverage

2019–2021: Microsoft Entra, Azure Synapse Analytics, and Azure Arc

Microsoft Azure matured into a full-fledged cloud ecosystem during these years as it expanded into the following areas:

Data and analytics
    Launch of Azure Synapse Analytics for big data and AI insights

Identity and security
> Strengthening cloud security with Microsoft Entra (formerly Azure Active Directory)

Hybrid cloud innovation
> Introduction of Azure Arc, allowing seamless management across on-premises, multi-cloud, and edge environments

2022–Present: AI Leadership and Sustainability

Azure has continued to lead in innovation while focusing on environmental sustainability. Recent years have brought:

AI integration
> A partnership with OpenAI, including hosting advanced AI models like ChatGPT, solidifies Azure as the leading cloud platform for cutting-edge AI and machine learning.

Sustainability commitments
> Microsoft (*https://oreil.ly/uo06s*) has pledged to run Azure entirely on renewable energy and achieve carbon negativity by 2030.

Benefits of Microsoft Azure

In Chapter 2, you learned about the general benefits of cloud computing. Let's take a moment to highlight the specific benefits that Microsoft Azure provides.

Cost Savings and Efficiency

One of the key advantages of Azure is its cost-effectiveness, driven by the shift from capital expenditures (CapEx) in on-premises environments to operational expenditures (OpEx) in the cloud. Azure operates on a pay-as-you-go pricing model, which allows organizations to scale resources based on demand, paying only for what they use. This eliminates the need for large up-front investments in infrastructure, reducing capital expenses. Azure's economies of scale offer competitive pricing, further lowering the total cost of ownership for cloud solutions. By optimizing resource utilization, Azure helps businesses maximize IT budgets and improve efficiency.

You'll learn more about this in Chapter 13.

Scalability, Elasticity, and Flexibility

Azure delivers powerful scalability, elasticity, and flexibility, allowing organizations to adapt instantly to changing demands while optimizing performance and costs.

Scalability
>Easily add more VMs to handle business growth—such as scaling from 10 to 100 VMs during a product launch—and ensure that your application stays responsive without delays.

Elasticity
>Automatically reduce VMs during off-peak hours (e.g., drop from 50 to 5 VMs overnight) to save costs and then scale back up seamlessly when traffic returns. This is a perfect solution for ecommerce sites or seasonal workloads.

With a global network of datacenters, Azure enables elastic scaling across compute, storage, and networking resources, maintaining high performance even during traffic spikes or geographic expansions.

Azure also offers unmatched flexibility through a broad ecosystem of services and tools:

- Build web apps using your preferred language: ASP.NET, Python, Java, or Node.js.
- Deploy and manage containers at scale with AKS.
- Run code without managing servers using Azure Functions (serverless).
- Seamlessly connect on-premises systems with the cloud via Azure Arc and Azure Hybrid Benefit for a unified hybrid experience.

This combination empowers businesses to innovate faster, respond to market changes, and maintain control—whether modernizing legacy systems or building cloud-native solutions.

Agility and Innovation

Azure accelerates time to market by enabling organizations to rapidly innovate. Developers can leverage Azure's extensive suite of tools and services to quickly build, deploy, and scale applications without managing the underlying infrastructure. GitHub and Azure DevOps services streamline the software development lifecycle, fostering collaboration and allowing teams to deliver high-quality software with speed. By supporting a culture of innovation, Azure helps businesses stay competitive and capitalize on emerging opportunities.

Reliability and Performance

Azure guarantees high availability and reliability, thanks to its extensive global datacenter network. Built-in redundancy and failover capabilities ensure resilience during outages, while Azure's SLAs guarantee uptime for core services. Azure's global footprint allows businesses to deploy resources closer to their users, reducing latency and enhancing the user experience.

Security and Compliance

Azure prioritizes security with a comprehensive portfolio that includes identity and access management, encryption, threat detection, and compliance certifications. Organizations can protect data and applications from evolving threats and ensure compliance with industry standards such as GDPR, HIPAA, SOC 1, SOC 2, and ISO 27001. By leveraging Azure's security capabilities, businesses can strengthen their security posture and mitigate risks associated with cloud adoption.

Ecosystem, Integration, and Interoperability

Azure boasts a vibrant ecosystem of partners, developers, and communities. It seamlessly integrates with Microsoft products, such as Microsoft Entra and Microsoft 365, as well as third-party solutions, allowing organizations to extend functionality and leverage existing investments. Azure provides a unified platform for building integrated solutions that drive business value and enable organizations to innovate faster.

Global Presence and Hybrid Capabilities

With over 70 regions worldwide, Azure ensures extensive coverage and compliance with data residency requirements. This global presence allows organizations to deploy resources closer to users, enhancing availability, fault tolerance, and reducing latency. Azure also offers robust hybrid capabilities, enabling seamless integration of on-premises infrastructure with cloud resources. Azure Arc extends management and governance across on-premises, multi-cloud, and edge environments, allowing organizations to maintain consistency and control over their entire infrastructure.

AI, Machine Learning, and IoT

Azure offers powerful AI and machine learning services to help organizations harness intelligence in their applications. Microsoft Foundry, Azure Machine Learning, Azure Databricks, and Microsoft Fabric provide tools to build custom models, extract insights from unstructured data, and train deep learning models. Additionally, Azure IoT Hub and Azure IoT Central offer comprehensive platforms for managing IoT devices, with end-to-end security provided by Azure Sphere.

Getting Started with Azure

Before you can dive into using Azure's powerful features, you'll need an Azure account and an Azure subscription.

The two terms *Azure account* and *Azure subscription* are often used interchangeably. However, they refer to distinct components in the Azure ecosystem. Let's demystify them.

What Is an Azure Account?

An *Azure account* is your identity for accessing Azure services. It's tied to a specific Microsoft identity, such as a personal Microsoft account (e.g., Outlook.com) or a work/school account from Microsoft Entra ID.

An Azure account acts as the primary identity and billing account for managing Azure subscriptions and resources. It lets you:

- Sign in to the Azure portal
- Manage multiple subscriptions associated with the account
- Access other Microsoft services, like Office 365 or Visual Studio, if they're enabled

What Is an Azure Subscription?

An *Azure subscription* is a logical container that organizes and provides access to Azure resources. It defines the customer's billing relationship, access permissions, and resource usage limits.

The key features of an Azure subscription include:

Billing
Each subscription is tied to a specific billing model, such as free trial, pay-as-you-go, or Enterprise Agreement. (You'll learn more about the Azure subscription types in the following section.)

Resource management
All Azure resources (VMs, storage, etc.) must reside within a subscription.

Access control
Permissions for users and groups to manage resources are assigned at the subscription level using RBAC.

Usage boundaries
Subscriptions have quotas or limits on resource consumption, like a maximum number of VMs or storage accounts.

Microsoft offers many Azure subscription types, and I'll explain some of the main ones a bit later in this chapter.

What Is the Relationship Between an Azure Account and a Subscription?

An Azure account is like a "parent" identity under which one or more subscriptions exist. Thus, a single Azure account can have multiple subscriptions, each with its own billing and resource management.

The distinction between Azure accounts and subscriptions affects many areas of business, including:

Billing segregation
  Multiple subscriptions under one account help separate billing for different projects or departments.

Access control
  Different teams or users can have specific roles and permissions at the subscription level.

Scalability
  Organizations can scale by adding subscriptions as needed for different workloads or environments.

By understanding this distinction, you can better manage resources, costs, and access within Azure.

Azure Subscription Types

Now that you understand the purpose of subscriptions at a high level, let's learn about the different types of Azure subscriptions that are available.

Free trial

Here's what you need to know about the free trial subscription (*https://oreil.ly/yJl-v*):

- Ideal for first-time users who want to explore Azure without up-front costs
- Includes $200 in credits for the first 30 days
- Provides access to 20+ popular services free for 12 months (new customers only)
- Provides access to 65+ always-free services with monthly usage limits
- After 30 days or upon exhausting your credits (whichever comes first), allows upgrading to pay-as-you-go pricing to continue using Azure

Pay-as-you-go

Here are the basics of the pay-as-you-go plan (*https://oreil.ly/Irs13*):

- Perfect for individuals or businesses needing cost flexibility
- No up-front fees, with payment only for the services actually used
- No termination fees, offering complete financial control

Enterprise Agreement

Microsoft Enterprise Agreement (EA) subscriptions (*https://oreil.ly/Uh9uF*) entail the following:

- Tailored for large organizations with substantial Azure usage (typically 500+ users/devices)
- Offer volume discounts and enterprise-level support for bulk purchases (custom terms negotiated via Microsoft Sales)
- Include features like Azure Prepayment for up-front commitments and centralized management through the EA portal

Microsoft Customer Agreement

The EA is Microsoft's legacy volume-licensing model, designed for large-scale commitments but increasingly outdated for today's agile cloud environments. For new customers, Microsoft strongly recommends transitioning to the Microsoft Customer Agreement (MCA) (*https://oreil.ly/w6wVg*) for the following reasons:

- MCA is a flexible, perpetual agreement that simplifies Azure procurement, billing, and management without rigid terms or minimum spends.
- It emphasizes digital onboarding, transparent pricing, and seamless integration across Microsoft products, making it ideal for businesses of all sizes that are adopting cloud-first strategies.
- It future-proofs your Azure investments while unlocking modern tools like enhanced cost analytics and unified invoicing.

Azure for Students/Azure for Students Starter

There are special subscriptions (*https://oreil.ly/klyoO*) available for certain students with verified academic credentials. Azure for Students is for full-time university students, and high school or secondary students can take advantage of Azure for Students Starter.

Here are the features of Azure for Students:

- Includes $100 in credits and free access to services
- Provides access to 20+ popular services free for 12 months
- Provides access to 65+ always-free services with monthly usage limits
- Offers the full catalog of services up to the free amounts
- Does not require a credit card

Azure for Students Starter also does not require a credit card and grants access to a free tier that includes Azure App Service, Azure Functions, Notification Hubs, Azure DevOps, and MySQL Database.

Microsoft Sponsorships

Finally, Microsoft chooses certain nonprofits, partners, events, and initiatives to receive sponsorships, where the recipient gets access to a certain amount of usage for a defined time period. This type of subscription:

- Is granted to organizations through special programs or grants (by email invitation only)
- Includes preallocated credits based on program eligibility

There are two types of Microsoft sponsorships:

- General information (*https://oreil.ly/P7ePc*)
- For customers already under a Microsoft EA plan (*https://oreil.ly/EtcP_*)

How to Create a Free Azure Account: A Step-by-Step Guide

In my experience, gaining hands-on practice is the key to successfully passing any Microsoft Azure certification exam, including the AZ-900 Azure Fundamentals exam. And to gain that practical experience, you'll need an active Azure account.

If you already have access to an Azure account through your workplace or another source, you're all set to dive in.

If you don't already have an Azure account, don't worry! This section will guide you through creating a free account and show you how to view your subscription details once your setup is complete.

Creating a Free Account if You're Not a Student

Once you activate your free Azure account, you'll get $200 in credits for the first 30 days to try out the Azure services mentioned in this book.

To create a free Azure account, follow these steps:

1. Navigate to Azure's free account page (*https://oreil.ly/yHi_s*) as shown in Figure 6-2.

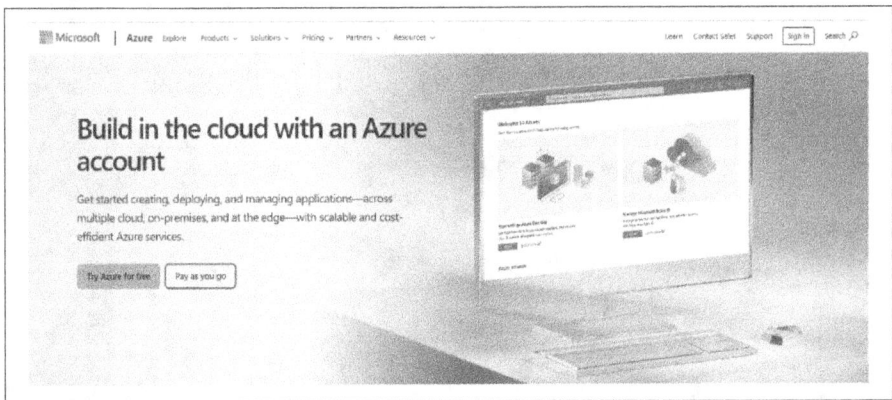

Figure 6-2. Azure's free account page (Note: The look of this landing page may be updated from time to time.)

2. Scroll down or click the "Free services" tab to see what you'll have access to once you have a free Azure account (Figure 6-3).

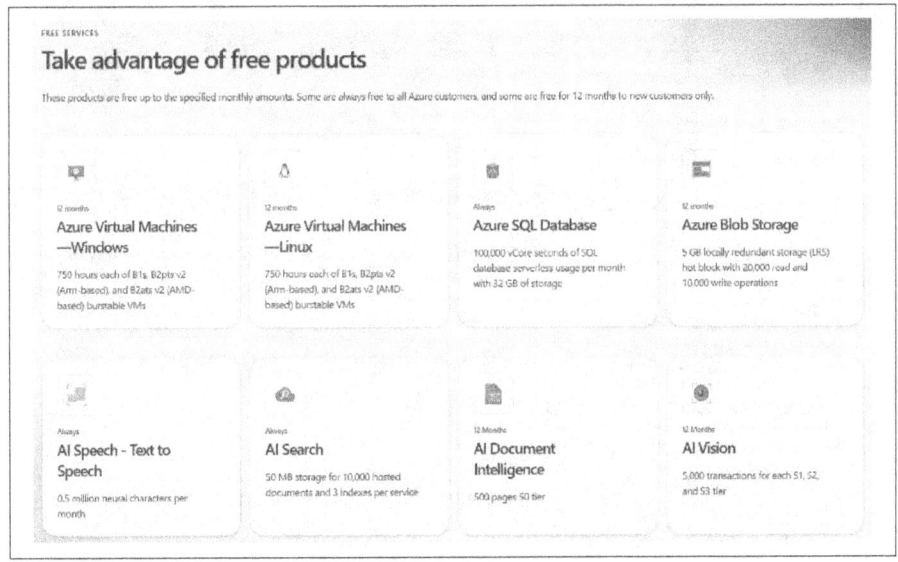

Figure 6-3. The Azure products that you can use with a free Azure subscription

3. Now, return to the top of the page and click **Try Azure for free** in the "Azure free account" tile to start creating your Azure account.

4. Sign in or create a Microsoft account, as shown in Figure 6-4:
   - If you already have a Microsoft account (e.g., from Outlook or Xbox) or a GitHub account, sign in.
   - Don't have one? Click **Create one!** and follow the prompts to set up an account.

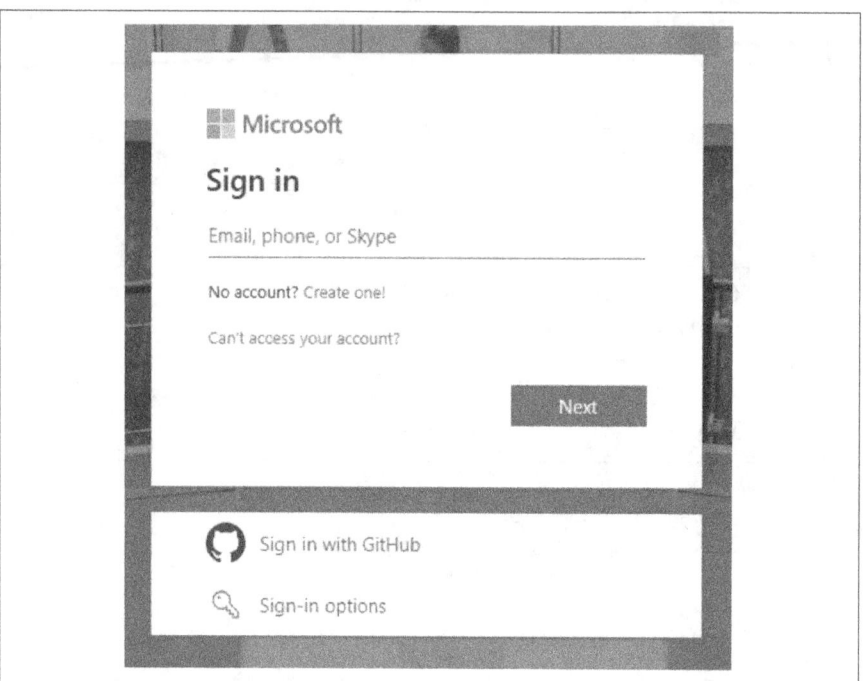

Figure 6-4. Signing in to your existing Microsoft Account or creating a new one

5. Verify your identity:
   - Provide a valid phone number to receive a verification code via SMS.
   - Enter the code on the verification page.

6. Provide your credit card information:
   - Azure requires a credit or debit card for identity verification.
   - Don't worry: you won't be charged unless you exceed the free tier or upgrade to a paid subscription.

7. Agree to the terms:
   - Review the terms and conditions and click **Agree**.
8. Activate your free account:
   - Click **Start Free**, and you'll be all set to explore Azure's free services!

Creating a Free Azure for Students Account

In the previous instructions, you're required to provide your credit card information in order to create the free Azure account. However, if you're a student, you can create a free Azure account without a credit card. Although the product is more limited in this tier, this is a great option for eligible students.

You can sign up at Azure for Students website (*https://oreil.ly/OOTcU*). Figure 6-5 shows the landing page for this free account type. To get started, click **Start free**.

Figure 6-5. The Azure for Students page (Note: The look of this landing page may be updated from time to time.)

Explore the Azure Portal

Once your Azure account is active, head over to the Azure portal (*https://oreil.ly/AXYjM*) to access all that Azure has to offer (see Figure 6-6).

The Azure portal is your main hub for deploying and managing Azure services, as shown in Figure 6-6. Familiarize yourself with the portal, learning how to navigate it, create resources, and perform basic management tasks.

In Chapter 15, you'll explore additional ways to work with Azure, including:

- Azure CLI
- Azure PowerShell
- ARM templates (JSON-based infrastructure as code)
- Bicep (simpler, declarative syntax for ARM)
- Terraform (multi-cloud infrastructure as code tool, supported in Azure)

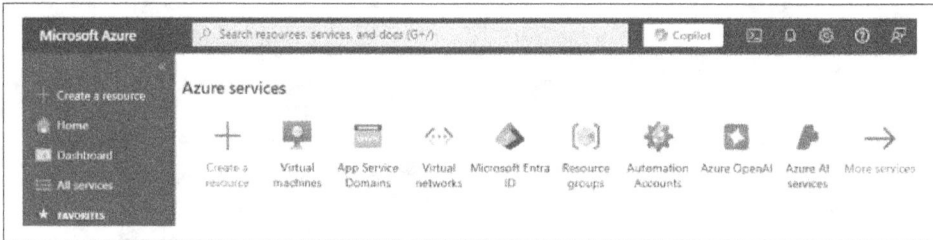

Figure 6-6. Azure portal

Upon logging in, you'll land on the Azure portal home page, which features:

Quick access
    Commonly used services, conveniently displayed at the top

Learning resources
    Links to documentation, tutorials, and other helpful materials

Additional tools
    A variety of widgets and options to customize your workspace and streamline your tasks

The Azure portal is your gateway to exploring and managing Azure's extensive cloud capabilities.

How to View Your Subscription Details

Keeping track of your Azure usage, billing, and service limits is essential for effective cloud management. By staying informed of your usage and charges, you stay in control of your budget.

Here's how to view and manage your subscription details:

1. Access the Subscriptions page, as shown in Figure 6-7:
   - Type **subscription** in the search bar at the top of the Azure portal and select the **Subscriptions** page from the dropdown.

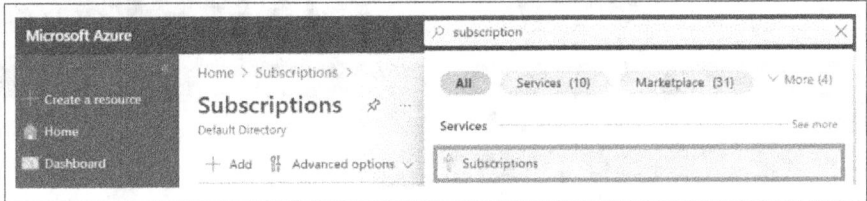

Figure 6-7. Navigating to the Subscriptions page

2. Select your subscription:
   - If you have multiple subscriptions, click on the one you wish to manage.
3. Explore the navigation bar to get key insights:
   - *Overview*: View your subscription name, ID, and current status at a glance.
   - *Cost management*: Access a cost analysis, set budgets, and configure cost alerts to monitor spending.
   - *Usage + quotas*: Check resource usage against available quotas to avoid hitting spending limits.
   - *Billing > Invoices*: Download detailed billing reports for a comprehensive breakdown of charges.

By regularly reviewing these details, you'll ensure that your subscription stays aligned with your needs and budget.

How to View the Azure Product Catalog

By now, you know that Azure offers an extensive range of products and services. But is there a way to explore everything available?

The answer is yes!

You can browse the entire Azure product catalog (*https://oreil.ly/7dmW1*) (see Figure 6-8). This catalog provides product descriptions and direct links to pricing details, helping you easily find the services you need.

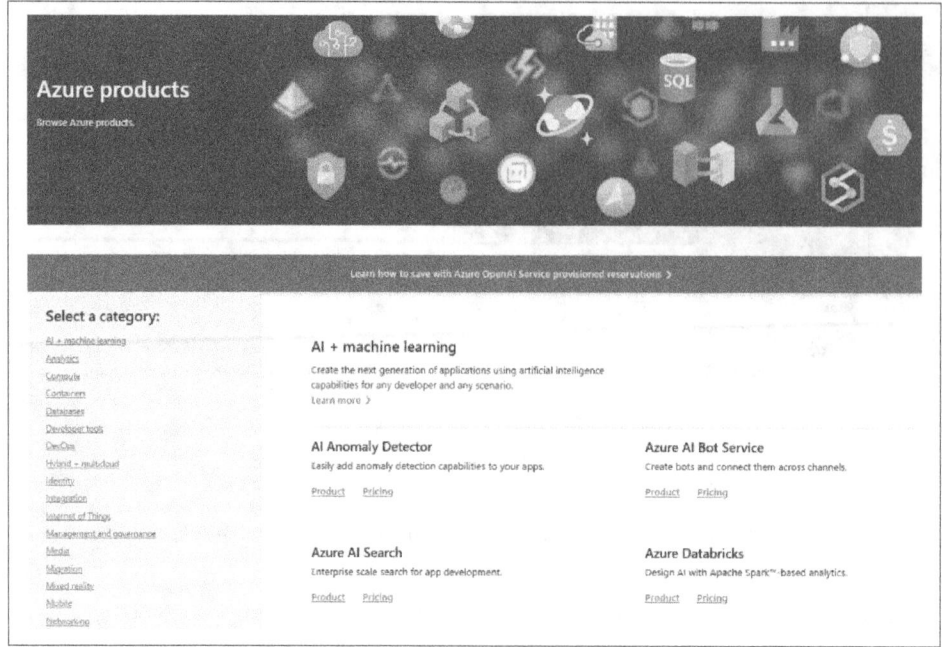

Figure 6-8. The official Azure product catalog

Summary

Now that you have a strong introduction to Microsoft Azure, the upcoming chapters will help you build a comprehensive understanding of this cloud platform by diving deeper into its powerful features and capabilities.

Here's a preview of what's coming up:

Core architectural components of Azure
  Learn about the foundational elements that make up Azure's infrastructure.

Azure management infrastructure
  Get familiar with Azure's tools for managing resources, from the portal to command-line interfaces.

Azure compute services
  Explore the compute options available in Azure, from VMs to managed services like App Services and Kubernetes.

Azure networking services
Understand networking essentials, including virtual networks, load balancing, and secure connectivity.

Azure storage services
Discover Azure's storage solutions for handling unstructured data, file storage, and more.

Azure identity, access, and security
Learn about identity and access management, along with Azure's robust security options.

Cost management in Azure
Gain insights into effectively managing and optimizing costs in Azure.

Azure governance and compliance
See how Azure supports governance and compliance to help you meet regulatory standards.

Managing and deploying Azure resources
Master the tools and best practices for deploying and managing resources in Azure.

Azure monitoring tools
Explore Azure's built-in monitoring services for ensuring performance and reliability.

Each chapter will expand on what you've learned, helping you complete your Azure Fundamentals knowledge.

Chapter 6 Quiz

To check your answers, please refer to the "Chapter 6 Answer Key" on page 302.

1. Your team wants to quickly deploy and test Azure resources through a graphical, browser-based interface without installing any software or writing code.

   Which tool should your team use?

   A. Azure CLI

   B. Azure PowerShell

   C. Azure portal

   D. ARM templates

2. Peter, who graduated from school several years ago, is preparing for the AZ-900 exam. He wants to experiment with hands-on labs using available credits instead of paying up-front.

   Which Azure subscription type would be the most suitable in this scenario?

   A. Pay-as-you-go

   B. Enterprise Agreement

   C. Free trial

   D. Azure for Students

3. Which of the following best describes the main purpose of Microsoft Entra?

   A. Web traffic management

   B. Identity and access management

   C. Virtual machine management

   D. Storage management

CHAPTER 7
Core Architectural Components of Azure

In the previous chapter, you were introduced to Microsoft Azure. Now, let's continue our journey by exploring the core architectural components of Azure.

Azure offers a suite of services that allows organizations to build, deploy, and manage applications and services through Microsoft-managed data centers.

Understanding the core architectural components of Azure and how they work together is key to preparing for the AZ-900 Azure Fundamentals exam. This foundational knowledge will also help you someday design scalable, reliable, and secure solutions.

In this chapter, we'll cover the core architectural components of Azure, which include:

- Azure datacenters
- Azure regions
- Availability zones
- Region pairs
- Sovereign regions

Let's dive in!

The Physical Infrastructure of Microsoft Azure

Azure is built on an extensive network of datacenters around the world. Each datacenter is fully equipped with racks of servers and resources supported by dedicated power, cooling, and networking infrastructure (see Figure 7-1).

Figure 7-1. Inside a Microsoft datacenter (photo credit: Microsoft (https://oreil.ly/rlvhs))

The Microsoft datacenters are highly secure. You can take a guided virtual tour of a Microsoft datacenter and learn more about the technology that powers Azure by visiting the official Microsoft site (*https://oreil.ly/sy8mY*).

Azure organizes these datacenters into regions and availability zones. This grouping enhances resiliency and reliability while ensuring that your business-critical workloads remain robust and accessible. You'll learn more about regions and availability zones in the next sections.

What Are Azure Regions?

In Azure, a *region* is a specific geographical area in the world that hosts one or more datacenters. When there's more than one datacenter, they're strategically located close to each other and interconnected via a high-speed, low-latency network. This design enables Azure to deliver services with high reliability, scalability, and performance. Azure continuously manages and optimizes resource allocation within each region to balance workloads efficiently and maintain service quality.

Azure offers an extensive network of 70+ regions worldwide (see Figure 7-2), enabling businesses to tailor solutions to meet their geographic regulatory compliance and operational requirements. You can explore an interactive map of Azure regions at the official Microsoft site (*https://oreil.ly/uWr0l*).

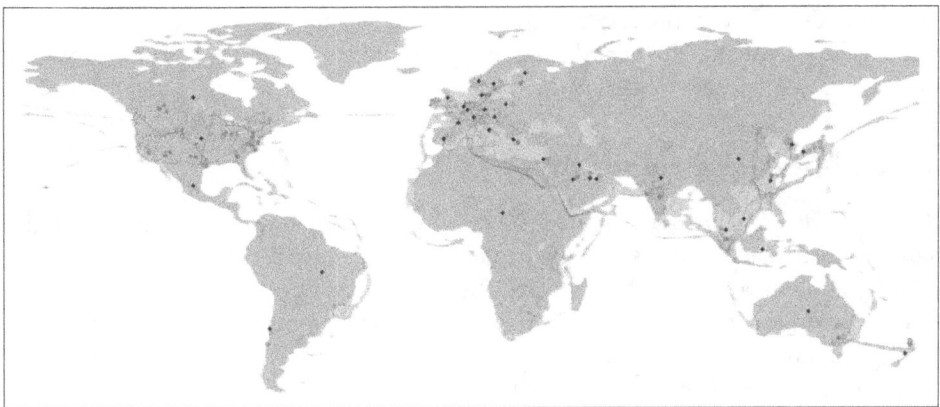

Figure 7-2. Azure's extensive network of 70+ regions worldwide

When deploying resources in Azure, choosing the right region is a critical decision that affects factors such as service availability, data residency, regulatory compliance, and latency.

Service Availability

Azure services and features aren't universally available in every region. For example, specific VM sizes, storage options, or advanced services may only be offered in select regions. It's important to verify the availability of your required services in your target region.

Data Residency and Regulatory Compliance

Azure regions play a critical role in meeting regulatory and compliance requirements. When you deploy resources in a specific region, your data stays within that region unless explicitly configured otherwise, helping you align with data residency laws.

Proximity and Latency

By selecting a region closer to your end users or your on-premises infrastructure, you can reduce latency and improve overall performance for your applications and services.

> While most Azure services are region specific and require you to select a deployment region, some are intentionally designed as *non-regional*. For example, as you'll see in Chapter 10, Azure Traffic Manager and Azure DNS are global services that operate across Azure's worldwide network and are not tied to any specific region.

Understanding Azure regions empowers you to make informed decisions about resource deployment, whether you seek to optimize for performance, meet regulatory needs, or access specialized services.

What Are Azure Availability Zones?

Azure availability zones (see Figure 7-3) are physically separated datacenters within a single region. Each zone is an independent facility equipped with its own power, cooling, and networking infrastructure. These zones are designed as isolation boundaries, ensuring that if one zone experiences a failure, the others remain operational. The zones are interconnected through high-speed, private fiber-optic networks to ensure seamless performance and low-latency communication.

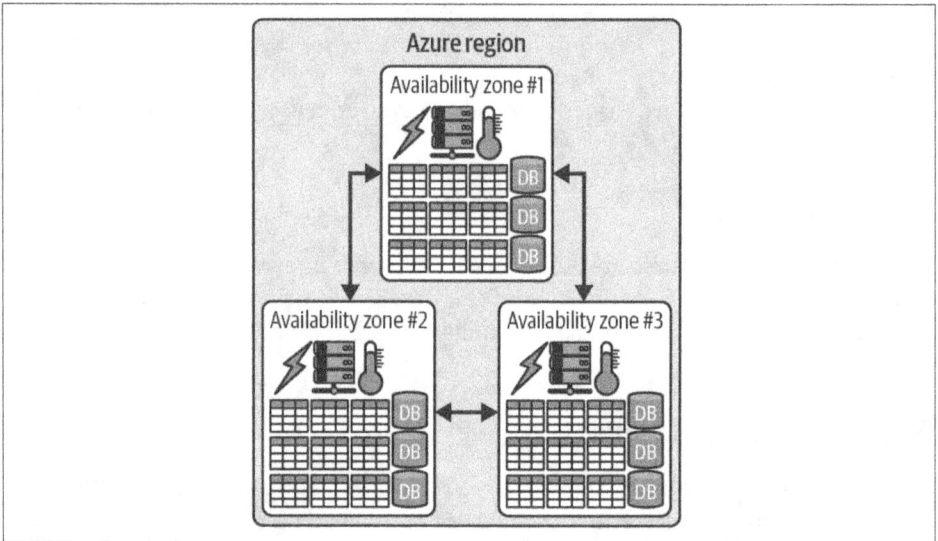

Figure 7-3. An example of three Azure availability zones in an Azure region

Key Features of Availability Zones

Let's review the key features of Azure's availability zones.

Physical separation
    Each availability zone is geographically isolated within a region to reduce the risk that a single event, such as a power outage or hardware failure, affects multiple zones.

High-speed connectivity
    The zones are linked by low-latency, high-speed private networks, ensuring that data transfer and application functionality are unaffected by physical separation.

Built-in resiliency
> Each Azure region that supports availability zones includes at least three zones to ensure redundancy and resiliency. If one zone fails, workloads can continue running in the other zones.

 As a best practice, always verify whether the Azure services you plan to deploy support availability zones. You can check the official Microsoft documentation (*https://oreil.ly/Ygowk*).

How to Use Availability Zones

Availability zones enable you to build robust, high-availability architectures for your applications. Let's look at how they can be leveraged.

Redundancy for mission-critical applications

By replicating your compute, storage, and networking resources across multiple zones, you can maintain operations even during localized failures.

Application design

Applications can colocate resources (such as VMs, managed disks, or databases) in specific zones and replicate them to other zones for redundancy.

Resilient services

Azure services that support availability zones fall into three categories:

Zonal services
> Resources are pinned to a specific zone (e.g., VMs, managed disks, IP addresses).

Zone-redundant services
> The platform automatically replicates data across zones (e.g., zone-redundant storage, Azure SQL databases).

Non-regional services
> These global (non-regional) services operate across Azure geographies and are resilient to outages in zones or even entire regions (e.g., Azure DNS, Microsoft Entra ID).

Key Considerations About Availability Zones

There are several things to consider when utilizing availability zones.

Cost implications

Increasing reliability by deploying across multiple availability zones can lead to higher costs, so it's important to understand the trade-offs. For example, if you run a single standard D4s v3 virtual machine in one zone, you might pay around $200 per month. Deploying the same VM in a multi-zone setup with redundant instances in two or three zones could increase the cost to $400–$600 per month, depending on the number of zones, the VM type, and any additional network or storage replication charges.

> **Exam Tip**
>
> Deploying resources across multiple availability zones generally increases costs because it requires additional compute instances, storage replication, and networking. The exact cost impact varies based on region, VM size, and architecture.

You can estimate costs for single-zone versus multi-zone architectures using the Azure pricing calculator, which lets you configure resources depending on the service, region, and deployment options you select. This helps you make informed decisions about balancing cost and resiliency. Costs can be tracked at the subscription, resource group, or individual resource level using Azure Cost Management + Billing, allowing fine-grained visibility into where your spend is going. You'll learn more about this in Chapter 13.

Limitations of zones

Although availability zones improve resiliency, extremely large-scale events might impact multiple zones within the same region. For even greater resilience, Azure provides region pairs (see the next section), enabling failover to a secondary region.

Regions without zones

It's worth noting that availability zones are available in many major regions such as North America, Europe, and Asia, but not all Azure regions have this support. You can check the most up-to-date list of regions that support availability zones through the Azure portal or official documentation, as it's regularly updated by Microsoft.

 If availability zones are crucial to your operations, it's essential to deploy resources in regions that offer them. Conversely, if your solution doesn't require this level of redundancy (for example, you're working on a proof-of-concept project), the choice of region becomes less critical.

Typical use cases

Availability zones are ideal for workloads requiring high uptime and low recovery time objectives (RTOs). Common scenarios include:

- Hosting critical applications
- Managing large-scale databases
- Implementing disaster recovery plans

By using availability zones, organizations can bolster resilience and maintain business continuity by protecting against localized outages.

What Are Azure Region Pairs?

Azure region pairs (see Figure 7-4) are strategically linked Azure regions within the same geography (such as the United States, Europe, or Asia) that work together to provide enhanced resilience, geo-replication, and disaster recovery capabilities for select Azure services. Microsoft defines these region pairs to enable prioritized recovery and minimize downtime during rare geography-wide outages and staggered system updates.

 Azure region pairs are strategically placed at least 300 miles (483 km) apart whenever feasible to reduce risk from large-scale events like natural disasters, power failures, or network disruptions.

Region pairs minimize the risk of large-scale outages because the regions' datacenters are at least 300 miles (483 kilometers) apart, whenever possible. This helps protect against events like natural disasters, civil unrest, power outages, or network failures that could affect an entire region.

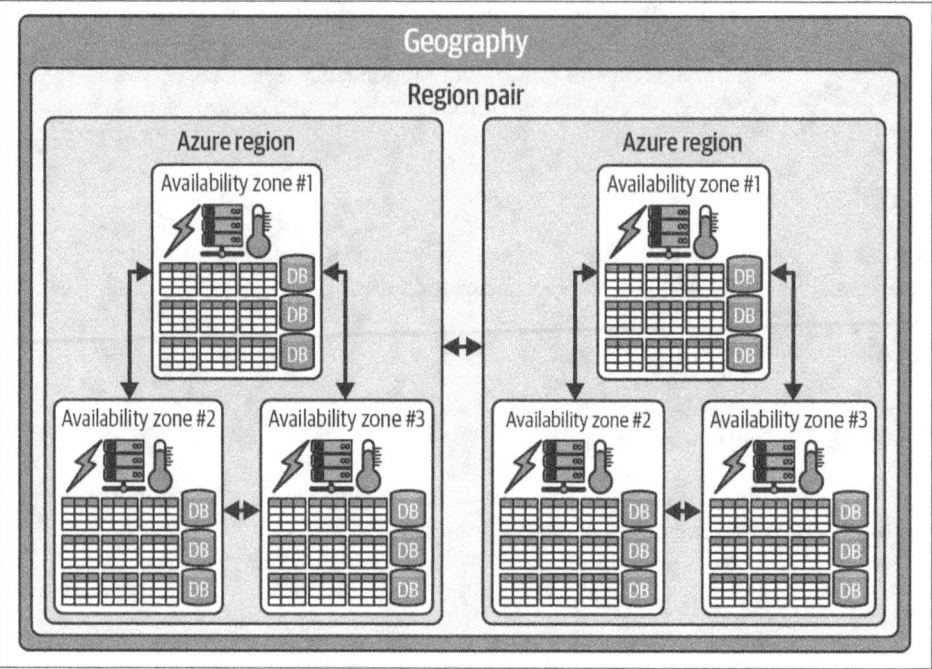

Figure 7-4. Azure region pairs linking Azure regions in the same geography

For example, the West US region is paired with East US, while Southeast Asia is paired with East Asia. These pairs are directly connected through high-speed networks, enabling resource replication and data redundancy across the pair.

Advantages of Region Pairs

Let's review some advantages of Azure's region pairs:

Enhanced disaster recovery
    In the event of a regional disaster, services and resources hosted in one region can fail over to its paired region, ensuring minimal downtime for mission-critical applications. For example, if West US is affected by an outage, workloads can automatically fail over to East US.

Planned maintenance coordination
    Azure performs planned updates to one region in the pair at a time, reducing the risk of simultaneous downtime and ensuring that applications remain available during maintenance windows.

Data residency and compliance
   Data replicated between paired regions remains within the same geography (with the exception of Brazil South, which is paired with South Central US) to comply with data residency, tax, and law enforcement jurisdiction requirements.

Prioritized recovery
   Azure uses prioritized recovery in its region pairs to protect against the rare outages which impact both regions in the same pair. In the event of a widespread Azure outage, Microsoft will prioritize one region in each pair for restoration to ensure that at least one becomes operational as quickly as possible.

How Region Pairs Work

Most region pairs are *reciprocal*, meaning that each region acts as a backup for the other. For example, West US backs up East US, and vice versa.

However, there are exceptions:

- Brazil South is paired with South Central US (located outside its geography), and this pairing operates in only one direction: Brazil South relies on South Central US for resilience and disaster recovery, but South Central US does not rely on Brazil South. Instead, South Central US is reciprocally paired with North Central US.

- West India is paired with South India, but South India is paired with Central India, making the pairing nonreciprocal.

> For an updated list of region pairings, please visit the Microsoft Learn page (*https://oreil.ly/g93fv*).

Key Considerations About Region Pairs

There are several considerations when thinking about regional pairs and your cloud computing:

Customer responsibilities
   Under Azure's shared responsibility model (*https://oreil.ly/Nu64Z*), Microsoft ensures baseline infrastructure reliability across regions, but not all services automatically replicate data or failover to the paired secondary region. For services that don't have automatic data replication or failover (e.g., IaaS VMs or certain PaaS workloads), customers must configure geo-replication and disaster recovery

themselves using tools like Azure Site Recovery or geo-redundant storage options.

Optimal pair selection
Azure region pairs are predefined by Microsoft, and customers can't change these pairings. However, understanding which regions are paired can help in designing resilient solutions.

Cost of redundancy
Replicating resources or data across regions may involve additional costs, especially for bandwidth usage and duplicated services.

Typical Use Cases for Region Pairs

Here are some use cases that show how organizations may leverage region pairs:

Disaster recovery solutions
Applications that require high availability and fast recovery times can leverage region pairs to implement failover mechanisms.

Compliance with data residency laws
Businesses that are bound by legal requirements to keep data within specific geographies can use region pairs to ensure compliance while maintaining redundancy.

Scalable architectures
Multiregion architectures can distribute workloads across region pairs to improve performance and provide failover capabilities.

By leveraging Azure region pairs, organizations can build resilient, compliant, and highly available solutions, ensuring that their critical workloads remain operational even during large-scale outages.

What Are Azure Sovereign Regions?

Azure sovereign regions are specialized instances of Azure that operate independently from the main Azure infrastructure. These regions are designed to meet unique compliance, security, and legal requirements for specific customer groups, such as governments or organizations operating in jurisdictions with strict data sovereignty laws. By offering isolated environments, sovereign regions provide enhanced controls, specialized certifications, and regulatory compliance capabilities.

Types of Azure Sovereign Regions

Here are some of the main types of sovereign regions.

US government regions

These regions, such as US Department of Defense (DoD) Central, US Gov Virginia, and US Gov Iowa, are specifically designed for US government agencies and their partners. Key characteristics include:

Physical and logical isolation
    These regions operate on dedicated physical infrastructure isolated from the public Azure instance.

Screened personnel
    They're managed by US government–screened personnel to ensure compliance with strict security standards.

Additional certifications
    They hold certain certifications to meet US government–mandated compliance standards.

China regions

Azure regions in China, such as China East and China North, are available through a partnership with 21Vianet, a Chinese data center operator:

Regulatory compliance
    These regions adhere to Chinese regulations regarding data sovereignty and privacy.

Independent operations
    While built on Azure technologies, these regions are operated independently by 21Vianet, and Microsoft does not directly manage the data centers.

Why Use Sovereign Regions?

Organizations may need to use Azure sovereign regions for several reasons:

Compliance with local laws
    Sovereign regions are essential for organizations subject to strict data sovereignty regulations, such as storing and processing sensitive data within specific geographic boundaries.

Enhanced security
    These regions offer additional safeguards, such as isolated networks and personnel screening, to protect sensitive information.

Regulatory mandates
    The use of sovereign regions is often required by government agencies or heavily regulated industries to meet legal and operational requirements.

Key Considerations About Sovereign Regions

Let's look at some considerations you should keep in mind when using sovereign regions:

Limited service availability
　Not all Azure services available in public regions are supported in sovereign regions. Organizations must verify which services are offered before deploying resources.

Operational independence
　Sovereign regions like those in China operate under independent management, which may introduce variations in policies, support, and availability from those offered by the main Azure instance.

Cost implications
　Deploying resources in sovereign regions may involve higher costs due to additional compliance requirements and operational overhead.

Integration challenges
　Connecting resources in sovereign regions to resources in public Azure regions may require additional configurations, such as using VPNs or ExpressRoute connections.

Use Cases for Sovereign Regions

Here are some use cases that show why an organization might use a sovereign region:

Government projects
　US government agencies can deploy secure workloads in Azure government regions, ensuring compliance with federal standards.

Regulated industries
　Financial institutions, healthcare providers, and defense contractors benefit from the enhanced security and compliance of sovereign regions.

Operations in China
　Organizations with operations in China can use Azure's partnership with 21Vianet to comply with local regulations while leveraging cloud technology.

Summary

In this chapter, you learned about Azure's physical infrastructure (datacenters, regions, availability zones, region pairs, and sovereign regions) and how Azure delivers reliability, performance, and geographic compliance around the world.

In the next chapter, you'll learn about the Azure management infrastructure, including resources, resource groups, subscriptions, and management groups, which together form the logical structure used to organize, govern, and manage cloud workloads.

Chapter 7 Quiz

To check your answers, please refer to the "Chapter 7 Answer Key" on page 303.

1. You are designing a high-availability web application. You want to ensure that if one physical datacenter fails, your application remains operational without downtime.

   Which Azure feature should you leverage?

   A. Availability zone

   B. Azure region

   C. Region pair

   D. Sovereign region

2. There is a major Azure outage affecting the West US region. Your organization has designed workloads to automatically failover to a secondary region in the same geography.

   Which Azure feature supports this failover strategy?

   A. Availability zone

   B. Azure region

   C. Region pair

   D. Sovereign region

3. A US government agency needs to deploy sensitive workloads that must comply with federal security standards and strict data residency mandates.

   Which Azure component should the agency use?

   A. Availability zone

   B. Azure region

   C. Region pair

   D. Sovereign region

CHAPTER 8
The Azure Management Infrastructure

In this chapter, you'll explore the Azure management infrastructure and learn how Azure organizes and governs cloud-based resources. You'll examine the four hierarchical layers that form the foundation for structuring, securing, and managing Azure deployments:

- Resources
- Resource groups
- Subscriptions
- Management groups

Understanding this hierarchy is essential not just for real-world Azure administration but also for success on the AZ-900 Azure Fundamentals exam. As you progress, pay close attention to:

- How each layer relates to the others
- Which layers are used for billing, policy, governance, and access control
- Why resource organization matters for scalability, cost management, security, and compliance

By the end of this chapter, you'll be able to clearly distinguish each management layer and understand how Azure's governance model supports secure and efficient cloud operations, knowledge that is frequently tested on the AZ-900 exam.

What Is the Azure Management Infrastructure?

Azure's management infrastructure is the organizational framework within Azure that governs how resources are structured, managed, and accessed. It establishes a hierarchy for organizing resources, applying policies, managing access, and controlling costs. This structure simplifies administration and ensures scalability, compliance, and security for projects and applications.

The management infrastructure resembles an onion (see Figure 8-1) with layers that build upon one another to create a cohesive hierarchy. Each layer serves a distinct purpose, yet they work together to form a unified management framework.

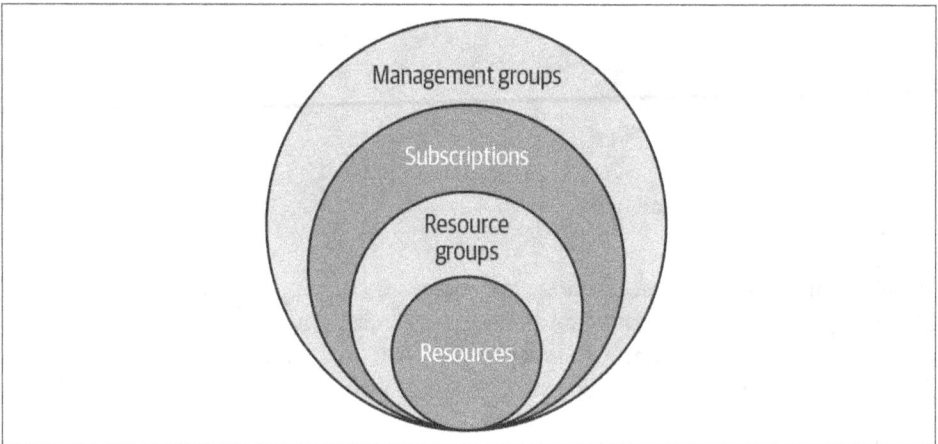

Figure 8-1. The layers of Azure's management infrastructure

The Core Layer: Azure Resources

At the core of the onion, you'll find Azure resources. *Resources*, which are the services that you create and manage, are the essential building blocks of any Azure project.

Here are some common examples of Azure resources:

- Azure Virtual Machines
- Azure Kubernetes Service
- Azure Functions
- Azure Storage Accounts
- Azure SQL Databases

Each resource provides specific functions within an application or service architecture.

The Second Layer: Azure Resource Groups

Encasing these resources are resource groups, analogous to the second layer from the onion's core. A *resource group* is a logical container for Azure resources that share a common lifecycle. By bundling related resources together, resource groups simplify management and streamline operations.

When you delete a resource group, both the resource group and all the resources within it are deleted.

Access control and other settings that are applied to a resource group cascade to all the resources it contains, simplifying administration. Note that if you delete a resource group, all resources inside are deleted in one action.

Exam Tip
Resource groups cannot be nested.

The resource group structure is intentionally flat, meaning that you can't put one resource group inside another resource group.

Structural Layers: Azure Subscriptions

Moving outward, the next layer is *Azure subscriptions*, which can contain multiple resource groups. Each subscription defines billing and access control boundaries:

Billing boundaries
  Subscriptions let you track costs independently for development, production, or department-specific workloads.

Access control boundaries
  Policies applied at the subscription level filter down to all resource groups and resources within the subscription.

You can create multiple subscriptions to separate environments, organizational structures, or billing needs, ensuring flexibility as your projects grow.

Exam Tip

Subscriptions cannot be nested.

Similar to resource groups, subscriptions can't be nested (i.e., you can't put one subscription inside another subscription).

The Outer Layer: Azure Management Groups

At the outermost layer of the onion lie the *Azure management groups*, which provide enterprise-grade governance by allowing you to apply policies and permissions across multiple subscriptions.

The management groups are used to:

- Apply policies that span multiple subscriptions, such as restricting VM deployments to a specific region
- Assign Azure RBAC at scale, giving users consistent access across subscriptions

Exam Tip

Management groups can be nested.

You can create a nested hierarchy of management groups (up to six levels deep) to align with your organizational structure.

By understanding and using this onion-like structure, you can build a robust Azure environment that's both easy to manage and capable of meeting your organizational needs. When designing your Azure management infrastructure, keep in mind that each layer serves a specific purpose, and together they form a cohesive, easy-to-manage system.

Benefits of a Well-Designed Azure Management Infrastructure

Let's look at the benefits of managing your resources appropriately in Azure's prescribed infrastructure.

Organized resource management

- Logical grouping makes it easier to manage related resources.
- Tasks like applying policies or tracking costs are greatly simplified.

Cost management

- Segregate costs by subscriptions for better tracking.
- Optimize spending by aligning billing with organizational units or projects.
- Perform detailed tracking of resource usage and spending via subscriptions.
- Budgets can be assigned at the subscription or resource group level to prevent overspending.

Governance and compliance

- Apply and enforce organizational policies at different levels of the hierarchy.
- Ensure that resources align with corporate or regulatory standards.

Scalability and flexibility

- Organize resources to adapt to organizational growth or evolving requirements.
- Simplify resource management through logical grouping.
- Leverage the hierarchical structure to support scalability by easily adding new resources, groups, or subscriptions.
- Flexibly adapt the structure to different organizational needs.

Access management and security

- Use Azure RBAC to define granular permissions.
- Inherit permissions across the hierarchy for consistent access management.
- Apply RBAC at different levels (subscription, resource group, or resource) to manage permissions efficiently.

Best Practices for Planning Your Azure Management Infrastructure

This listing describes best practices for designing an effective management structure:

Define naming conventions
  Establish clear and consistent naming for management groups, subscriptions, resource groups, and resources to enhance clarity and ease of management.

Align with business needs
  Organize your hierarchy according to operational requirements, such as by separating environments, organizational units, or projects.

Monitor and optimize
  Use tools like Azure Cost Management and Azure Monitor to track usage, performance, and costs for ongoing optimization. We'll talk more about this in Chapter 13.

Leverage policies
  Use Azure Policy, Blueprints, and infrastructure as code (IaC) to streamline governance and resource provisioning. We'll talk more about IaC in Chapter 15.

Real-World Example: Hierarchical Integration of Management Groups, Subscriptions, and Resource Groups

Earlier, I used an onion analogy to explain the four layers of the Azure management infrastructure. Now, let's bring that analogy to life with a real-world example.

The diagram in Figure 8-2 illustrates how Azure's management structure can be organized in a business environment, showcasing nested management groups and subscriptions. For simplicity, resource groups and individual resources are not shown, but they are understood to exist within their respective subscriptions.

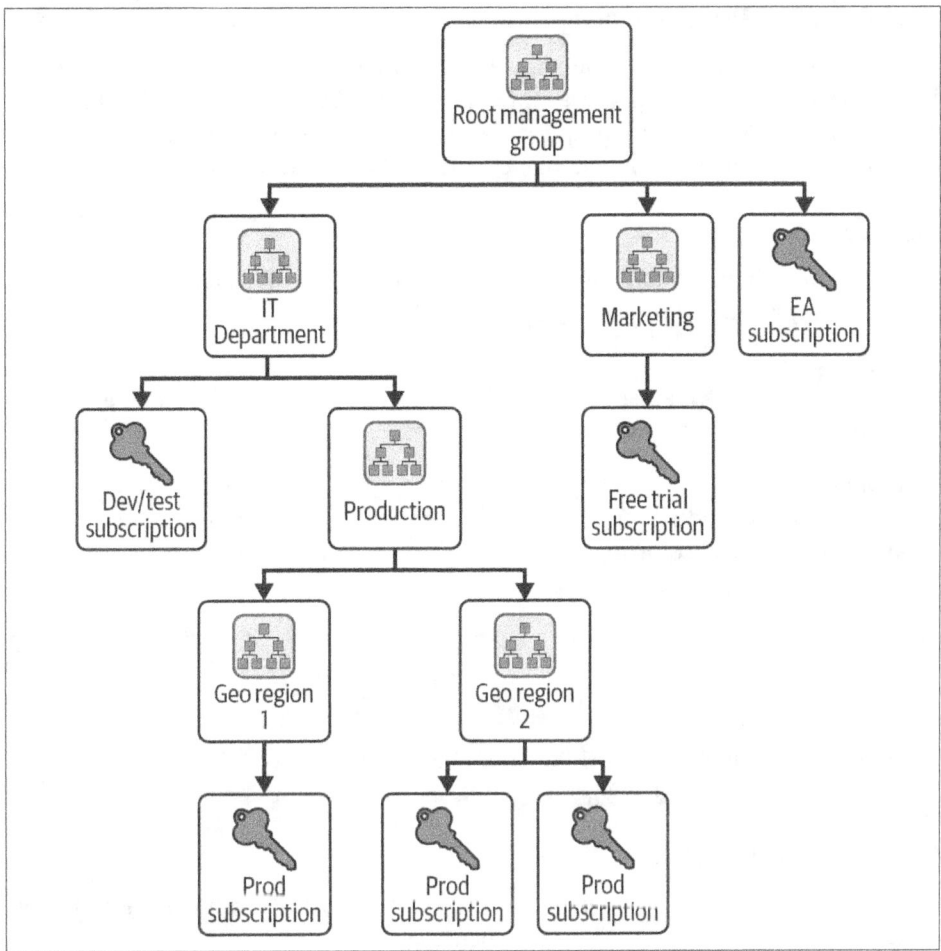

Figure 8-2. Example of the Azure management structure in an organization

Breaking Down the Azure Management Structure

Let's walk through each level of the diagram, starting at the top.

Root management group

At the top of the hierarchy is the root management group, which is the pinnacle of the management group structure. It acts as a container for all other management groups, enabling the application of governance and policies across all the entire hierarchy.

IT Department and Marketing management groups

Below the root management group are two departmental management groups: the IT Department and Marketing. These represent different business units within the organization. Each management group can enforce its own set of policies, such as access control, cost management, or compliance rules, tailored to its specific needs.

Subscriptions

Subscriptions are linked to their respective management groups and serve as logical containers for resource groups. Examples include:

An EA subscription
   An enterprise agreement subscription for larger-scale billing and enterprise management

Prod subscriptions
   Dedicated to production workloads, supporting both customer-facing applications and internal company use

A dev/test subscription
   Used for non-production environments where the focus is on development and testing activities

A free trial subscription
   Created for short-term testing or marketing research with limited resources under the Marketing management group

Resource groups and resources

Resource groups act as containers for related resources within a subscription, simplifying resource organization and management.

For example:

- The dev/test subscription under the IT Department contains resources for development and testing environments.
- Geo Region 1 and Geo Region 2 in the Production management group represent geographically distributed subscriptions and resource groups. These are designed for disaster recovery and to ensure high availability of production workloads in different regions.

How the Structure Works

Let's take a look at how the Azure management structure works:

Policies and governance
    Policies set at the root management group level are inherited by all sub-management groups, such as IT Department and Marketing, enabling consistent, centralized governance across the organization.

Cost management
    Subscriptions tied to specific departments (e.g., IT Department and Marketing) can operate under distinct billing models. This separation allows for detailed cost tracking and accountability by the organizational unit.

Access control
    Each management group and subscription can enforce tailored access control policies. For instance, the Production team within the IT Department may have exclusive access to production resources, while the Development team within the IT Department is restricted to its dev/test subscription.

As you can see, each layer of the Azure management infrastructure is interconnected. Policies and permissions set at the outer layers cascade inward, flowing through management groups, subscriptions, resource groups, and individual resources.

This hierarchical structure provides flexible, scalable governance that evolves with your organization's needs.

Summary

In this chapter, you learned about the Azure management infrastructure, which is the hierarchical framework used to organize, govern, and manage cloud resources.

The management infrastructure has four layers:

Resources
    Individual services or components such as virtual machines, databases, or storage accounts

Resource groups
    Containers for grouping related resources to simplify management, deployment, and access control

Subscriptions
    Logical units for billing, policy application, and access management across multiple resource groups

Management groups
    Higher-level containers that organize subscriptions, enabling governance, policy enforcement, and consistent access control across large-scale environments

Understanding this hierarchy is essential for effective governance, cost management, security, and compliance in Azure, and thus the hierarchy is frequently tested on the AZ-900 exam.

In the next chapter, we'll look at Azure's compute services.

Chapter 8 Quiz

To check your answers, please refer to the "Chapter 8 Answer Key" on page 303.

1. You are cleaning up your Azure environment and decide to delete a resource group that contains multiple virtual machines, storage accounts, and databases.

   You understand that this will happen to the resources inside the group:

   A. Only the resource group will be deleted; all resources will remain intact.

   B. The resource group and all its contained resources will be deleted.

2. What is the purpose of Azure subscriptions?

   A. To organize individual resources

   B. To manage virtual networks

   C. To provide boundaries for billing and access control

   D. To create nested resource groups

3. Which of the following can be nested in Azure?

   A. Resource group

   B. Subscription

   C. Management group

   D. Management groups, resource groups, and subscriptions can all be nested.

CHAPTER 9
Azure Compute Services

Modern applications must be capable of scaling globally, handling unpredictable traffic, integrating with diverse services, and operating reliably without interruption. To make this possible, Azure provides a broad portfolio of compute services designed for different application architectures, skill levels, and operational models.

Whether you want full control over virtual machines, a fully managed platform for web apps, container-based solutions for microservices, or event-driven serverless functions, Azure Compute gives you the flexibility to choose the right tool for each workload.

Understanding these options is essential for success on the AZ-900 Microsoft Azure Fundamentals exam and even more important for designing efficient, cost-effective cloud solutions.

In this chapter, we'll explore the key Azure compute services, organized into five main categories:

Infrastructure as a service (IaaS)

- Azure Virtual Machines
- Azure Virtual Machine Scale Sets
- Azure availability sets
- Azure Virtual Desktop

Platform as a service (PaaS)

- Azure App Service

Serverless computing (PaaS)

- Azure Functions

Container services (PaaS)

- Azure Kubernetes Service
- Azure Container Instances

Managed container services (PaaS)

- Azure Container Apps

Choosing the appropriate compute service is crucial for optimizing performance, managing cost, and ensuring scalability. By understanding the features, use cases, advantages and limitations of each option, you can make more informed decisions tailored to your specific workload requirements.

Let's start with the first category: IaaS!

Infrastructure as a Service

As described in Chapter 3 of this book, IaaS is a cloud computing model that provides on-demand access to fundamental computing resources such as VMs, storage, and networking. With IaaS, you can deploy and manage applications without the burden of purchasing or maintaining physical hardware, giving you flexibility, scalability, and control over your environment. In this section, we'll explore key IaaS offerings in Azure, including:

Azure Virtual Machines
    Build and run fully customizable virtual servers.

Azure Virtual Machine Scale Sets
    Automatically scale VM instances to match demand.

Azure Availability Sets
    Improve VM uptime across hardware and maintenance events.

Azure Virtual Desktop
    Provide secure, cloud-hosted Windows desktops.

IaaS is ideal when you need maximum control or need to lift and shift traditional workloads to the cloud.

Azure Virtual Machines

Azure Virtual Machines, commonly known as Azure VMs, enable you to create and manage virtualized computing environments where you can run applications and services on virtual machines that emulate physical computers. This means you don't need to invest in or maintain physical hardware; instead, Azure provides the infrastructure. Azure VMs offer scalable and flexible computing power, with a variety of operating systems, configurations, and sizes available to meet your specific needs.

Networking for Azure VMs is flexible and robust, supporting private and public IP addresses, virtual networks, subnets, network security groups, and load balancers. For higher control over physical hardware, Azure offers the Dedicated Host service, which gives you single-tenant servers ideal for compliance or licensing requirements, including Windows Server and SQL Server licensing considerations.

For cost-sensitive or interruptible workloads, *Azure Spot VMs* provide deep discounts by using unused capacity, though they may be evicted if demand increases. Licensing considerations are important, as some VMs include bundled licenses while others allow you to bring your own licenses (BYOL).

Azure VMs combine flexibility, scalability, and a variety of deployment options, making them suitable for everything from development and testing to high-performance production workloads.

To better understand Azure VMs, think of using one as being like renting a fully furnished apartment in a high-rise building. When you rent an apartment, you don't worry about constructing the building, installing utilities, or handling maintenance. Your focus is solely on your personal living space, and you pay rent to the landlord, who ensures that the building is well maintained.

Similarly, with Azure VMs, you don't need to worry about the underlying physical hardware or infrastructure. Azure takes care of all that, allowing you to concentrate on your virtualized environment and applications.

In this analogy:

- The building represents the Azure data center, where all the underlying infrastructure is housed.
- Your apartment symbolizes your VM, where you have full control over the contents including the operating system, software, and files.
- The landlord (Azure) handles the maintenance of the building, provides essential utilities such as electricity (compute power) and water (networking and storage), while you pay for what you use.

Just as you pick an apartment based on the number of rooms (CPU cores) and amenities (RAM, storage), you can configure your VM to match your needs. If you find that you'll be using more or less space, you can easily upgrade or downgrade your VM to fit your requirements.

Key features

Customizable hardware
> Offers a range of sizes and configurations, including CPU, memory, and storage options, to match your workload requirements.

Operating system flexibility
> Supports various operating systems, including Windows, Linux, and custom images, allowing you to run a diverse set of applications.

Scalability
> Easily scales up or down based on your workload demands, because you can add or remove VMs as needed.

Integration with Azure services
> Seamlessly integrates with other Azure services such as storage, networking, and security services, enhancing functionality and security.

Pay-as-you-go pricing
> Offers flexible pricing models, including pay-as-you-go or reserved instances, to help manage costs based on usage.

Common use cases

Running legacy applications
> Azure VMs are ideal for running older applications that require a full operating environment.

Lift-and-shift migration
> They can facilitate the migration of legacy applications to the cloud without a need for major modifications.

Full control services
> They are suitable for hosting services where you need complete control over the operating environment.

Disaster recovery
> A VM can serve as a backup solution for disaster recovery, allowing you to replicate your on-premises environment to the cloud.

Key advantages

Flexibility
Offers a wide range of VM sizes and configurations to meet diverse workload requirements, with the ability to customize and scale resources as needed

Cost management
Provides various pricing options and cost management tools to help control and optimize spending

High availability
Ensures high availability through features like availability sets, availability zones, and disaster recovery options

Integration
Integrates with other Azure services for enhanced functionality, including storage, networking, and security

Limitations

Management overhead
Requires more effort to manage than other solutions do. The customer's responsibility for maintaining the operating system, applications, and updates can add administrative workload.

Cost
Ongoing costs can accumulate based on usage, including compute, storage, and network resources, and large-scale deployments can become expensive.

Resource overprovisioning
If not properly configured, the VM has the potential for inefficient resource use.

Slower scaling
Scaling up or down may be slower than for containers, because VMs run a full operating system that takes time to boot up and initialize. (You'll learn more about containers when we discuss container services with PaaS.)

In summary, Azure VMs provide a versatile and controllable environment, perfect for many traditional applications and scenarios, while also presenting some challenges in management and scaling.

Resources Required for Azure VMs

To effectively deploy and manage an Azure VM, you'll need to make some decisions about resources and configurations to ensure that the VM operates efficiently and meets your requirements for performance, availability, and security.

Compute resources
- *VM size:* Choose from various VM sizes based on the number of CPUs and amount of RAM you'll need and other hardware specifications. The size should match the workload requirements of your application.
- *VM series:* Select the VM series based on your needs. Examples include general purpose, compute-optimized, memory-optimized, storage-optimized, or GPU-based VMs.

Storage resources
- *OS disk:* An operating system disk is required to install and run the operating system. It can be based on Standard HDD, Standard SSD, or Premium SSD, depending on your performance and cost requirements.
- *Data disks:* These additional disks for storing application data, databases, or logs can also be based on Standard HDD, Standard SSD, or Premium SSD, and their performance should align with your application needs.
- *Temporary disk:* This disk provides temporary storage for data that isn't persistent, such as when working with temporary files and caching, and it's reset if the VM is deallocated.

Networking resources
- *Azure Virtual Network (VNet):* This virtual network provides isolated and secure communication between your VMs and other Azure resources. You must configure subnets within the VNet to organize and control network traffic.
- *Network security group (NSG):* An NSG defines inbound and outbound traffic rules to control network access to and from your VM, enhancing security.
- *Public IP address:* Optionally, a public IP address accesses your VM from outside the Azure network. It can be dynamic or static depending on whether you need a consistent IP address.

Security resources
- *Azure Firewall or NSGs:* Implement additional network security measures to protect your VM from unauthorized access.
- *Microsoft Defender for Cloud:* This provides advanced security management and threat protection for your VMs, helping to detect and respond to potential security threats.

Backup and recovery
- *Azure Backup:* This service backs up and restores VM data, including OS and data disks, providing protection against data loss and accidental deletion.
- *Azure Site Recovery:* By replicating VM data to another Azure region or on-premises environment, this service ensures business continuity in case of a regional outage.

Monitoring and management
- *Azure Monitor*: Monitors VM performance, collects metrics, and generates alerts for operational insights and troubleshooting. The Log Analytics tool provides detailed logging and analysis of VM operations and performance, helping to diagnose issues and optimize performance.

Licensing and compliance
- *Operating system licenses*: Ensure that you have appropriate licenses for the operating system running on the VM. Azure offers licensing options for Windows Server and supports various Linux distributions.
- *Compliance requirements*: Use Azure's compliance offerings and certifications to adhere to compliance and regulatory requirements relevant to your industry or region.

By properly configuring these resources, you can ensure that your Azure VM is optimized for performance, security, and availability while meeting your specific operational requirements.

Virtual Machine Deployment

Now that you've learned about configuring Azure VMs, we'll explore several options for deploying and managing them.

Azure Virtual Machine Scale Sets

Azure Virtual Machine Scale Sets (VMSS) is a service that allows you to deploy and manage a group of identical, load-balanced VMs in a scalable and highly available manner. VMSS enables you to automatically scale the number of VMs up or down based on demand, ensuring that your applications maintain optimal performance and availability.

If you think of a single VM as a single apartment unit, then a VMSS is like an entire apartment building, housing identical units that can grow or shrink based on demand.

Key features

Autoscaling
 Automatically adjusts the number of VM instances based on predefined rules, such as CPU utilization or custom metrics, to handle varying workloads efficiently.

Load balancing
 Integrates with Azure Load Balancer to distribute incoming traffic evenly across the VMs in the scale set, improving application availability and performance.

High availability
: Distributes VM instances across multiple availability zones or fault domains to ensure that your application remains available even in the event of a hardware failure or data center outage.

Integrated management
: Simplifies the management of VM configurations and updates through rolling upgrades, allowing you to deploy changes across all VMs without downtime.

Customizable VM images
: Allows you to use custom VM images or predefined images from the Azure Marketplace, enabling tailored configurations for your applications.

Common use cases

Web applications
: Is ideal for hosting web applications that require automatic scaling to handle varying traffic loads while maintaining high availability.

Microservices
: Is suitable for running microservices architectures where multiple instances of services are needed to scale out and manage workloads effectively.

Batch processing
: Provides a scalable environment for batch-processing jobs or large-scale computations that require varying amounts of compute resources.

Development and testing
: Proves useful for creating and managing environments for development and testing that need to scale dynamically based on testing needs.

Key advantages

Scalability
: Automatically scales the number of VMs up or down based on demand, improving resource utilization and performance without manual intervention.

High availability
: Ensures high availability and fault tolerance through distribution across multiple availability zones or fault domains.

Cost efficiency
: Helps optimize costs by scaling resources based on actual demand, thereby avoiding overprovisioning and underutilization.

Simplified management
: Streamlines the management of VM configurations, updates, and deployments through integrated tools and automation features.

Limitations

Configuration complexity
: Requires careful configuration of autoscaling rules and load-balancing settings to ensure optimal performance and cost-efficiency.

Cost variability
: Costs can vary based on the number of VM instances and the scaling policies in place, potentially leading to unpredictable expenses.

Limited customization
: While VMSS provides automated scaling and management, it may not support all custom configurations or advanced scenarios in the way that is possible with individual VM management.

Azure availability sets

Azure availability sets handle uptime by protecting VMs against hardware failures and maintenance events within a single datacenter. They're designed to ensure the high availability of your applications and services by distributing VMs across multiple fault domains and update domains. This approach helps safeguard your applications from both planned and unplanned outages, improving the overall reliability and resilience of your deployments.

Key features

Fault domains
: Grouping VMs into fault domains to spread them across different physical hardware ensures that different VMs are not affected by the same hardware failure.

Update domains
: Distributing VMs into update domains helps manage the impact of planned maintenance and updates. During maintenance, Azure updates VMs in one update domain at a time, minimizing downtime and ensuring that not all VMs are impacted simultaneously.

Load balancer integration
: When used with Azure Load Balancer, availability sets help distribute traffic evenly across VMs to improve availability and performance.

Common use cases

High-availability applications
  Provide essential resilience for applications that require continuous availability and minimal downtime, such as web services, databases, and critical business applications.

Disaster recovery
  Provide a foundation for disaster recovery by distributing VMs across fault and update domains, ensuring that applications remain operational in the event of failures or maintenance activities.

Mission-critical services
  By offering resilience against both hardware and software issues, they're ideal for mission-critical services that cannot afford to experience downtime.

Key advantages

Enhanced availability
  Improve application availability by ensuring that VMs are distributed across multiple fault and update domains, protecting against hardware failures and maintenance impacts.

Cost-effective
  Provide high availability without the need for additional infrastructure or significant changes to application design.

Automatic load balancing
  Ensure even distribution of traffic across VMs, helping to maintain performance and reliability.

Seamless integration
  Work with other Azure features and services, such as Azure Load Balancer and Virtual Network, to enhance overall application resilience.

Limitations

Configuration complexity
  Require careful planning and configuration to effectively distribute VMs across fault and update domains, an operation that can be complex for large-scale deployments.

Limited to single region
  Being confined to a single Azure region, they don't provide cross-region redundancy or disaster recovery.

No automatic scaling
    Unlike Azure VMSS, availability sets don't automatically scale VMs based on demand; manual intervention is required to adjust the number of VMs.

Azure Virtual Desktop

Azure Virtual Desktop (AVD) provides full Windows desktops hosted in Azure, accessible from virtually anywhere. AVD provides users with a complete Windows experience on any supported device, while Azure takes care of the underlying infrastructure, scaling, security, and maintenance.

Key features

Virtualized desktops and applications
    Access virtually a full Windows desktop experience or specific applications from any device.

Scalability
    Easily scale up or down based on user demand without worrying about the underlying infrastructure.

Cost-effective
    Pay only for the resources used, with options to optimize costs through features like Windows 10 or Windows 11 Enterprise multi-session deployments.

Security
    Rely on built-in security features such as MFA and compliance with industry standards.

Integration with Microsoft 365
    Leverage seamless integration with Microsoft 365 applications and services.

Common use cases

Remote work
    Enables employees to access their work desktops from any location, supporting remote and hybrid work setups.

Business continuity
    Provides secure remote access to desktops during emergencies or disruptions, ensuring continuous operations.

Temporary workforce
    Enables quick provisioning of desktops for temporary or seasonal workers.

Application access
> Allows you to run specific applications without installing them on local devices, simplifying application management.

Training and development
> Provides a controlled environment for training sessions or software testing without affecting the main infrastructure.

Key advantages

Accessibility
> Allows users to access their virtual desktops from any device with an internet connection, making remote work and mobility easy.

Cost savings
> Reduces the need for physical hardware and maintenance, with a pay-as-you-go pricing model.

Centralized management
> Simplifies management and deployment by centralizing control in the cloud.

Scalability
> Easily scales the number of virtual desktops up or down based on the organization's needs, without hardware limitations.

Security
> Uses Azure's security features to protect data and comply with regulatory requirements, reducing risks associated with local device management.

Limitations

Dependency on internet
> Requires a stable and fast internet connection for optimal performance, a condition that is challenging to meet in areas with poor connectivity.

Latency
> May have latency issues depending on users' geographic location relative to the Azure data center.

Performance
> Can experience varying levels of performance that impact user experience depending on cloud infrastructure quality and the complexity of applications.

Platform as a Service

As you'll recall from Chapter 3, PaaS is a cloud computing model that provides a fully managed environment for building, deploying, and running applications without worrying about the underlying infrastructure. PaaS handles servers, storage, networking, and runtime environments, allowing developers to focus on writing code and delivering functionality faster.

In this section, you'll learn about Azure App Service, one of the most widely used PaaS offerings in Azure.

Azure App Service

Azure App Service is a fully managed platform for building, deploying, and scaling web applications, APIs, and mobile backends. It simplifies the development process by managing the infrastructure, server maintenance, and scaling, allowing developers to focus on writing code and delivering features. Azure App Service supports multiple programming languages and frameworks, providing built-in capabilities for monitoring, continuous integration, and deployment.

Think of using Azure App Service as renting a party room to host a kids' birthday party. Suppose you want to host a birthday party for your child but lack the space or resources to set up a party venue yourself. Instead of decorating your home, pitching tents in your yard, or building a special space, you rent a party room from a venue that specializes in hosting such events. This room comes fully equipped with decorations, tables, chairs, entertainment options, and refreshments. Your focus is on planning and enjoying the party, while the venue provider ensures everything is set up and ready for the celebration.

In this analogy:

- The party room represents Azure App Service. Just as the party room provides a ready-to-use space for your event, Azure App Service provides a ready-to-use platform for hosting web applications, APIs, and mobile backends.
- The birthday party is akin to the application you deploy. You focus on developing and running your application, while Azure App Service handles the underlying infrastructure, including server maintenance, scaling, and security.

Key Features

Web apps
    Hosts web applications and APIs with support for .NET, Java, PHP, Node.js, and Python.

App service plans
> Defines the compute resources, pricing tier, and scaling options for your apps, enabling you to balance cost and performance.

Deployment slots
> Creates separate environments, like staging and production, to safely test new versions before swapping them into live use.

App service environments
> Enables high-security and high-performance environments for hosting apps in a virtual network.

Continuous integration and deployment (CI/CD)
> Integrates with tools like GitHub, Azure DevOps, and Bitbucket to automate the deployment process.

Scaling and load balancing
> Automatically scales applications based on demand and balances traffic across instances.

Security and compliance
> Offers built-in security features, including SSL certificates, managed identities, and compliance with industry standards.

Common use cases

Web applications
> With features like autoscaling and load balancing, Azure App Service is ideal for hosting and scaling web applications.

APIs
> Provides a scalable and secure environment for backend services and is thus suitable for creating and managing APIs.

Mobile backends
> Provides a perfect solution for building backends for mobile apps, as it offers authentication, data storage, and integration with other services.

Key advantages

Managed environment
> Provides a fully managed platform so you don't need to worry about server maintenance, updates, or infrastructure management.

Autoscaling
> Automatically adjusts resources based on demand, ensuring that your application performs well during traffic spikes without manual intervention.

Integrated services
> By offering integration with other Azure services, such as Azure Application Insights, databases, monitoring tools, and DevOps pipelines, it simplifies application development and deployment.

Limitations

Limited customization
> Gives you less control over the underlying infrastructure and configurations than if you managed your own VMs or servers.

Cost
> Can become expensive as your application scales or if you require advanced features and higher performance tiers.

Platform constraints
> May not support all custom configurations or technologies, limiting some advanced use cases or specific requirements.

PaaS: Serverless Computing

Serverless computing is a cloud model where you run code without provisioning or managing servers; the underlying infrastructure is fully managed by the cloud provider. This doesn't mean there are no servers. Azure still runs your code on compute resources. However, you don't have to worry about scaling, patching, or maintaining them.

Azure Functions is Microsoft's serverless compute service that lets you run discrete pieces of code, called functions, in response to events such as HTTP requests, message queue updates, or timers. Functions automatically scale based on demand, and you only pay for the time your code executes. For more advanced scenarios, *Durable Functions* allows you to orchestrate long-running workflows and stateful operations across multiple function executions.

Azure Functions supports different hosting options, including the Premium Plan, which provides features like VNET integration, unlimited execution duration, pre-warmed instances to mitigate cold starts, and enhanced scaling. Developers can also use custom handlers to run code in languages or runtimes not natively supported by Azure Functions.

As an analogy, think of Azure Functions as being like an on-demand plumber who fixes a water leak only when needed. Imagine you have a house, and every now and then, a water leak occurs. Instead of having a plumber at your house at all times, you call the plumber only when a leak occurs. The plumber arrives, fixes the issue, and then leaves once the job is done. You pay only for the time and effort needed to fix the leak, not for having the plumber on standby all the time.

In this analogy:

- The on-demand plumber represents Azure Functions. Just as the plumber addresses specific issues as they arise, Azure Functions runs small pieces of code in response to particular events or triggers, such as when a file is uploaded or a new message arrives.
- The water leak symbolizes the event that triggers a function. The function performs a specific task related to that event and then completes its job, similar to how the plumber fixes the leak and then departs.

Azure Functions allows you to execute code in response to events without needing to maintain or manage servers continuously. You only pay for the execution time and resources used, just like you only pay the plumber for the time spent fixing the leak.

Key features

Serverless architecture
    Means there's no need to provision or manage servers, since Azure Functions run in a fully managed environment, scaling automatically based on the workload.

Event-driven
    Enables functions to be triggered by a wide range of events, such as HTTP requests, timer schedules, changes to data in storage, or messages from queues.

Flexible development
    Supports multiple programming languages including C#, JavaScript, Python, Java, and PowerShell, allowing developers to use the language they're most comfortable with.

Integrated development tools
    Works seamlessly with development tools like Visual Studio, Visual Studio Code, Azure Application Insights, and Azure DevOps for development, testing, and deployment.

Common use cases

Event-driven processing
    Ideal for processing data or handling tasks in response to events, such as processing files uploaded to a cloud storage or handling messages from a queue

Scheduled tasks
    Running scheduled tasks like nightly data backups, report generation, or system maintenance

API backends
Creating serverless APIs, handling HTTP requests and providing responses without managing a dedicated server

Key advantages

Cost-efficiency
Makes you pay only for the compute time and resources used by the function, similar to paying the plumber only for the time spent on the job.

Scalability
Automatically scales to handle varying loads, so you don't have to worry about provisioning or managing servers.

Reduced management overhead
Lets you focus on writing code for specific tasks without managing infrastructure or server maintenance.

Limitations

Cold starts
Functions may experience latency during initial invocations if they haven't been used recently, giving you an experience similar to waiting for the plumber to arrive.

Execution time limits
Execution time limits depend on the hosting plan. On the Consumption plan, functions have a default timeout of 5 minutes (extendable to 10 minutes). Premium and Dedicated plans support long-running executions without a fixed timeout.

Complexity of state management
Managing state between function executions can be challenging, as each function execution is stateless by design.

Containers and Azure Kubernetes Services

Containers represent a modern approach to deploying applications, packaging an application and its dependencies into a lightweight, portable container that can run consistently across different environments.

In this section, I'll introduce you to containers and Azure Kubernetes Services.

Kubernetes is an open source system for automating the deployment, scaling, and management of containerized applications. It orchestrates and manages containers, ensuring that they run smoothly across a cluster of machines.

Docker is a popular platform for building, running, and managing these containers. It ensures that each application behaves the same way, no matter where it's deployed.

Azure Kubernetes Service (AKS) is Microsoft's managed Kubernetes offering, often categorized as container orchestration as a service (CaaS), where Azure manages the control plane while you manage workloads and cluster configuration. In AKS, *pods* are the smallest deployable units that host one or more containers, while *nodes* are the virtual or physical machines that run these pods. AKS automates deployment, scaling, and management, ensuring that containers run reliably across a cluster, while Docker focuses on creating and running individual containers.

Imagine this scenario: You're at a grocery store, picking up a variety of items (fruits, vegetables, dairy, and meats). When you get home, you carefully place each type of food into its own container to keep them fresh and prevent cross-contamination, and you label these containers. You then store them in your fridge, where everything is kept at the right temperature, neatly organized, and easy to access when needed.

In this analogy:

- Containers in Azure are like the individual food containers you use. Each container holds a specific type of food, just as a software container packages a specific application or service along with everything it needs to run. By keeping different foods (applications) in separate containers, you ensure they don't spoil each other and stay fresh (run consistently) no matter where you place them.

Docker is one of the most popular platforms for building, deploying, and managing containers. Docker provides tools to package an application and its dependencies into a container, which ensures that it runs consistently across different environments.

- Your refrigerator symbolizes AKS. It keeps all the containers organized, maintains the right environment (temperature and humidity) for them, and makes sure everything is easily accessible. AKS helps you manage, deploy, and scale your containers efficiently, just as your fridge ensures that your food stays fresh and ready to use whenever you need it.

Key features

Managed Kubernetes
Provides a managed Kubernetes control plane, including automated updates, monitoring, and scaling.

Integrated development tools
   Works with Azure DevOps and other CI/CD tools to streamline the development, testing, and deployment processes.

Scaling and load balancing
   Automatically scales applications based on demand and distributes traffic across multiple instances.

Security and compliance
   Offers built-in security features such as integration with Microsoft Entra ID, RBAC, and network policies. You'll learn more about RBAC in Chapter 12.

Monitoring and diagnostics
   Provides integrated monitoring and logging through Azure Monitor and Azure Log Analytics for tracking the health and performance of applications.

Common use cases

Microservices architecture
   Containers are ideal for deploying microservices, where each service can be developed, tested, and deployed independently. AKS helps manage these services, ensuring that they work together seamlessly.

CI/CD
   Containers support CI/CD pipelines by providing consistent environments for testing and deployment. AKS automates the deployment process, making it easier to integrate new code changes quickly and efficiently.

Dev/test environments
   Developers use containers to create isolated environments for development and testing. Because containers package the application along with all its dependencies, the same container that runs on a developer's laptop can also run reliably in the cloud, ensuring consistency and eliminating the "it works on my machine" problem that tends to occur among development, testing, and production.

Hybrid cloud and multi-cloud deployments
   Containers make it easier to deploy applications across different cloud environments or on-premises infrastructure. AKS simplifies managing these deployments across Azure and other cloud providers.

Key advantages

Managed service
   Reduces the operational overhead of managing Kubernetes clusters by handling infrastructure, updates, and scaling.

Integration with Azure Services
> Seamlessly integrates with other Azure services such as Microsoft Entra ID, Azure Monitor, and Azure Container Registry.

Faster deployment
> Enables rapid deployment by packaging applications and their dependencies together in containers, reducing setup time.

Lower resource overhead
> Leads to more efficient use of resources, because containers are lightweight compared to traditional VMs.

Consistency across environments
> Through the use of containers, ensures that applications run consistently across different environments, from development to production.

Scalability
> Automatically scales applications and infrastructure based on demand, improving resource utilization and performance.

Security
> Leverages Azure's security features to protect applications and data, ensuring compliance with industry standards.

Limitations

Complexity
> Kubernetes itself can be complex, and understanding its concepts and configurations may require a learning curve.

Cost
> Costs can accumulate based on usage, scaling, and the number of nodes, which may become significant depending on the deployment size.

Azure Container Instances

Azure Container Instances (ACI) is a compute service that enables you to run containerized applications in a serverless environment. It provides a quick and easy way to deploy and manage containers without needing to manage the underlying infrastructure. ACI is designed for scenarios where you need to run containers without the complexity of orchestrating them, making it suitable for various use cases, including development, testing, and simple production workloads.

To better understand ACI, let's imagine that you're organizing a user group event and need to rent various equipment—tables, chairs, a microphone, and a projector. You go to a rental service where you can choose and rent these items for the duration of the event. The rental service delivers the equipment to your event location, sets it up, and after the event, they come back to pick up the equipment. They will also clean and see to any needed maintenance of the used equipment. You pay only for the rental period and use the equipment as needed.

In this analogy:

- Rental equipment represents the container instances. Each item you rent serves a specific purpose during the event, just as each container instance runs a specific application or service.
- The rental service represents Azure container instances. Just as the rental service provides and manages the equipment, ACI provides and manages the containers.
- The event's duration symbolizes the ephemeral nature of containers in ACI. Just as you use the rental equipment only for the duration of your event, containers in ACI are temporary and used only for the duration of the task.

Key features

Serverless containers
   Provides a serverless model for running containers, meaning that you don't need to manage or provision the underlying virtual machines or infrastructure.

On-demand
   Allows deployment of containers quickly on a pay-per-use basis, allowing you to run containers for short durations without long-term commitments.

Simple deployment
   Enables deployment of containers using Docker Images from any container registry, including Azure Container Registry, Docker Hub, or private registries.

Flexible resources
   Allows you to specify CPU and memory resources based on your application's needs, with the ability to scale resources up or down as required.

Networking and storage
   Supports virtual network integration, enabling secure communication with other Azure resources, and provides options for mounting Azure File Shares for persistent storage.

Common use cases

Development and testing
   Ideal for running development and test environments where you need quick, isolated containers without infrastructure management

Batch jobs and scheduled tasks
> Suitable for running batch-processing jobs, data processing, or scheduled tasks that don't require long-term infrastructure

Single-container deployments
> Effective for scenarios where a simple, single-container application is required without the need for orchestration or complex configurations

Microservices
> Can be used for lightweight microservices that don't require the full capabilities of Kubernetes or other orchestration platforms

Key advantages

Quick deployment
> Enables rapid deployment of containerized applications without the need for complex orchestration or infrastructure management.

Cost-effective
> Offers a pay-as-you-go pricing model, allowing you to pay only for the compute and storage resources you use, with no long-term commitments.

Flexibility
> Supports a wide range of container images and configurations, with the ability to adjust CPU and memory resources based on workload requirements.

Integration
> Integrates with other Azure services, including Azure Virtual Networks, Azure Storage, and Azure Monitor, to provide a comprehensive solution for your containerized applications.

Limitations

Scalability
> While ACI is suitable for single-container or small-scale workloads, it doesn't provide the advanced orchestration capabilities of services like AKS.

Limited persistence
> Containers in ACI are ephemeral, which means that data stored locally within a container is lost if the container is stopped or deleted. Persistent storage options are available but may require additional configuration.

No built-in orchestration
> ACI lacks the built-in orchestration features for managing complex container deployments, scaling, and load balancing that are available in more advanced container platforms.

PaaS: Managed Container Services and Azure Container Apps

Azure Container Apps is a fully managed serverless container service that allows you to deploy and run containerized applications without managing the underlying infrastructure. With Azure Container Apps, you can focus on developing and deploying your containerized applications while Azure takes care of the operational aspects such as scaling, patching, and infrastructure management.

To illustrate what an Azure Container App offers, suppose you're planning a series of outdoor fitness classes in your local park. Instead of investing in a permanent fitness center, you rent portable exercise stations equipped with yoga mats, dumbbells, and resistance bands from a rental service. The rental company provides a fully managed service by delivering and setting up the equipment at the park for each class and taking it down afterward. You pay only for the equipment while the classes are going on and have no need to worry about long-term storage or maintenance.

In this analogy:

- Portable exercise stations represent the containerized applications deployed in Azure Container Apps. Each piece of equipment (container) serves a specific purpose during the fitness classes.
- The rental company represents Azure Container Apps. Just as the company manages the delivery, setup, and removal of the equipment, Azure Container Apps handles the deployment, scaling, and management of your containers.
- Class duration symbolizes the flexible and scalable nature of Azure Container Apps. Just as you use the equipment only during the classes, Azure Container Apps manages containers that run for as long as needed, automatically scaling based on demand.

Key features

Serverless containers
    Automatically scales container instances based on demand without requiring manual intervention or management of the underlying infrastructure.

Event-driven
    Supports integration with various event sources such as Azure Event Grid, Azure Service Bus, and HTTP triggers, enabling you to build event-driven architectures.

Flexible scaling
    Offers built-in scaling options based on CPU usage, memory, or custom metrics, ensuring that applications can handle varying loads efficiently.

Managed environment
> Provides a fully managed platform that abstracts away infrastructure concerns, including server management, patching, and scaling.

Integration with Azure Services
> Seamlessly integrates with other Azure services, including Azure Key Vault for secrets management, Azure Monitor for logging and monitoring, and Azure Logic Apps for workflow automation.

Common use cases

Microservices
> Ideal for deploying microservices architectures where containers can be scaled independently based on demand

Serverless workloads
> Executing workloads that benefit from automatic scaling and a pay-as-you-go pricing model

Event-driven applications
> Suitable for applications that respond to events from various sources such as message queues, webhooks, or timers

Web applications
> Useful for hosting web applications and APIs that require automatic scaling and are built using containerized environments

Batch jobs and background tasks
> Effective for running batch jobs or background tasks that can benefit from scalable container execution

Key Advantages

Serverless model
> Eliminates the need to manage and provision infrastructure, allowing you to focus solely on your applications and code.

Automatic scaling
> Automatically scales container instances up or down based on workload demands, optimizing resource usage and cost.

Ease of deployment
> Simplifies deployment of containerized applications with built-in CI/CD integration and streamlined configuration.

Integration
 Works well with Azure's ecosystem of services, providing seamless integration with tools for security, monitoring, and automation.

Limitations

Limited to container workloads
 It's primarily suited for containerized applications and may not be ideal for workloads that require traditional virtual machines or other infrastructure.

Complexity of event-driven architectures
 While it supports event-driven scenarios, managing complex event flows and integrations may require additional configuration and setup.

Feature scope
 While Azure Container Apps is production-ready, it container may not provide the same level of low-level control and advanced customization available in AKS.

Choosing the Right Compute Service

Choosing the right Azure compute service depends on various factors, including the specific needs of your application, workload characteristics, budget, and management preferences.

Here's a guide to help you select the most suitable Azure compute service:

Azure Virtual Machines
 Best for applications requiring full control over the operating system and infrastructure with flexibility in configurations

Azure Virtual Machine Scale Sets
 Perfect for large-scale deployments needing automatic scaling and high availability

Azure App Service
 Ideal for web applications and APIs requiring a managed platform with built-in scaling and deployment features

Azure Functions
 Optimal for event-driven and background tasks that benefit from a serverless model and automatic scaling

Azure Kubernetes Service
 Best for complex containerized applications requiring orchestration and scaling with Kubernetes

Azure Container Instances
  Useful for quick deployments of single containers or batch jobs with minimal management

Azure Container Apps
  Suitable for running scalable, event-driven containerized applications in a serverless environment

Table 9-1 provides a quick reference to help you choose the right Azure compute service based on your application needs, management preferences, and scaling requirements.

Table 9-1. Quick reference for choosing the right Azure compute service

Feature/ Service	Azure VMs	Azure VMSS	Azure App Service	Azure Functions	AKS	ACI	Azure Container Apps
Deployment model	IaaS	IaaS with autoscaling	PaaS	Serverless	Container orchestration as a service	Serverless containers	Serverless containers
Management overhead	High	Medium	Low	Very low	Medium to high	Very low	Very low
Scaling	Manual or autoscaling via VMSS	Autoscaling	Autoscaling	Autoscaling	Autoscaling	Manual scaling	Autoscaling
Networking	Virtual networks, NSGs	Virtual networks, NSGs	Integrated networking and load balancing	Integration with event sources	Virtual networks, NSGs, load balancing	Optional VNet integration, limited NSG support	Virtual networks, NSGs
Integration	Integrates with Azure services	Integrates with Azure services	Integrates with CI/CD, monitoring, etc.	Integrates with event-driven services	Integrates with Azure services and tools	Integrates with Azure services	Integrates with Azure services
Use cases	Legacy apps, custom configurations	Large-scale deployments, autoscaling	Web apps, APIs, mobile backends	Event-driven apps, background tasks	Microservices, complex deployments	Quick deployments, batch jobs, testing	Microservices, event-driven applications
Cost model	Pay-as-you-go or reserved instances	Pay-as-you-go, scaling affects cost	Pay-as-you-go	Pay-per-execution	Pay-as-you-go, based on cluster resources	Pay-per-use	Pay-per-use
Advantages	Full control, flexible configurations	Autoscaling, high availability	Managed environment, ease of use	Serverless, cost-effective, simple	Managed Kubernetes, scalable, flexible	Fast deployment, low management overhead	Serverless, easy deployment, autoscaling

Feature/ Service	Azure VMs	Azure VMSS	Azure App Service	Azure Functions	AKS	ACI	Azure Container Apps
Limitations	High management, scaling complexity	Configuration complexity	Limited control over infrastructure	Stateless, limited for long-running tasks	Complex setup and management	Limited orchestration features	Limited to containerized workloads

By carefully evaluating these factors, you can select the Azure compute service that best aligns with your application requirements, operational preferences, and budget constraints.

Bonus Material: Azure Application and Integration Services (Optional)

Now that we've explored the core Azure compute services, it's useful to take a look at Azure App Service and Azure Integration Services.

This section is included as bonus material to give you a complete picture of how Azure supports modern, connected cloud solutions.

Modern cloud applications rarely work in isolation. They often need to interact and communicate with other apps, services, or systems, both inside and outside of Azure. Azure offers a set of application and integration services designed to simplify this communication, automate workflows, and ensure reliable messaging between components.

While these are not traditional compute resources, they complement compute by enabling applications to communicate, automate workflows, and handle messaging reliably.

The key services that we'll cover in this bonus section include:

API Management
  Management of APIs and control access to connect disparate systems

Logic Apps
  Automation of repetitive workflows and business processes

Event Grid
  Enablement of event-driven messaging for reactive applications

Service Bus
    Reliable, asynchronous communication between applications

Let's start by having a look at API Management.

Azure API Management

Azure API Management (APIM) is a fully managed service that helps organizations publish, secure, monitor, and scale APIs. It acts as a gateway between your backend services and the clients (developers, apps, or partners) consuming those APIs. APIM is part of Azure's integration services, which allow different systems and applications to communicate securely and efficiently.

Key features

API gateway
    Acts as a single entry point for all API calls.

Security and access control
    Protects APIs with authentication, rate limiting, and quotas.

Monitoring and analytics
    Track usage patterns and performance of your APIs.

Developer portal
    Provides a central location for developers to discover and test APIs.

Modernization of legacy services
    Exposes older systems through standardized APIs without rewriting them.

Key benefits

- Centralizes API management for your organization
- Secures APIs and ensures controlled access
- Provides insights into API usage and health
- Supports hybrid and multi-cloud environments

Common use cases

- A company wants to share internal services with external partners securely. APIM acts as the gateway and manages authentication and rate limits.
- An enterprise is modernizing legacy applications, exposing them as APIs without changing the underlying system.
- Developers need a central place to explore the APIs provided by an organization for building apps.

Azure Logic Apps

Azure Logic Apps is a fully managed workflow automation service that helps you connect apps, data, and services across cloud and on-premises environments. It enables you to automate tasks and orchestrate processes without writing custom code.

Key features

Workflow automation
Automates business processes with visual designers.

Connectors
Uses prebuilt integrations for hundreds of services like Office 365, Dynamics 365, SAP, and custom APIs.

Triggers and actions
Allows workflows to start automatically based on events or to run on schedules.

Scalability
Handles anything from simple tasks to complex enterprise workflows.

Key benefits

- Automates repetitive processes, saving time and reducing errors
- Connects cloud services and on-premises systems seamlessly
- Reduces the need for custom integration code

Common use cases

- Automatically send an email notification when a new file is uploaded to Azure Blob Storage.
- Integrate Salesforce and Dynamics 365 to synchronize customer data.
- Automate approval workflows for document management in an organization.

Azure Event Grid

Azure Event Grid is a fully managed event routing service that enables reactive, event-driven architectures. It allows applications to react to events in near real time by pushing messages to subscribers.

Key features

Event routing
Routes events from sources (e.g., storage, custom apps) to destinations (e.g., Azure Logic Apps, Azure Functions, webhooks).

High scalability
  Handles millions of events per second.

Reliability
  Ensures delivery of events with retry policies.

Serverless integration
  Works well with Functions and Logic Apps for event-driven automation.

Key benefits

- Decouples event producers from consumers, reducing complexity
- Supports serverless and reactive architectures
- Enables real-time notifications and automated responses

Common use cases

- Notify an application when a new blob is uploaded to Azure Storage.
- Trigger a Logic App workflow whenever a new user signs up.
- Send alerts to monitoring tools when infrastructure events occur.

Azure Service Bus

Azure Service Bus is a fully managed messaging service that allows reliable communication between decoupled applications. It ensures that messages are delivered even if the receiver is temporarily offline.

Key features

Message queues
  Store messages until they are processed by the receiving application.

Topics and subscriptions
  Use a publish/subscribe model for multiple receivers.

Guaranteed delivery
  Messages are reliably stored and delivered at least once, with support for duplicate detection to help achieve effectively once-only processing.

Integration across systems
  Connects cloud and on-premises applications.

Key benefits

- Enables asynchronous communication between applications
- Decouples components to improve reliability and scalability
- Supports complex messaging patterns like publish/subscribe and request/reply

Common use cases

- Decouple order processing systems from inventory management to handle high volumes reliably.
- Enable communication between microservices without direct dependencies.
- Implement retry and dead-letter mechanisms for critical message delivery.

Summary

This chapter provided an overview of Azure's compute offerings, covering services across IaaS, PaaS, serverless, and container-based solutions. It explained key services such as Virtual Machines, Azure App Service, Azure Functions, and Azure Kubernetes Service, highlighting their features, use cases, and benefits. Understanding these compute options helps you choose the right service to optimize performance, cost, and scalability for your specific workloads.

As a bonus, we've also included a section on Azure App Service and Azure Integration Services to show how Azure enables applications to communicate, automate workflows, and handle messaging reliably. This material gives you a more complete view of cloud application capabilities.

In the next chapter, we'll talk about Azure's networking services.

Chapter 9 Quiz

To check your answers, please refer to the "Chapter 9 Answer Key" on page 304.

1. Your company needs to deploy a custom legacy application that requires installing specialized third-party components and configuring system files. Your team wants full administrative access to the underlying operating system.

    Which Azure compute service meets this requirement?

    A. Azure Kubernetes Service

    B. Azure App Service

    C. Azure Virtual Machines

    D. Azure Functions

2. Your development team wants to deploy microservices that automatically scale based on HTTP requests and messages, but they don't want to manage container orchestration or the underlying infrastructure.

   Which Azure service is most appropriate for running scalable, event-driven containerized applications in a fully managed serverless environment?

   A. Azure Virtual Machines

   B. Azure Container Instances

   C. Azure Container Apps

   D. Azure Kubernetes Service

3. A retail application must handle fluctuating workloads, especially high seasonal traffic. The solution requires automated scaling of multiple identical VM instances, without manually provisioning additional servers.

   Which Azure service should be used?

   A. Availability sets

   B. Azure Firewall

   C. Azure Kubernetes Service

   D. Azure Virtual Machine Scale Sets

CHAPTER 10

Azure Networking Services

In the last chapter, we explored Azure compute services; as the foundation of any cloud-based application, these provide the necessary computational resources. However, Azure compute alone (especially in modern cloud-native and hybrid architectures) is not enough to build scalable, resilient solutions. That's where Azure networking comes in.

Azure networking is the backbone that connects, secures, and optimizes how resources communicate, both within the cloud and with the outside world. It ensures seamless interaction between application components, enabling efficiency, security, and performance.

In this chapter, we'll dive into the core principles of Azure networking that are essential for success on the AZ-900 Azure Fundamentals exam. We'll break down key concepts along with common use cases and best practices to help you understand their practical applications.

We'll start with the Open Systems Interconnection (OSI) model as it's mapped to Azure services, move to the foundational Azure Virtual Network (VNet), and then explore security, connectivity, and traffic management. By the end, you'll have a solid grasp of Azure networking and how it integrates with other Azure services to create complete, cloud-ready solutions.

There's a lot to cover, so let's get started!

The OSI Model

The *OSI model* is a conceptual framework that standardizes how computers communicate. It organizes communication into seven layers, each performing a specific role and interacting with the layers above and below it.

 The OSI model is a conceptual framework that standardizes the functions of a networking system into seven layers. It helps us understand how different networking protocols interact and communicate across networks.

Table 10-1 summarizes these layers. Don't worry if it doesn't all make sense yet. By the end of the chapter, each layer will become clear as we map it to Azure services. You can revisit this table anytime for a concise overview of each layer, its purpose, and corresponding Azure service examples.

Table 10-1. The OSI model in relation to Azure services

Layer	Name	Purpose	Protocols	Azure services
7	Application	Interfaces with end user apps; supports web, email, file transfer	HTTP, DNS, SMTP, REST APIs	App Gateway, Front Door, Traffic Manager, CDN, DNS, Bastion, Firewall (App Rules)
6	Presentation	Translates, encrypts, compresses data	TLS/SSL, JSON, XML	App Gateway (SSL termination), Front Door (TLS offloading), Key Vault (certificates)
5	Session	Manages sessions between endpoints	Session tokens, RPC	Apps Service (session affinity), App Gateway (cookie affinity)
4	Transport	Provides end-to-end communication; TCP/UDP	TCP, UDP	Load Balancer, network security groups (NSGs; port rules), ExpressRoute encapsulation, Firewall (network rules)
3	Network	Handles IP addressing, routing, forwarding	IP, routers	VNets, subnets, VNet peering, VPN Gateway, ExpressRoute, Firewall
2	Data link	Node-to-node delivery, MAC addressing	Ethernet, VLANs	ExpressRoute circuits, virtual network interface cards (NICs)
1	Physical	Sends raw bits over physical mediums	Fiber, WiFi, cabling	Datacenter network, ExpressRoute physical cross-connects

Understanding the OSI model helps you identify where Azure networking services operate and what problems they solve as you can see in Table 10-2.

Table 10-2. Mapping Azure networking services to OSI Layers

Azure networking service	OSI Layer
Azure Firewall	Layers 3–7
Network security groups	Layers 3–4
Azure Load Balancer	Layer 4
Azure Application Gateway	Layer 7
Azure ExpressRoute	Primarily Layer 3 for the core operation (Layer 2 applies to the underlying provider circuit in some cases)

This foundation helps you see how networking services form a hierarchical, secure architecture.

Azure Networking

Azure networking refers to the suite of services and features provided by Microsoft Azure to enable communication among Azure resources, on-premises infrastructure, and the internet. Azure networking encompasses a wide range of services, including virtual networks, load balancers, VPN gateways, and more, all designed to provide secure, reliable, and scalable networking solutions.

Azure networking can be explained using a simple analogy. Imagine that you're building a house where each room serves a specific function—a kitchen for cooking, a bedroom for sleeping, and a living room for relaxing. Each room's function represents an Azure compute resource, designed to perform a specific task.

However, without hallways and doors, these rooms would be isolated, making it impossible to move between them. That's where Azure networking comes in. Azure networking acts as the hallways and doorways, seamlessly connecting different rooms of your house and allowing you to move freely between them.

Your house itself represents the *Azure Virtual Network (VNet)*, a private, secure space where everything inside belongs to you. Similar to how your house is divided into rooms, your VNet is segmented into *subnets*. Your subnets allow you to organize and isolate your Azure resources (like databases, web servers, or applications) for better security and management.

And just like doors can have locks to control who can enter, Azure networking has network security groups (NSGs) and firewalls to secure access and protect your resources from unwanted visitors.

Why Is Azure Networking Important?

In the context of cloud computing, Azure networking enables:

Communication between Azure resources
> Azure VMs, databases, and other services need to communicate with each other to function as a cohesive application solution.

Connectivity to on-premises infrastructure
> Many organizations operate in a hybrid environment, where some resources are hosted on-premises and others in the cloud. Azure networking provides the necessary connectivity to bridge these two worlds.

Access to the internet
> Applications hosted in Azure often need to be accessible to users over the internet. Azure networking ensures that this access is secure and reliable.

Key Services in Azure Networking

Let's start by familiarizing ourselves with some key services that underpin Azure networking in Table 10-3.

Table 10-3. Key services in Azure networking

Azure networking service	Purpose	Example use case
VNet	A virtual network is a logically isolated section of the Azure cloud where you can deploy and manage Azure resources. It's similar to a traditional network in an on-premises data center but with the added flexibility and scalability of the cloud.	Creating a VNet to host application tiers such as web servers, application servers, and databases in separate subnets
Subnet	A subnet is a segmented portion of a virtual network. Subnets allow you to organize and secure your resources by grouping them into smaller, more manageable sections.	Splitting a VNet into frontend and backend subnets so only the frontend subnet is internet facing while the backend subnet remains private
NSG	An NSG is a firewall that controls inbound and outbound traffic to and from Azure resources. It allows you to define security rules to permit or deny traffic based on source, destination, port, and protocol.	Applying an NSG to block all inbound traffic except HTTPS (443) to a web server subnet
Public and private IP addresses	Azure resources can be assigned public IP addresses (accessible over the internet) or private IP addresses (accessible only within the virtual network).	Assigning a public IP to an Azure VM running a web server while backend VMs use only private IPs
Azure Load Balancer	A load balancer distributes incoming network traffic across multiple resources to ensure high availability and reliability.	Using Azure Load Balancer to spread traffic across multiple VMs running an application
Azure VPN Gateway	A VPN gateway enables secure, encrypted connections between virtual networks and on-premises networks over the internet.	Connecting an on-premises data center to Azure for secure hybrid communication using a site-to-site VPN
Azure ExpressRoute	ExpressRoute provides a private, dedicated connection between Azure and on-premises infrastructure, bypassing the public internet for enhanced security and performance.	A financial institution using ExpressRoute for low-latency, private connectivity to Azure for compliance-sensitive workloads

We'll do a deep dive into each of these Azure networking services in the next section.

Core Infrastructure: Azure VNet and Subnets

An Azure Virtual Network is the foundation of Azure networking, providing a private, secure environment for your cloud resources.

What Is a VNet?

As we discussed in our analogy, a VNet is like your house—a private space where everything inside belongs to you. It allows you to create an isolated network in the cloud, where you can deploy and manage VMs, databases, web applications, and other resources.

Exam Tip

A VNet is isolated from other VNets, by default.

Just as each house in a neighborhood is separate from the others, a VNet is isolated from other VNets, ensuring that your resources remain secure and protected from unauthorized access.

What Is a Subnet?

Within your house, different rooms serve specific purposes, and similarly, a VNet can be divided into subnets, organizing and isolating different resources to improve security, traffic management, and performance.

By using a VNet, you can connect, secure, and manage your cloud environment efficiently. It's just like designing a well-structured house with the proper layout, doors, and security measures to keep everything running smoothly.

Key Features of Azure VNet

Following are the key features of Azure VNet:

Isolation
   Each VNet is isolated from other VNets, providing a secure environment for your resources.

Subnetting
   You can divide a VNet into multiple subnets to organize and segment your resources.

IP addressing
   You can define your own IP address range for the VNet and assign private IP addresses to resources within the VNet.

DNS resolution
  Azure provides built-in DNS resolution for resources within a VNet, allowing them to communicate using domain names.

Connectivity
  You can connect VNets to each other, to on-premises networks, and to the internet.

Best Practices for Using Azure VNet

Here are some best practices for using Azure VNet:

Plan IP addressing carefully
  Use non-overlapping IP address ranges and adhere to Classless Inter-Domain Routing (CIDR) best practices.

Use subnets for segmentation
  Organize resources logically using subnets for better security and traffic control.

Enable NSGs
  Apply NSGs at both subnet and network interface card (NIC) levels to restrict traffic for enhanced security.

Monitor network traffic
  Enable Azure Network Watcher (you'll learn more about Azure Network Watcher later in this chapter) to track and diagnose network issues.

Use Cases for Azure VNet

Here are some use cases for Azure Virtual Network:

Hosting VMs
  Connect and manage Azure VMs securely within a private network.

Microservices and container networking
  Connect AKS or Azure App Service securely within a VNet.

How to Create an Azure VNet

Creating a VNet in Azure is a straightforward process. Here's a step-by-step guide:

1. Log in to the Azure portal (*https://portal.azure.com*) and sign in with your credentials.

2. Click on **Create a resource**, search for "Virtual network," and click **Create**, as shown in Figure 10-1.

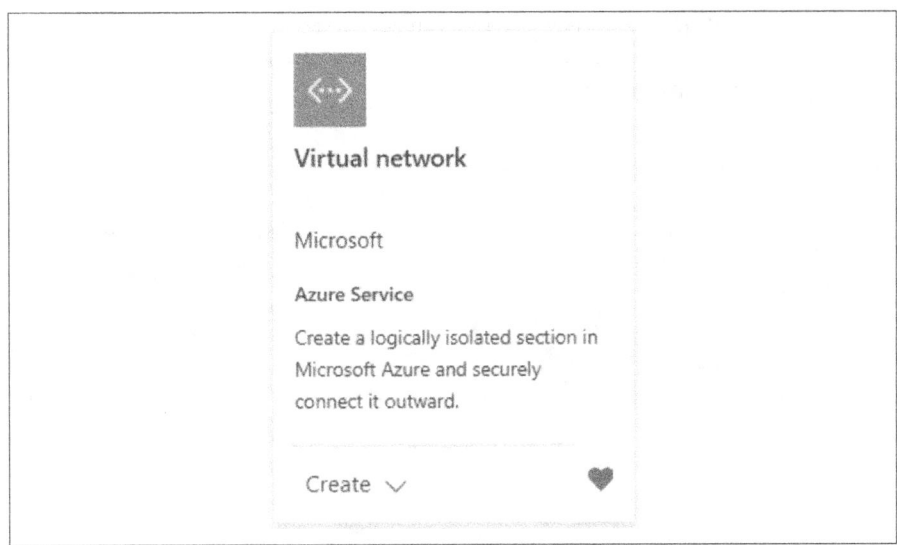

Figure 10-1. Creating a virtual network

3. Configure the VNet: Provide a name for your VNet and select the region, as shown in Figure 10-2.

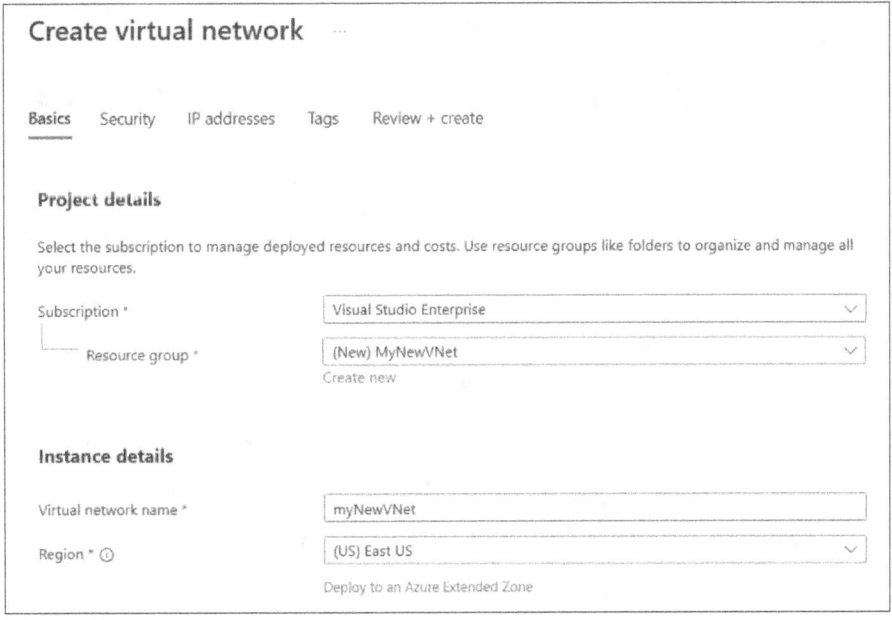

Figure 10-2. Configuring the VNet

Core Infrastructure: Azure VNet and Subnets | 145

4. Define the IP address range, as shown in Figure 10-3.

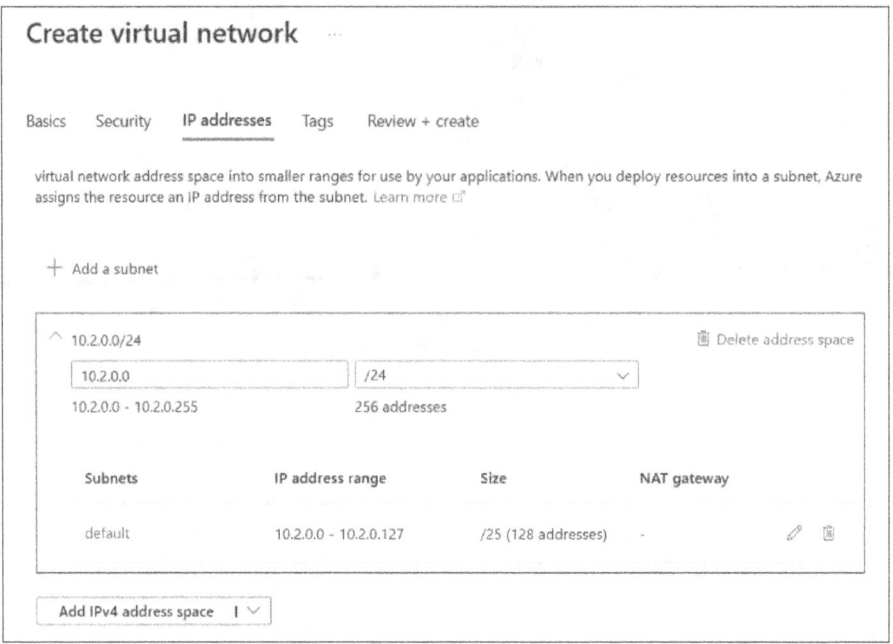

Figure 10-3. Defining the IP address range

5. Add subnets: Divide the VNet into subnets by specifying each subnet name and IP address range, as shown in Figure 10-4.

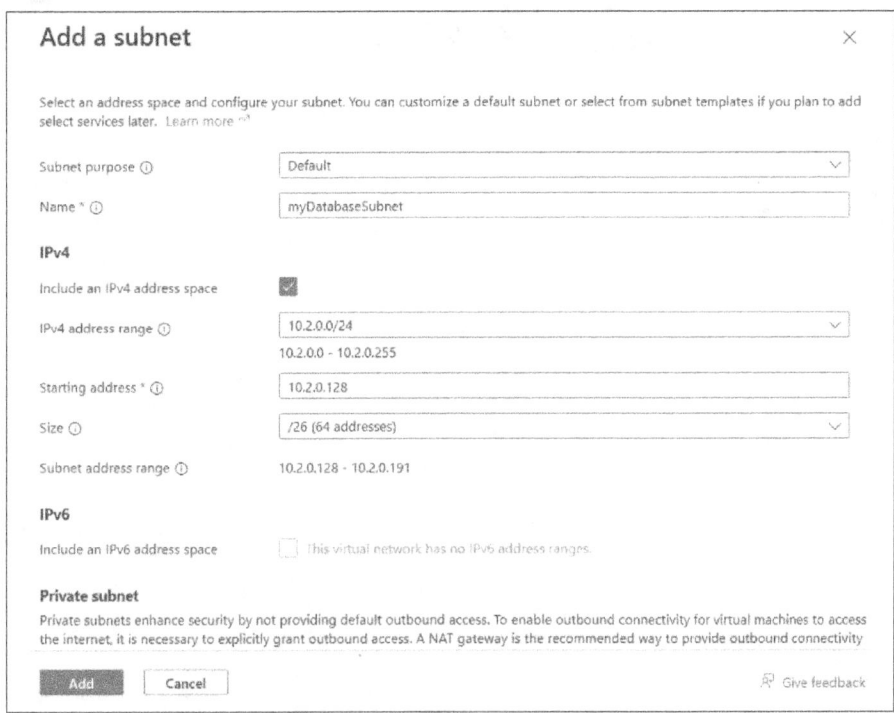

Figure 10-4. Adding a subnet

6. Review and create: Review the configuration and click **Create** to deploy the VNet, as shown in Figure 10-5.

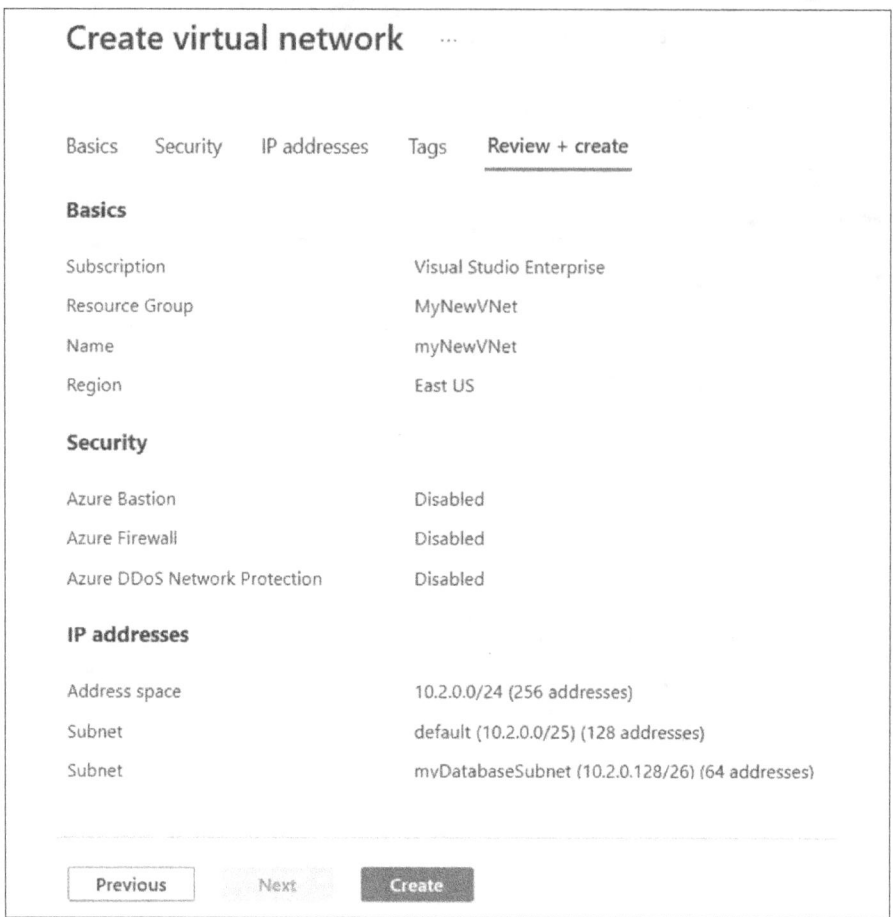

Figure 10-5. Reviewing the VNet's configuration before creating it

Virtual Network Peering

As you learned in the previous section, by default resources in one Azure VNet can't communicate with those in another VNet because each VNet is isolated for security and network segmentation.

To enable communication between VNets, you can use virtual network peering. *Virtual network peering* connects two VNets, whether in the same region or across different regions, allowing resources to interact securely and efficiently.

Key Features of Virtual Network Peering

These are the key features of virtual network peering:

Seamless connectivity
> Enables resources in different VNets to communicate as if they were on the same network, with low latency and high bandwidth.

Cross-region peering
> Supports peering between VNets in the same region (*intra-region*) or in different regions (*global peering*) for expanded network reach.

Private and secure communication
> Traffic between peered VNets stays within the Microsoft backbone network, avoiding exposure to the public internet.

Minimal latency
> Provides near-instant communication between VNets with negligible latency compared to VPN-based solutions.

Resource sharing
> Allows services like Azure VMs, databases, and application services in one VNet to access resources in another VNet.

Best Practices for Using Virtual Network Peering

Here are some best practices for using virtual network peering:

- Use virtual network peering within the same region whenever possible: Peering within the same region is faster and avoids extra costs.
- Consider bandwidth and latency: Cross-region peering incurs additional costs and higher latency.

Use Cases for Virtual Network Peering

One use case for virtual network peering involves peering two VNets. Suppose you have two VNets: VNet1 is for your development environment, and VNet2 is for QA. Both VNets are in the same region. By peering these VNets, developers can securely access QA resources for testing and troubleshooting, ensuring seamless collaboration while maintaining network security.

Another use case, centralizing network security and traffic routing through a hub VNet, involves developing a hub-and-spoke architecture.

Securing Azure Networking

This section covers key methods for securing your Azure network, including:

- Network security groups
- Azure Firewall
- Azure Bastion
- Public endpoints versus private endpoints

These tools and configurations help control access, protect resources, and ensure secure communication within and outside your Azure environment.

Network Security Groups

A *network security group* is a firewall that controls inbound and outbound traffic to and from Azure resources. It primarily operates at layer 3 (network layer) and layer 4 (transport layer) of the OSI model, filtering traffic based on IP addresses, ports, and protocols.

Think of an NSG as the security checkpoint at an airport. Before boarding a flight, you must pass through security, where your belongings are checked and you're screened for prohibited items. Similarly, an NSG inspects incoming and outgoing traffic to ensure that only authorized traffic is allowed through.

An NSG consists of a set of rules that control traffic based on source, destination, port, and protocol, ensuring that only approved connections are established while unauthorized traffic is denied.

Key Features of NSGs

Here are the key features of NSGs:

Security rules
 NSGs allow you to define rules that permit or deny traffic based on various criteria.

Association with subnets or NICs
 NSGs can be associated with subnets or individual NICs to control traffic at different levels.

Default rules
 NSGs come with a set of default rules that allow essential traffic, such as communication within the VNet and outbound internet access, to get through.

Best Practices for Using NSGs

Here are some best practices for using NSGs:

Follow the principle of least privilege
    Apply the principle of least privilege by allowing only necessary traffic and denying everything else.

Deny all traffic by default
    Allow only explicitly required traffic in order to reduce the potential attack surface.

Follow rule prioritization
    NSG rules are evaluated in order of priority. Ensure that higher-priority rules do not inadvertently block essential traffic.

Enable logging and monitoring
    Enable *NSG flow logs* to monitor and analyze traffic patterns for security and troubleshooting purposes.

Use Cases for NSG

Here are some use cases for NSG:

Restrict inbound and outbound traffic
    Control access to resources using fine-grained security rules.

Secure web applications
    Block unwanted IPs while allowing specific inbound/outbound connections.

Segment internal traffic
    Apply different security rules for subnets that host databases, applications, and frontends.

Block malicious traffic
    Prevent unauthorized access and block traffic from suspicious sources.

Azure Firewall

Azure Firewall is a managed, cloud-based network security service that protects your Azure VNet resources from unauthorized access. It primarily operates at layer 4 (transport layer) and layer 7 (application layer) of the OSI model, enabling both network-level and application-level traffic filtering.

Think of Azure Firewall as a security checkpoint at the entrance of a secure facility. Before anyone is allowed to enter, they must pass through the checkpoint. The guard verifies their identity and checks their belongings for forbidden items. Similarly,

Azure Firewall inspects all incoming and outgoing traffic, allowing only authorized connections while blocking potential threats.

Key Features of Azure Firewall

Here are the key features of Azure Firewall:

Stateful firewall
: Provides stateful inspection of network traffic, allowing or denying traffic based on defined rules.

Threat intelligence
: Integrates with Microsoft Defender Threat Intelligence to block traffic from known malicious IP addresses and domains.

SNAT support
: Provides outbound Source Network Address Translation (SNAT) support to hide the internal IP addresses of resources behind the firewall.

High availability
: Built-in high availability ensures that the firewall is always available to protect your resources.

What Is SNAT?

Source Network Address Translation (SNAT) is a networking technique that allows devices in a private network to access the internet using a single public IP address. In simpler terms, it's a mechanism that "masks" the private IP addresses of your internal servers so they can "go out" to the internet, without the internet knowing exactly who they are.

Best Practices for Using Azure Firewall

Here are some best practices for using Azure Firewall:

Use application and network rules
: Define rules to allow only essential traffic.

Enable threat intelligence
: Block traffic from known malicious IPs.

Centralize your firewall management
: Manage multiple firewalls via the Azure Firewall manager.

Monitor and log traffic
: Enable Azure Monitor logs to track network activity.

Use Cases for Azure Firewall

Here are some use cases for Azure Firewall:

Network security
   Protect Azure VNets from unauthorized access and malicious traffic.

Compliance
   Meet compliance requirements by enforcing strict network security policies.

Centralized management
   Centralize the management of network security policies across multiple Azure subscriptions and virtual networks.

Azure Bastion

Azure Bastion is a fully managed service that provides secure and seamless Remote Desktop Protocol (RDP) and Secure Shell (SSH) access to VMs directly from the Azure portal. It primarily operates at layer 7 (application layer) of the OSI model, as it facilitates application-level remote access over secure protocols.

Imagine that you're working from home and need to access your office computer. Instead of exposing your office computer to the internet, you use a secure remote access solution that allows you to connect directly to your computer, without exposing it to potential threats.

Key Features of Azure Bastion

This listing describes the key features of Azure Bastion:

Secure access
   Provides secure RDP and SSH access to VMs without exposing them to the public internet.

No public IP required
   Eliminates the need for a public IP address on the VMs, reducing the attack surface.

Integrated with Azure portal
   Allows you to connect to VMs directly from the Azure portal without additional clients or software.

High availability
   Built-in high availability ensures that the service is always available for secure access.

Best Practices for Using Azure Bastion

Here are some best practices for using Azure Bastion:

Avoid public IPs on VMs
   Use Azure Bastion instead of exposing VMs to the public internet.

Enable IP-based access restrictions
   Restrict Azure Bastion access to specific IP ranges.

Use RBAC
   Limit access to Azure Bastion by assigning Azure RBAC roles.

Use Cases for Azure Bastion

Here are some use cases for Azure Bastion:

Secure remote access
   Provide secure RDP and SSH access to Azure VMs for administrators and developers.

Compliance
   Meet compliance requirements by ensuring that VMs are not exposed to the public internet.

Simplified management
   Simplify the management of remote access by integrating it directly into the Azure portal.

Public Endpoints Versus Private Endpoints

Azure networking supports both public and private endpoints for various services:

- *Public endpoints* are accessible over the internet and are associated with a public IP address. They allow global access, provided security rules permit it.
- *Private endpoints* use a private IP address within a VNet and are accessible only within that VNet or through connected networks (e.g., peered VNets, VPN, or ExpressRoute).

Think of a public endpoint as the front door of a shop on a busy street—it's visible and accessible to anyone walking by. Customers from anywhere may enter, provided they follow the store's rules.

A private endpoint, on the other hand, is like a door to a private office inside a gated building—only people who are already inside the building (or have special access through a connected corridor) can reach it. It keeps the space secure and restricted from the general public.

When to Use Public Endpoints Versus Private Endpoints

Use Table 10-4 to help you determine when to use public endpoints and when you should use private ones.

Table 10-4. Public endpoint or private endpoint?

Scenario	Use public endpoint	Use private endpoint
Hosting a public website or API	Yes	No
Running internal business applications	No	Yes
Securely connecting PaaS services (Storage, SQL) within Azure	No	Yes
Allowing external users to access a service globally	Yes	No
Ensuring compliance and security (e.g., in the financial or healthcare sector)	No	Yes

Comparison of Public and Private Endpoints

Table 10-5 shows a comparison of public and private endpoints on a variety of features.

Table 10-5. Comparison of public and private endpoints

Feature	Public endpoints	Private endpoints
IP type	Public IP	Private IP (from VNet)
Accessibility	Available over the internet	Only accessible within the VNet or connected networks (e.g., VNet peering, VPN, ExpressRoute)
Security risks	Exposed to potential internet threats (DDoS, unauthorized access)	More secure as it avoids internet exposure
Use case	Hosting public-facing apps, websites, APIs	Connecting PaaS services securely to a VNet
Common Azure services	Azure App Service, Azure Load Balancer, Azure Storage (public access)	Azure Storage, Azure SQL Database, Azure Key Vault (via private link)
Internet dependency	Yes, requires internet access	No, remains within the private Azure backbone
DNS resolution	Public fully qualified domain name (FQDN) Example: mystorage.blob.core.windows.net	Private fully qualified domain name (FQDN) Example: mystorage.privatelink.blob.core.windows.net
Network security integration	Can be restricted using NSGs, Azure Firewall, and web application firewall (WAF)	Uses private link, NSGs, and custom DNS for security

Controlling Traffic: Load Balancing

Azure offers several load-balancing services, each designed to operate at different layers of the OSI model.

The four primary load-balancing services covered in this section are:

- Azure Load Balancer (layer 4)
- Azure Application Gateway (layer 7)
- Azure Traffic Manager (DNS level)
- Azure Front Door (layer 7, global)

Each service helps distribute traffic, improve performance, and ensure high availability for your applications.

Azure Load Balancer

Azure Load Balancer is a service that distributes incoming network traffic across multiple resources to ensure high availability and reliability. It operates at layer 4 (transport layer) of the OSI model and can handle both inbound and outbound traffic for your applications.

Imagine that you're managing a theme park with multiple entrances. To prevent long lines at any single entrance, you deploy staff members to direct visitors to the least crowded entrances. The Azure Load Balancer works in a similar way, evenly distributing incoming traffic across multiple resources to ensure optimal performance and availability.

Key Features of Azure Load Balancer

Following are the key features of Azure Load Balancer:

Load balancing
    Distributes traffic evenly across multiple resources to prevent overloading any single resource.

High availability
    Ensures your application remains available even if one or more resources fail.

Health probes
    Monitors the health of resources and routes traffic only to healthy instances.

Scalability
    Scales to handle large volumes of traffic and integrates with autoscaling services such as VM Scale Sets and AKS.

Types of Azure Load Balancers

Azure offers two types of load balancers:

Public load balancer
 Distributes traffic from the internet to Azure resources.

Internal load balancer
 Distributes traffic within a VNet, typically for internal applications that are not exposed to the internet.

Best Practices for Using Azure Load Balancer

Here are some best practices for using Azure Load Balancer:

Choose the right load balancer type
 Use a public load balancer for internet-facing traffic and an internal load balancer for private traffic.

Ensure that health probes are configured
 Set up health probes to detect and reroute failed backend instances.

Use load balancing rules efficiently
 Configure rules that match your application's needs.

Enable high-availability zones
 Distribute traffic across availability zones for better resilience.

Use Cases for Azure Load Balancer

Here are some use cases for Azure Load Balancer:

Web applications
 Distribute incoming web traffic across multiple web servers to ensure high availability and scalability.

Database replication
 Balance read traffic across multiple database replicas to improve performance.

Virtual desktop infrastructure (VDI)
 Distribute user connections across multiple VDI hosts to ensure a smooth user experience.

Azure Application Gateway

Azure Application Gateway is a web traffic load balancer that operates at layer 7 (application layer) of the OSI model.

Think of Azure Application Gateway as a restaurant menu. When you visit a restaurant, the menu provides different options for appetizers, main courses, and desserts. Based on your selection, the waiter directs your order to the appropriate kitchen station. Similarly, Azure Application Gateway intelligently routes incoming traffic to the correct backend pool based on the URL path and other routing rules.

Azure Application Gateway also offers advanced traffic management features such as SSL termination, URL-based routing, and web application firewall (WAF) to enhance security and performance.

Key Features of Azure Application Gateway

This listing highlights the key features of Azure Application Gateway:

SSL termination
    Offloads SSL decryption from backend servers, improving performance and reducing latency.

URL-based routing
    Routes traffic based on the URL path, allowing you to direct traffic to different backend pools.

WAF
    Provides protection against common web vulnerabilities, such as SQL injection and cross-site scripting (XSS).

Autoscaling
    Automatically scales to handle increased traffic without manual intervention.

Best Practices for Using Azure Application Gateway

Here are some best practices for using Azure Application Gateway:

Enable WAF
    Protect against common web threats like SQL Injection and XSS attacks.

Use URL-based routing
    Direct traffic based on request URLs for better traffic segmentation.

Enable SSL termination
    Offload SSL encryption to reduce backend server load.

Configure autoscaling
    Ensure sufficient capacity by scaling up/down based on traffic needs.

Use Cases for Azure Application Gateway

Here are some use cases for Azure Application Gateway:

Web applications
    Load balance web traffic across multiple backend servers while providing SSL termination and URL-based routing.

API management
    Route API traffic to different backend services based on the API endpoint.

Security
    Protect web applications from common vulnerabilities using the built-in WAF.

Azure Traffic Manager

Azure Traffic Manager is a DNS-based global traffic distribution service that directs incoming client requests to the most appropriate Azure regions or endpoints.

Imagine that you're an air traffic controller responsible for managing the arrival and departure of flights at a busy airport. Your goal is to ensure that flights are routed to the most suitable runways based on factors such as weather, runway availability, and flight priority. Azure Traffic Manager works in a similar way, routing incoming traffic to the most suitable endpoint based on predefined rules and conditions.

Azure Traffic Manager helps improve availability and responsiveness of applications by routing traffic to the optimal endpoint based on various routing methods.

Key Features of Azure Traffic Manager

These are the key features of Azure Traffic Manager:

Global load balancing
    Distributes traffic across multiple Azure regions to ensure high availability and performance.

Routing methods
    Supports various routing methods, including priority, weighted, performance, and geographic routing.

Health monitoring
    Continuously monitors the health of endpoints and routes traffic only to healthy endpoints.

Scalability
    Automatically scales to handle high volumes of traffic without manual intervention.

Best Practices for Using Azure Traffic Manager

Here are some best practices for using Azure Traffic Manager:

Choose the proper routing method

- Use performance-based routing for user proximity.
- Use priority routing for failover.
- Use weighted routing for load balancing.
- Use geographic routing to direct users to region-specific services based on their location.

Enable endpoint monitoring

- Set up health checks to ensure that only healthy endpoints receive traffic.

Use traffic manager for multi-region deployments

- Improve availability and failover readiness.

Use Cases for Azure Traffic Manager

Here are some use cases for Azure Traffic Manager:

Global applications
    Distribute traffic across multiple Azure regions to ensure high availability and low latency.

Disaster recovery
    Route traffic to a secondary region in the event of a failure in the primary region.

A/B testing
    Distribute traffic between different versions of an application for A/B testing and canary deployments (i.e., releasing in production to only a small group of users).

Azure Front Door

Azure Front Door operates at layer 7 (application layer) and provides a global entry point for web applications, ensuring fast, secure, and reliable user experiences. It combines global load balancing, SSL offloading, caching, and a WAF to optimize performance, enhance security, and maintain high availability across regions.

Think of Azure Front Door as a global airline hub for your web applications. Imagine passengers (users) from all over the world trying to reach various airports (your application endpoints in different regions). Front Door acts like the airline's central operations center, determining the fastest, safest, and most efficient route for each passenger. It directs them to the nearest or healthiest airport, handles security checks (like a WAF), and ensures smooth travel with minimal delays (caching and SSL offloading).

Just like a global airline hub keeps flights efficient, secure, and reliable, Azure Front Door ensures that your users get a fast, safe, and consistent experience no matter where they are in the world.

Key Features of Azure Front Door

Here are some key features of Azure Front Door:

Global load balancing
    Directs users to the nearest or fastest backend endpoint.

Application acceleration
    Uses caching and anycast-based routing (i.e., having multiple servers with the same IP address and sending data to the one closest to the user) to reduce latency.

WAF
    Protects against common web threats.

SSL offloading
    Terminates SSL at the edge, reducing backend load.

Best Practices for Using Azure Front Door

Best practices for using Azure Front Door include:

- Integrate WAF policies for security.
- Use caching to accelerate content delivery.
- Combine Front Door with Application Gateway for regional traffic management if needed.

Use Cases for Azure Front Door

Consider these example use cases for Azure Front Door:

- Deliver web applications globally with low latency.
- Provide secure, fast access for users across multiple regions.
- Improve resilience by automatically routing traffic away from unhealthy endpoints.

Comparison of the Load-Balancing Services

The various load-balancing services we've discussed operate at different layers of the OSI model and are most appropriate for different use cases. Table 10-6 offers a quick reference to the information in this section.

Table 10-6. Comparison of load-balancing services

Service	Layer	Scope	Main use case
Azure Load Balancer	4	Regional	Distributing network traffic to multiple VMs or services
Azure Application Gateway	7	Regional	HTTP/HTTPS routing with WAF and URL-based routing
Azure Traffic Manager	DNS	Global	Routing users to an optimal endpoint based on performance or priority
Azure Front Door	7	Global	Fast, secure web traffic delivery with WAF, SSL offload, and caching

Hybrid Connectivity

In this section, we'll focus on hybrid connectivity solutions. In particular, we'll look at:

- Azure VPN Gateway
- Azure ExpressRoute

Azure VPN Gateway

Azure VPN Gateway is a service that enables secure, encrypted connections between Azure virtual networks and on-premises networks over the internet.

Think of Azure VPN Gateway as a secure tunnel that connects two separate locations, such as your home and your workplace. This tunnel is encrypted, ensuring that no one can intercept or tamper with the data as it travels between the two locations.

Azure VPN Gateway supports both point-to-site and site-to-site VPN connections, allowing an organization to extend its on-premises network to the cloud for secure and reliable communication.

Key features of Azure VPN gateway

Here are the key features of the Azure VPN Gateway:

Secure connectivity
    Encrypts data in transit to ensure secure communication between Azure and on-premises networks.

Site-to-site VPN
> Establishes a secure connection between an on-premises network and an Azure VNet.

Point-to-site VPN
> Allows individual devices to connect securely to an Azure VNet.

High availability
> Supports active-active configurations for high availability and redundancy.

Best practices for Azure VPN Gateway

Azure VPN Gateway best practices include:

Select the right SKU
> Choose the VPN Gateway SKU based on bandwidth and connection requirements.

Use active-active mode
> Improve redundancy by enabling multiple tunnels.

Optimize routing
> Use Border Gateway Protocol (BGP) for dynamic routing between networks.

Monitor connection health
> Enable Azure Monitor to track connection stability and performance.

Use cases for Azure VPN Gateway

Here are some use cases for Azure VPN Gateway:

Hybrid cloud
> Connect on-premises data centers to Azure VNets for hybrid cloud deployments.

Remote access
> Allow remote employees to securely access Azure resources over a VPN connection.

Disaster recovery
> Establish secure connections between Azure and on-premises disaster recovery sites.

Azure ExpressRoute

Azure ExpressRoute is a service that provides a private, dedicated connection between Azure and on-premises infrastructure, ensuring faster, more reliable, and secure connectivity.

Imagine that you're commuting to work. Instead of using public roads, which can be slow and congested, you have access to a private highway that offers a smoother, faster, and more secure journey. Azure ExpressRoute works the same way, creating a direct, high-speed connection between your on-premises network and Azure.

Unlike VPN connections, which rely on the public internet, ExpressRoute bypasses the internet, providing enhanced security, greater reliability, and consistent performance for enterprise workloads. ExpressRoute works at the lower layers of networking: OSI layer 2 (data link layer) and layer 3 (network layer). This means it uses a dedicated private connection (like a private highway) to route private IP traffic between your on-premises network and Azure, avoiding the public internet.

Key features of Azure ExpressRoute

Following are the key features of Azure ExpressRoute:

Private connectivity
    Establishes a private connection between Azure and on-premises networks, bypassing the public internet.

High bandwidth
    Supports high-bandwidth connections, ranging from 50 Mbps up to 100 Gbps, depending on the ExpressRoute SKU and provider.

Global reach
    Provides connectivity to Azure regions worldwide, enabling global deployments.

Redundancy
    Offers built-in redundancy for high availability and reliability.

Best practices for using Azure ExpressRoute

Here are some best practices for using Azure ExpressRoute:

Use ExpressRoute circuits
    Deploy multiple ExpressRoute circuits in different locations for high availability.

Leverage global reach
    Connect multiple ExpressRoute circuits across regions for better connectivity.

Monitor and optimize bandwidth
    Use Azure Monitor to check bandwidth utilization.

Plan for failover
    Have a backup VPN connection for redundancy in case issues arise with ExpressRoute.

Use Cases for Azure ExpressRoute

Some example use cases for Azure ExpressRoute include:

Enterprise connectivity
　　Connect large enterprise networks to Azure for secure and reliable cloud access.

Data-intensive applications
　　Support data-intensive applications that require high bandwidth and low latency.

Compliance and security
　　Meet compliance requirements by ensuring that data does not traverse the public internet.

Azure Domain Name System

Azure Domain Name System (DNS) is a hosting service for DNS domains that provides name resolution using Microsoft Azure infrastructure. Operating at layer 7 (application layer) of the OSI model, it translates human-readable domain names (e.g., *www.oreilly.com*) into machine-readable IP addresses, allowing users and applications to locate and connect to resources in Azure or on the internet.

DNS is a distributed directory that translates human-friendly domain names (like (*https://www.oreilly.com*)) into machine-readable IP addresses (like 23.34.45.56).

Think of Azure DNS as a phone directory for the internet. When you want to call someone you don't talk to very often, you usually haven't memorized their phone number. Instead, you look up their unique name to find the correct phone number. Similarly, when you enter a website domain name, Azure DNS translates it into the corresponding IP address, directing your request to the right destination.

With Azure DNS, you can manage DNS records directly in Azure, ensuring fast and reliable DNS resolution for your applications.

Key Features of Azure DNS

Following are the key features of Azure DNS:

High availability
　　Ensures high availability and reliability because it's built on Azure's global network of data centers.

Scalability
　　Automatically scales to handle high volumes of DNS queries.

Integration with Azure services
   Seamlessly integrates with other Azure services, such as VNets and Traffic Manager.

Security
   Provides secure DNS resolution with support for DNS Security Extensions (DNSSEC).

Best Practices for Using Azure DNS

Here are some best practices for using Azure DNS:

- Use Private DNS zones for internal name resolution: Avoid using public DNS for private services.
- Enable autoregistration for private DNS zones: Simplify hostname management for the VMs in a VNet.
- Enable redundant DNS servers: Avoid having a single point of failure by using multiple DNS servers.
- Monitor DNS queries: Track DNS resolution logs for troubleshooting and security analysis.

Use Cases for Azure DNS

Consider these example use cases for Azure DNS:

Domain hosting
   Host your domain in Azure DNS for reliable and scalable name resolution.

Custom domains
   Use Azure DNS to manage custom domains for Azure services, such as Azure App Service and Azure Functions.

Traffic management
   Integrate Azure DNS with Azure Traffic Manager to route traffic based on DNS queries.

Azure Content Delivery Network

Azure Content Delivery Network (CDN) is a global network of servers that delivers content to users with high availability and low latency. It operates at layer 7 (application Layer) of the OSI model, optimizing the delivery of web content, media files, and applications by caching content closer to users and improving performance, reliability, and security.

Think of it as being like a library system with a central library and multiple branch locations. Instead of requiring users to visit the central library for every book, the system stores copies of popular books at the branch libraries, allowing users to access them faster and with less effort.

By offloading requests from origin servers, Azure CDN enhances speed, scalability, and reliability for applications and media delivery.

Key Features of Azure CDN

Here is a summary of the key features of Azure CDN:

Global reach
    Delivers content from edge locations worldwide, ensuring low latency for users regardless of their location.

Caching
    Caches static and dynamic content at edge locations to reduce the load on origin servers.

Optimization
    Provides optimization features for different types of content, such as images, videos, and web applications.

Security
    Offers security features, such as DDoS protection and HTTPS support, to protect content delivery.

Best Practices for Using Azure CDN

Here are some best practices for using Azure CDN:

Cache static content
    Use CDN caching for faster load times.

Use compression
    Enable Gzip compression to reduce data transfer sizes.

Enable custom domains and HTTPS
    Achieve secure content delivery with SSL/TLS.

Monitor CDN performance
    Use Azure CDN Core Analytics to track traffic patterns and cache performance.

Use Cases for Azure CDN

Azure CDN has a number of use cases, including:

Media delivery
: Deliver high-quality video and audio content to users with low latency and high availability.

Software distribution
: Distribute software updates and patches to users worldwide.

Web acceleration
: Accelerate the delivery of web content, such as images, CSS, and JavaScript files, to improve website performance.

Azure Network Watcher

Azure Network Watcher is a suite of tools that provides monitoring, diagnostics, and analytics for Azure networking resources. It operates across multiple OSI layers: from layer 3 (network layer) for IP-level monitoring and routing diagnostics up to layer 7 (application layer) for analyzing traffic patterns and application connectivity, helping to ensure network performance, security, and reliability.

Think of Azure Network Watcher as a network health checkup tool. Just as you visit a doctor for a regular checkup to monitor your vital signs and detect any potential issues, Azure Network Watcher continuously monitors your network's health and provides insights to help you detect and resolve issues before they impact your applications.

Key Features of Azure Network Watcher

Here are descriptions of the key features of Azure Network Watcher:

Network monitoring
: Provides real-time monitoring of network traffic, latency, and packet loss.

Diagnostics
: Offers diagnostic tools, such as IP flow verify, next hop, and packet capture, to troubleshoot network issues.

Topology visualization
: Visualizes the topology of your virtual network, including resources and their connections.

Security group view
: Provides a view of the effective security rules applied to a VM, helping you troubleshoot connectivity issues.

Best Practices for Using Azure Network Watcher

Here are some best practices for using Azure Network Watcher:

Enable Network Watcher for every region
　Ensure that monitoring tools are active in all regions your applications are using.

Use Azure's connection monitor
　Continuously track network connectivity between resources.

Analyze NSG flow logs
　Monitor inbound/outbound traffic for security insights.

Use packet capture
　Troubleshoot network latency and connectivity issues efficiently.

Use Cases for Azure Network Watcher

Here are some use cases for Azure Network Watcher:

Performance monitoring
　Monitor network performance and detect issues such as high latency or packet loss.

Troubleshooting
　Diagnose and resolve connectivity issues between Azure resources.

Security analysis
　Analyze network traffic to detect potential security threats and vulnerabilities.

Summary

In this chapter, we explored the key components of Azure networking, including virtual networks, network security groups, load balancers, VPN gateways, ExpressRoute, DNS, Traffic Manager, Application Gateway, CDN, Firewall, Bastion, and Network Watcher. Each of these services plays a vital role in building secure, reliable, and scalable cloud solutions.

This listing offers a quick reference to the services that we've covered:

Azure Virtual Network (VNet)
　Provides a secure, isolated environment for deploying and managing Azure resources.

Virtual network peering
　Enables communication between VNets.

Network security groups (NSGs)
Acts as a firewall to control inbound and outbound traffic to Azure resources.

Azure Firewall
Protects Azure VNets from unauthorized access and malicious traffic.

Azure Bastion
Provides secure RDP and SSH access to Azure VMs without exposing them to the public internet.

Azure Load Balancer
Distributes incoming traffic across multiple resources to ensure high availability and reliability.

Azure Application Gateway
Provides advanced traffic management features, including SSL termination and URL-based routing.

Azure Traffic Manager
Distributes traffic across multiple Azure regions to ensure high availability and performance.

Azure Front Door
Provides global, application-level routing, caching, acceleration, and WAF.

Azure VPN Gateway
Enables secure, encrypted connections between Azure and on-premises networks.

Azure ExpressRoute
Provides a private, dedicated connection between Azure and on-premises infrastructure.

Azure DNS
Offers reliable and scalable DNS resolution for your applications.

Azure CDN
Delivers content to users with high availability and low latency.

Azure Network Watcher
Offers monitoring, diagnostics, and analytics for Azure networking resources.

By understanding these services and how they integrate with each other, you can design and implement robust networking solutions that meet the needs of your applications and users. Whether you're preparing for the AZ-900 exam or building real-world cloud solutions, a solid foundation in Azure Networking is essential.

Chapter 10 Quiz

To check your answers, please refer to the "Chapter 10 Answer Key" on page 305.

1. What is the primary function of an Azure Virtual Network?

    A. To host .NET applications on Azure

    B. To enable secure communication between Azure resources

    C. To provide identity and access management services in Azure

    D. To store and process large datasets in the cloud

2. Your organization wants a high-performance, private connection between its on-premises datacenter and Azure, bypassing the public internet.

    Which service should you choose?

    A. Azure ExpressRoute

    B. Azure VPN Gateway

    C. Azure Load Balancer

    D. Azure Firewall

3. What is the purpose of Azure VPN Gateway?

    A. Load-balancing traffic

    B. Managing firewall rules

    C. Connecting on-premises networks to Azure over an encrypted tunnel

    D. Providing DNS name resolution

CHAPTER 11
Azure Storage Services

In the previous chapter, we explored Azure networking and how it connects Azure resources, on-premises networks, and the internet to enable secure and scalable communication. Now, we shift our focus to Azure Storage services, which serve as the backbone of data management in the cloud.

Azure Storage provides a scalable, secure, and cost-effective way to store and manage data, making it one of the key topics on the AZ-900 Azure Fundamentals exam.

Unlike traditional on-premises storage solutions, Azure Storage offers high availability, redundancy, and flexible access options that allow businesses to efficiently manage their data while optimizing costs and performance.

To build a strong understanding of Azure Storage services, we'll cover the following topics and more:

Various Azure Storage services options
    Learn about different storage solutions, including Blob Storage, File Storage, Table Storage, and Queue Storage.

Storage access tiers for Azure Blob Storage
    Explore how Azure Storage access tiers (Hot, Cool, Cold, and Archive) can help manage costs and performance for Azure Blob Storage.

Redundancy and replication options
    Discover how Azure ensures data availability with various redundancy models.

Storage account types and storage options
    Understand the different types of storage accounts and how to choose the right one for your use case.

Moving files in Azure Storage
> Learn about file transfer tools, including AzCopy, Azure Storage Explorer, and Azure File Sync.

Migration tools
> Explore how Azure Migrate and Azure Data Box help move large datasets to Azure.

This chapter will give you a solid foundation in Azure Storage, helping you understand how to choose the right storage solution for various workloads. By the end of this chapter, you'll be well equipped to tackle Azure Storage–related questions on the AZ-900 Azure Fundamentals exam.

We have lots to cover, so let's get started!

Introduction to Azure Storage Account

Azure Storage is a cloud service that empowers organizations to store and manage all data types (structured, semi-structured, and unstructured) in a scalable and secure way.

At the core of Azure Storage is the *Azure Storage account*, which provides a centralized, highly available, and secure environment for managing various storage services. A storage account simplifies management and billing while ensuring seamless integration across different storage solutions.

A storage account provides access to multiple storage types, including:

- Azure Blob Storage
- Azure File Storage
- Azure Table Storage
- Azure Queue Storage
- Azure Data Lake Storage Gen2

Think of an Azure Storage account as a secure, globally accessible filing cabinet that lets you store and access data from anywhere in the world within a unified environment. Whether you need to store documents, databases, or application logs, Azure ensures that your data remains safe and highly available and accessible if you need to handle massive workloads at scale.

Next, we'll explore why so many organizations choose Azure Storage over traditional on-premises data centers.

Benefits of Azure Storage Versus On-Premises Storage

Migrating from an on-premises data center to Azure Storage unlocks significant advantages in terms of cost, scalability, security, performance, and management.

Let's take a closer look at the key benefits.

Some of the terms mentioned in this section will be further explained later in this chapter.

Cost-Efficiency

Azure Storage offers lower costs and a pay-as-you-go model:

- No large up-front capital expenses (CAPEX), since you pay only for what you use
- No hardware maintenance, since Azure handles infrastructure, power, cooling, and repairs
- Storage access tiers (*https://oreil.ly/aeUz1*) (Hot, Cool, Cold, and Archive) that reduce costs by aligning storage pricing with data access frequency:
  - *Hot tier*: Highest storage cost, lowest access cost; best for frequently accessed data
  - *Cool tier*: Lower storage cost than Hot, higher access cost; 30-day minimum retention (early deletion penalty applies)
  - *Cold tier*: Even lower storage cost, higher access cost than Cool; 90-day minimum retention (early deletion penalty applies)
  - *Archive tier*: Lowest storage cost, highest retrieval cost; data is offline and must be rehydrated before access; 180-day minimum retention (early deletion penalty applies)
- Leverages the elastic nature of Azure Storage to increase capacity as your data requirements grow, eliminating the need to overprovision storage upfront

On the other hand, on-premises storage often requires high up-front and maintenance costs:

- Expensive hardware (SAN/NAS devices, RAID controllers) required
- Ongoing maintenance costs for backups, security, and upgrades
- Storage that must be preprovisioned, leading to wasted capacity

Scalability and Elasticity

Azure Storage is instantly scalable:

- Virtually unlimited storage, meaning that there's no need to predict future demand
- Autoscaling up/down to handle traffic spikes seamlessly
- Global redundancy options that store copies of data in different regions

On-premises storage is limited by its physical hardware:

- Fixed storage capacity that requires new hardware purchases for expansion
- Scaling up that is complex, often requiring downtime
- Long lead times for ordering, installing, and configuring new storage

High Availability and Disaster Recovery Capacity

Azure Storage offers built-in replication and failover capabilities to support high availability, disaster recovery, and very high data durability, with multiple redundancy options designed to balance resiliency and cost.

Durability refers to the likelihood that your stored data will not be lost. These durability numbers represent the annual probability of object loss, with higher "nines" indicating extremely low likelihood of data loss.

Locally redundant storage

- Data is synchronously replicated three times within a single datacenter in the primary region.
- Locally redundant storage (LRS) protects against local hardware failures and offers at least 99.999999999% (11 nines) durability over a year.

Zone-redundant storage

- Data is synchronously replicated across three or more availability zones within the same region, providing resilience to zone failures.
- Zone-redundant storage (ZRS) offers at least 99.9999999999% (12 nines) durability over a year.

Geo-redundant storage

- Data is asynchronously replicated to a secondary region hundreds of miles away.
- Geo-redundant storage (GRS) provides at least 99.99999999999999% (16 nines) durability over a year.

Read-access geo-redundant storage

- Extends GRS by allowing read access to the secondary region in the event of a primary region outage.
- Read-access geo-redundant storage (RA-GRS) provides the same 99.99999999999999% (16 nines) durability as GRS.

Geo-zone-redundant storage and read-access geo-zone-redundant storage

- Combines ZRS within the primary region with geo-replication to a secondary region.
- Both geo-zone-redundant storage (GZRS) and read-access geo-zone-redundant storage (RA-GZRS) offer at least 99.99999999999999% (16 nines) durability.

In contrast, on-premises storage environments can carry a higher risk of data loss and downtime due to:

- Risk of hardware failures that can lead to permanent data loss if redundancy is insufficient
- Expensive disaster recovery solutions that require additional data centers or off-site backups
- Manual failover and recovery processes, which can increase downtime and complexity

Security and Compliance

Azure Storage offers enterprise-grade security:

Encryption by default
    Data that's encrypted at rest and in transit (AES-256)

RBAC
    Granular access control using Microsoft Entra ID

Advanced threat protection
    Ability to detect unusual access patterns and unauthorized activity

Compliance ready
    Meets ISO, SOC, HIPAA, GDPR, FedRAMP, and other regulatory standards

With on-premises storage, the responsibility for security falls on the organization's IT teams:

- Encryption that must be manually configured and managed
- Compliance enforcement that's manual and complex
- A higher risk of insider threats and unauthorized access

Performance and Accessibility

With Azure Storage, you get global reach and high-speed access:

- Fast, low-latency data access from anywhere
- Optimization for cloud workloads, including Azure Virtual Machines, AI, big data, and IoT
- Hybrid connectivity with Azure ExpressRoute or VPN Gateway for secure on-premises integration

On-premises storage offers only limited accessibility and constraints on performance:

- Remote access only via VPN or direct network access
- Performance bottlenecks due to hardware limitations
- High latency for global users due to lack of built-in content delivery

Backup and Retention Policies

Azure Storage provides automated backup and retention:

- Built-in snapshots and point-in-time recovery
- Azure Backup and Azure Site Recovery for long-term retention
- Immutable storage (WORM, or write once, read many) ensures data integrity for compliance

An on-premises solution will require manual backup management:

- A need for dedicated backup hardware (tapes, NAS, external drives)
- Risk of human errors in scheduling and verification
- Physical backups that are vulnerable to natural disasters and theft

Comparison of Azure Storage Versus On-Premises Storage

Table 11-1 summarizes how Azure Storage stacks up against on-premises storage.

Table 11-1. Comparison of Azure Storage and on-premises storage

Factor	Azure Storage (strengths)	On-premises storage (weaknesses)
Up-front Cost	Low (pay as you go)	High (hardware purchase needed)
Scalability	Instantly scales	Requires manual upgrades
Availability	99.999999999% durability	Dependent on hardware uptime
Disaster recovery	Geo-redundant options	Requires separate DR planning
Security	Built-in encryption and compliance	Manual security enforcement
Performance	Low-latency global access	Limited by local network
Backup and recovery	Automated with Azure Backup	Manual with risk of failure

Supported Data Types

Azure storage services support three major data types:

- Structured data
- Semi-structured data
- Unstructured data

Table 11-2 lists each data type along with its definition, examples, and key characteristics.

Table 11-2. Comparison of the three data types

Data type	Definition	Examples	Characteristics
Structured data	• Highly organized data that follows a fixed schema, typically stored in relational databases • Best for relational databases and transactional systems	• SQL databases • Financial transactions • Customer records	• Stored in tables with rows and columns • Enforces relationships between data (e.g., foreign keys) • Uses SQL for querying
Semi-structured data	• Data that doesn't fit into traditional relational tables but still has some organizational structure (e.g., key-value pairs, JSON, XML) • Offers flexibility for NoSQL databases and big data analytics	• JSON documents • XML • CSV files (context-dependent) • IoT sensor logs	• Doesn't require a strict schema (schema-on-read) • More flexible than structured data but still has recognizable formats
Unstructured data	• Data that doesn't follow a predefined format or schema (e.g., images, videos, audio, and backups) • Ideal for object storage, media files, and backups	• Photos, videos, PDFs, audio files • Server logs, email archives • Machine learning training datasets	• No fixed schema or structure • Can be text based (logs, emails) or binary (images, media) • Requires specialized storage solutions for indexing and retrieval

Understanding the three broad categories of data will help you choose the right service for your workload.

Next, we'll explore and compare the different Azure Storage services to help you choose the best option for your data storage needs.

Azure Storage Services

Azure Storage provides a variety of services to accommodate different data storage needs. When creating an Azure storage account, you select an account type, which determines the available Azure Storage services (such as Blob, Files, Queues, or Tables), backup redundancy options, and best use cases. However, you don't need to specify an individual storage service at the time of storage account creation, since all supported storage services can be added later within the same Azure Storage account.

Azure Storage Services and Data Types

Azure offers multiple storage services within a single Azure Storage account. Each storage service is optimized for a specific data type (structured, semi-structured, or unstructured). See Table 11-3 to learn more.

Table 11-3. Comparing Azure storage services and data types

Storage service	Data type	Description
Azure Blob Storage	Unstructured	• Stores large volumes of unstructured data (text and binary) • Ideal for images, videos, documents, and log files • Supports storage access tiers (Hot, Cool, Cold, and Archive) for cost optimization
Azure Data Lake Storage Gen2	Unstructured and semi-structured	• Optimized for big data analytics • Supports hierarchical namespace for efficient file organization • Built on top of Blob Storage, offering high-performance analytics for large datasets
Azure Files	Unstructured	• Provides fully managed file shares accessible via Server Message Block (SMB) and Network File System (NFS) protocols • Enables seamless migration of on-premises file shares to the cloud • Supports Azure File Sync for hybrid storage scenarios
Azure Queues	Semi-structured	• A message-queuing service that enables asynchronous processing and decouples application components for scalability and reliability • Supports messages up to 64 KB, with unlimited queue storage
Azure Tables	Semi-structured	• A NoSQL key-value store for applications requiring fast lookups at scale • Schema-less design makes it ideal for scenarios like IoT, logging, and metadata storage

Globally Unique Namespace for Azure Storage Account

Each Azure Storage account must have a globally unique namespace, because that name serves as the base for its storage service endpoint URL and must be unique to ensure distinct identification for your data.

Here are the naming rules for Azure Storage accounts:

- Must be between 3 and 24 characters in length, inclusive
- Can contain only numbers and lowercase letters
- Must be globally unique within Azure (no two storage accounts can have the same name)

Storage Service Endpoints

Each storage service within an account has a unique endpoint format, as shown in Table 11-4.

Table 11-4. Storage services and their endpoint formats

Storage service	Endpoint format
Azure Blob Storage	https://<storage-account-name>.blob.core.windows.net
Azure Data Lake Storage Gen2	https://<storage-account-name>.dfs.core.windows.net
Azure Files	https://<storage-account-name>.file.core.windows.net
Azure Queue	https://<storage-account-name>.queue.core.windows.net
Azure Tables	https://<storage-account-name>.table.core.windows.net

Azure Managed Disks: A Separate Storage Service

Azure managed disks are stored on Azure's storage platform. However, unlike the other Azure Storage services mentioned earlier, Azure managed disks are not stored within your Azure Storage account.

Instead, *Azure managed disks* are a separate block-level storage service specifically designed for Azure VMs. They're optimized for performance, durability, and lifecycle management.

Azure managed disks handle virtual hard disks (VHDs) and integrate with VM deployments, providing features such as automatic scalability, built-in redundancy, and security.

Comparing Azure Storage Services

We've covered a lot of key concepts about Azure Storage services in this section. Table 11-5 offers a concise summary of the Azure Storage services that we've discussed.

Table 11-5. Comparison of Azure Storage services

Storage service	Data type(s)	Description	Common use cases	Cost considerations
Azure Blob Storage	Unstructured	Object storage for massive amounts of unstructured data (binary and text)	Storing images, videos, backups, logs, and big data analytics	Costs vary by access tier (Hot, Cool, Cold, Archive), and you pay for storage + egress. The Archive tier is cheapest but has high retrieval costs.
Azure Data Lake Storage Gen2	Unstructured and semi-structured	Advanced data lake built on Azure Blob Storage, optimized for big data analytics and hierarchical file organization	Storing large-scale datasets for analytics, AI/ML processing, and data warehousing	Pricing follows Azure Blob Storage cost model, with additional charges for hierarchical namespace operations and metadata.
Azure Files	Unstructured	Fully managed SMB/NFS file shares in the cloud	Enterprise file sharing for applications, user documents, and app configurations	Charges are based on provisioned or used storage. • The Premium tier is SSD based and more expensive. • The Standard tier is cheaper but slower.
Azure Table Storage	Semi-structured	NoSQL key-value store for structured, non-relational data	Storing logs, metadata, IoT data, and user profiles	Low-cost storage: you are charged per GB stored + transactions. Cheaper than Cosmos DB but less flexible.
Azure Queues	Semi-structured	Message queue storage for async communication between apps	Decoupling microservices, handling background jobs, and event-driven workflows	Very low-cost: you are charged per storage used and operations performed. Cost structure is ideal for large-scale messaging.
Azure Managed Disks	Unstructured	Block storage for VMs and databases	Storing VM OS/data disks, databases, and persistent workloads	Charges are based on disk size + performance tier (Standard HDD, Standard SSD, Premium SSD, Ultra Disk), and higher input/output operations per second (IOPS) and throughput cost more.

As you can see, selecting the appropriate Azure Storage service depends on the type of data you need to store. In the next section, we'll learn about Azure Storage account types and options.

Choosing the Right Storage Account Types and Options

Azure storage accounts provide scalable and secure storage solutions for various data types, and there are different options available. Selecting the appropriate storage account type is crucial for optimizing performance, cost, and redundancy based on your specific workload requirements.

This section introduces the available storage account types and redundancy options. You'll find a detailed discussion of redundancy in "Azure Redundancy Options" on page 185.

Types of Azure Storage Accounts

There are different accounts you can utilize in Azure Storage Accounts.

General-purpose v2 storage accounts

General-purpose v2 (GPv2) storage accounts support a number of Azure services:

- Blob Storage (including Data Lake Storage)
- Queue Storage
- Table Storage
- Azure Files

Redundancy options include:

- LRS
- GRS
- RA-GRS
- ZRS
- GZRS
- RA-GZRS

GPv2 is recommended for general-purpose storage needs.

- Most scenarios involve blobs, file shares, queues, and tables.

Premium block blob storage accounts

Premium block blob storage accounts support the following service:

- Blob Storage (including Data Lake Storage)

Their redundancy options include:

- LRS
- ZRS

These storage accounts are best suited for:

- Scenarios requiring high transaction rates, handling smaller objects, or necessitating consistently low storage latency

Premium file shares storage accounts

Premium file shares storage accounts support the following service:

- Azure Files

These redundancy options are available:

- LRS
- ZRS

This type of storage account supports both Server Message Block (SMB) and Network File System (NFS) and is best suited for:

- Enterprise or high-performance scale applications

Premium page blobs storage accounts

Premium page blobs storage accounts support only this service:

- Page blobs

These redundancy options are available:

- LRS
- ZRS

The best use case for these storage accounts involves:

- Specialized workloads that require high-performance storage for page blobs

Choosing the Right Storage Account Type

When selecting a storage account type, consider the following factors:

Supported services
 Ensure that the account type supports the Azure Storage services your application requires.

Performance requirements
    Premium accounts offer the lower latency and higher throughput that are suitable for performance-sensitive applications.

Redundancy needs
    Choose a redundancy option that aligns with your data durability and availability requirements.

Cost considerations
    Balance performance and redundancy features against budget constraints to select a cost-effective solution.

Table 11-6 offers a concise comparison that summarizes this section's discussion.

Table 11-6. Comparison of storage types

Storage account type	Supported services	Redundancy options	Best for
GPv2	Blob Storage (including Data Lake), Queue Storage, Table Storage, Azure Files	LRS, GRS, RA-GRS, ZRS, GZRS, RA-GZRS	Most general-purpose workloads, including blobs, file shares, queues, and tables
Premium block blob storage	Blob Storage (including Data Lake)	LRS, ZRS	High transaction rates, low latency, and small object workloads
Premium file shares storage	Azure Files	LRS, ZRS	High-performance file sharing for enterprise applications; supports SMB and NFS
Premium page blobs storage	Page Blobs only	LRS	High-performance workloads requiring fast disk storage, such as VM disks

By understanding the features and ideal use cases of each storage account type, you can make informed decisions that align with your organization's objectives and workload demands.

As noted, redundancy options are a key factor to consider, since redundancy ensures data availability and durability as well as disaster recovery capability. Let's take a closer look at Azure redundancy options next.

Azure Redundancy Options

Selecting the right Azure redundancy option is important to ensuring data availability, durability, and disaster recovery. Azure provides several redundancy options that protect your data from hardware failures, datacenter outages, and regional disasters. These options range from local resiliency to cross-region failover. Understanding these models is essential for the AZ-900 exam.

Types of Redundancy Options

Let's explore these redundancy options in detail.

Locally redundant storage

Locally redundant storage (LRS) maintains three copies of data within a single Azure datacenter. If a hardware failure occurs, Azure automatically recovers data from the remaining copies.

LRS is best suited for:

- Cost-effective storage for noncritical workloads
- Scenarios in which data durability within a single region is sufficient

It has some limitations:

- If the entire datacenter fails (e.g., due to a natural disaster or power outage), data could be lost.
- It doesn't provide protection against regional outages.

Zone-redundant storage

Zone-redundant storage (ZRS) distributes three copies of your data across multiple availability zones within the same Azure region, ensuring high availability and resiliency. If one availability zone experiences a failure, your data remains accessible from the other zones, minimizing downtime. ZRS uses synchronous replication between zones, which maintains low-latency access while keeping all copies consistent.

ZRS is best suited for:

- Mission-critical applications that require high availability
- Workloads such as shared file storage, databases, or application data that need zone resilience

The limitations of ZRS are:

- If the entire region experiences an outage, data may be lost.
- It doesn't provide cross-region disaster recovery.

Geo-redundant storage

Geo-redundant storage (GRS) replicates your data across two geographically separated Azure regions, with three copies stored in the primary region and three copies in a secondary region. Data is initially written to the primary region using LRS, and Azure asynchronously replicates it to the secondary region to ensure durability. In the event of a failure in the primary region, Microsoft can initiate a failover to the secondary region, allowing continued access to your data.

The most suitable use cases for GRS are:

- Disaster recovery scenarios requiring cross-region failover
- Business continuity for applications with global users

Keep in mind these limitations:

- The secondary copy isn't accessible unless a failover is initiated.
- GRS incurs higher costs than LRS or ZRS do.

Read-access geo-redundant storage

Read-access geo-redundant storage (RA-GRS) works similarly to GRS by replicating data across two geographically separated regions. The key difference is that RA-GRS allows read access to the secondary region even before a failover occurs, providing additional flexibility and availability. Because it ensures that users can access data reliably from multiple locations, it's ideal for applications that require high availability and global data distribution.

RA-GRS is well-suited for:

- Applications that need a globally distributed, highly available backup
- Workloads where data can be read from the nearest region to reduce latency

Here are the limitations of this approach:

- Writes are still only possible in the primary region.
- Secondary region access is read-only until failover.

Geo-zone-redundant storage

Geo-zone-redundant storage (GZRS) combines the benefits of ZRS and GRS, providing both intra-region zone redundancy and cross-region disaster recovery. Data is first synchronously written across multiple availability zones in the primary region, ensuring high durability and low-latency access. It's then asynchronously replicated to a geographically distant secondary region, allowing Microsoft to initiate a failover if the primary region experiences an outage.

GZRS is ideally suited for:

- Mission-critical applications that need both zone redundancy and cross-region failover protection
- Business-critical workloads that require high availability and the potential for disaster recovery

Keep these limitations in mind:

- The secondary copy remains inaccessible until failover occurs.
- GZRS incurs higher costs than other methods due to its dual redundancy mechanisms.

Read-access geo-zone-redundant storage

Read-access geo-zone-redundant storage (RA-GZRS) extends GZRS by allowing read access to the secondary region even before a failover occurs. Data is first written across multiple availability zones in the primary region, providing high durability and low-latency access. It's then asynchronously replicated to a geographically distant secondary region, which can serve read requests for distributed workloads, ensuring both disaster recovery and improved global availability.

Consider RA-GZRS for these use uses:

- Global applications that require real-time read access from multiple regions
- Where there is the potential for disaster recovery scenarios in which an immediate failover is not needed but secondary data access would be beneficial

RA-GZRS has some limitations:

- Writes can only occur in the primary region.
- Secondary access is read-only until failover.

Choosing a Redundancy Option

The best redundancy option depends on your workload requirements, as shown in Table 11-7.

Table 11-7. Choosing the optimal redundancy option

Redundancy type	Protects against	Use cases	Read access before failover?
LRS	Hardware failure in a single datacenter	Cost-effective storage for noncritical workloads	No
ZRS	Datacenter or availability zone failure	High-availability applications within a single region	No
GRS	Regional failure	Disaster recovery, business continuity	No
RA-GRS	Regional failure	Global applications requiring a backup region for read access	Yes
GZRS	Zone and regional failure	Mission-critical workloads needing maximum redundancy	No
RA-GZRS	Zone and regional failure	Business-critical applications with high availability and global reach	Yes

By selecting the appropriate redundancy option, you can ensure that your data remains available and durable while optimizing for cost and performance.

In the next section, we'll talk about how to move files from an on-premises environment to Azure Storage.

Options for Transferring Files to Azure Storage

Azure offers multiple tools for transferring files between on-premises environments, Azure storage accounts, and other cloud services. The best choice depends on factors such as data size, frequency, automation needs, and ease of use.

Different Tools for File Transfer

In this section, you'll learn about AzCopy, Azure Storage Explorer, and Azure File Sync.

AzCopy

AzCopy is a command-line tool designed for fast, high-performance transfers of large files to and from Azure Storage. It supports one-time or scheduled automated transfers and works with Azure Blob Storage, Azure Files, and Azure Data Lake Storage Gen2. By leveraging parallel transfers, AzCopy maximizes throughput and reduces transfer times, making it ideal for large-scale bulk data transfers and scenarios where speed and efficiency are critical.

Here are some common use cases for AzCopy:

- Bulk file uploads to Azure Blob Storage
- Syncing large datasets from on-premises to Azure
- Automated or scripted data transfers
- Moving files between different Azure storage accounts

This is an example AzCopy command:

```
azcopy copy "C:\AZ-900-demo\" "https://teststracctv1.blob.core.windows.net/mycontainer" --recursive
```

This command uploads all files and subfolders from `C:\AZ-900-demo\` to the Azure Blob container `mycontainer` using AzCopy.

Benefits of using AzCopy include:

- Makes large data transfers fast and efficient
- Supports automation via scripting
- Works with Azure Blob Storage, Azure Files, and Azure Data Lake Storage Gen2

Limitations to consider when working with AzCopy include:

- It's command-line based and thus may not be user-friendly for beginners.
- It has no graphical interface.

Azure Storage Explorer

Azure Storage Explorer is a GUI-based tool designed for managing Azure Storage, making it ideal for manual, visual file transfers. It supports drag-and-drop file operations and works with a variety of Azure storage types, including Blob Storage, Files, Tables, and Queues. Users can also access and manage multiple storage accounts from a single interface; thus, Azure Storage Explorer provides a convenient way to browse, organize, and interact with storage resources without using command-line tools.

Here are some use cases for Azure Storage Explorer:

- Easily doing manual uploads/downloads
- Managing storage across multiple Azure accounts
- Viewing and editing stored data
- Ideal for small-scale or one-time transfers

Benefits include the following:

- A user-friendly graphical interface
- No need for scripting or CLI commands
- Works across Windows, macOS, and Linux

Limitations when working with Azure Storage Explorer include:

- It's slower than AzCopy for bulk transfers because AzCopy uses optimized network protocols and retry logic for bulk transfers, which improves speed and reliability.
- It's not ideal for automated transfers.

Azure File Sync

Azure File Sync is a hybrid cloud solution designed for continuous syncing between on-premises Windows Server and Azure Files. It supports multisite synchronization, allowing multiple file servers to stay in sync, and offers cloud tiering, which keeps frequently accessed files on-premises while offloading less-used files to Azure. This makes Azure File Sync ideal for hybrid cloud storage scenarios where it can enable seamless access to files across locations while reducing on-premises storage requirements.

Here are some use cases for Azure File Sync:

- Syncing on-premises file servers to Azure
- Disaster recovery via backing up on-premises data to the cloud
- Reducing on-premises storage costs with cloud tiering
- Keeping files synchronized across multiple locations

Benefits of Azure File Sync include:

- Seamless integration with Windows Server
- Cloud tiering to help reduce on-premises storage needs
- Ability to keep multiple file servers in sync

There are some limitations when working with Azure File Sync:

- It works only with Azure Files (not Blob Storage).
- It requires Windows Server 2016+.

Comparison of File Transfer Options

See Table 11-8 for a summary of the transfer options discussed in the previous sections.

Table 11-8. Comparison of AzCopy, Azure Storage Explorer, and Azure File Sync

Tool	Best for	Interface	Storage types supported	Automation support	Speed	Ideal use case
AzCopy	Large-scale transfers	CLI	Blob, Files, Tables	Yes (scripting)	Very fast	Bulk uploads
Azure Storage Explorer	Manual transfers	GUI	Blob, Files, Tables, Queues	No	Moderate	Small-scale uploads
Azure File Sync	Hybrid file storage	Windows Server integration	Azure Files	Yes (continuous sync)	Fast	On-premises file server sync

Given the different strengths of these tools:

- *For fast, automated, large-scale transfers, use AzCopy.* AzCopy is optimized for bulk data movement and can be scripted or scheduled for repeated operations. It's ideal when you need high-performance uploads or downloads, but it isn't designed for continuous real-time syncing.

- *For small, manual, GUI-based transfers, use Azure Storage Explorer.* Azure Storage Explorer provides an intuitive interface for browsing and managing files, performing drag-and-drop transfers, and accessing multiple storage accounts. It's best for ad hoc or interactive file management rather than large-scale or automated transfers.

- *For ongoing synchronization with on-premises servers, use Azure File Sync.* Azure File Sync continuously keeps your on-premises Windows Server and Azure Files in sync. It supports multisite synchronization and cloud tiering, automatically keeping frequently accessed files local while offloading less-used files to Azure. Unlike AzCopy, File Sync is designed for continuous, real-time replication, not just one-time bulk transfers, making it ideal for hybrid cloud scenarios.

This wraps up our discussion of file transfer options. Now, suppose you're interested in migrating your existing data from your on-premises data center to Azure Storage. Fortunately, there are several options. We'll go through each migration option in the next section.

Migration Options to Azure Storage

When migrating data to Azure, the best approach depends on data size, speed requirements, network limitations, and automation needs.

Types of Migration Solutions

Two primary migration solutions are:

Azure Migrate
   A cloud-based migration service

Azure Data Box
   An offline migration appliance

Let's take a closer look at both of these.

Azure Migrate

Azure Migrate is a cloud-based migration service designed for large-scale migrations from on-premises environments or other cloud platforms. It provides a centralized hub for assessment, tracking, and planning, supporting servers, databases, applications, and storage. Azure Migrate offers performance-based recommendations to help determine the right size and configuration for workloads, and it facilitates real-time replication to enable migrations with minimal downtime, making it an essential tool for organizations moving workloads to Azure efficiently and safely.

Use cases for Azure Migrate include:

- Migrating on-premises file servers to Azure Files
- Moving VM disk data to Azure managed disks
- Replicating databases to Azure SQL
- Achieving live migration with minimal disruption

Following are the key features of Azure Migrate:

- Agent-based and agentless migration options
- Dependency mapping to analyze workloads before migration
- Integration with third-party tools (e.g., Zerto, Carbonite)
- Built-in cost estimates for Azure storage and compute

Azure Migrate offers these benefits:

- Real-time replication and live migration support
- Automation of migration planning and tracking
- No need for physical hardware

Be aware of the following limitations of Azure Migrate:

- Need for a stable internet connection (bandwidth can be a bottleneck)
- Not ideal for petabyte-scale data transfers

Azure Data Box

Azure Data Box is a Microsoft-managed physical appliance designed for offline data migration, making it ideal for transferring terabytes or even petabytes of data when network bandwidth is limited or impractical. It supports Azure storage types such as blob, files, and managed disks, allowing organizations to securely move large volumes of data to Azure without relying solely on online transfers.

Use cases for Azure Data Box include:

- Data center migrations (e.g., large file servers, backups, archives)
- Big data transfers (e.g., media, genomics, IoT data)
- Air-gapped environments with no direct internet access
- Disaster recovery data imports

Review Table 11-9 to see the types of options available for Azure Data Box.

Table 11-9. Azure Data Box options

Azure Data Box type	Capacity	Transfer speed	Use case
Data Box Disk	Up to 8 TB per disk	USB 3.0, SATA	Small migrations and backups
Data Box	100 TB	1 Gbps / 10 Gbps network	Large file server migration
Data Box Heavy	1 PB	40 Gbps network	Massive datasets

The benefits of Azure Data Box include:

- Fast, secure data transfer without network dependency
- Support of encryption for data security
- Ability to work in air-gapped environments

Azure Data Box has the following limitations:

- Physical handling required (shipping time adds delay)
- Not ideal for real-time or ongoing sync

Here are the steps for migrating data using the Azure Data Box:

1. Order a Data Box device from the Azure portal.
2. Microsoft ships the device to your data center.
3. Copy data to the device via local high-speed network.
4. Ship it back to Microsoft.
5. Azure uploads the data to your storage account.

Comparison of Azure Migration Options

See Table 11-10 for a comparison of the various Azure migration options.

Table 11-10. Comparison of Azure Migrate and Azure Data Box

Feature	Azure Migrate	Azure Data Box
Best for	Online migrations	Offline bulk data transfer
Data size	TBs to PBs (depends on bandwidth)	8 TB to 1 PB per appliance
Speed	Depends on network	1–40 Gbps (faster than most networks)
Use cases	VMs, databases, storage	Large-scale file and object storage
Internet required	Yes	No
Downtime	Minimal (real-time sync possible)	Higher (physical shipping involved)
Security	End-to-end encryption	Hardware encryption (AES-256)

To summarize this info even more succinctly:

- For cloud-based migrations with minimal downtime, use Azure Migrate.
- For large-scale, offline data transfers, use Azure Data Box.
- For hybrid scenarios (ongoing sync + bulk data), combine both for efficiency.

Summary

In this chapter, we explored Azure Storage services, covering the different storage types, tiers, redundancy options, and account types you can use to help optimize performance, cost, and reliability. We also reviewed tools for managing and migrating data, including AzCopy, Azure Storage Explorer, Azure File Sync, Azure Migrate, and Azure Data Box. Understanding these concepts is key for effective cloud data management and success on the AZ-900 Azure Fundamentals exam.

In the next chapter, you'll learn about managing identity, access, and security in Azure.

Chapter 11 Quiz

To check your answers, please refer to the "Chapter 11 Answer Key" on page 305.

1. A media company needs a cloud storage solution for storing large volumes of high-resolution marketing assets such as photos, promotional videos, PDFs, and design files. The data formats vary and do not follow a structured schema. The company needs highly scalable and cost-effective storage.

   Which Azure Storage service best meets this requirement?

   A. Azure Table Storage

   B. Azure Blob Storage

   C. Azure Queue Storage

   D. Azure File Storage

2. A financial reporting system will store archived reports that, while accessed infrequently, must remain quickly retrievable. The team plans to use Azure Blob Cool tier to save on storage costs. The team must comply with the tier's minimum retention policy to avoid early deletion charges.

   What is the minimum required retention period for the Cool tier?

   A. 7 days

   B. 14 days

   C. 30 days

   D. 180 days

3. A startup wants to store application data in Azure but needs to keep costs as low as possible. High availability across multiple regions is not a requirement. The company is comfortable with redundancy only within a single Azure datacenter.

   Which redundancy option should the company choose?

   A. Read-access geo-redundant storage

   B. Locally redundant storage

   C. Geo-redundant storage

   D. Zone-redundant storage

CHAPTER 12
Azure Identity, Access, and Security

In the previous chapter, we explored how Azure securely stores and manages data in Azure Storage. Now, we turn our focus to another essential pillar of cloud computing: identity, access, and security.

At its core, "identity, access, and security" refers to the systems and practices that ensure only authorized users or services can access the right resources at the right time, and nothing more. This is vital for maintaining trust, protecting sensitive data, preventing unauthorized access, and complying with industry regulations. In cloud computing, where resources are accessible from anywhere, these protections become even more critical.

Azure embeds identity, access, and security into the core of its platform, providing a built-in framework for managing users, controlling access to resources, and protecting against cyberthreats. At the heart of this framework is *Microsoft Entra ID* (formerly Azure Active Directory), which acts as the central identity provider. It enables organizations to authenticate users and devices, enforce multifactor authentication (MFA), set Conditional Access policies, and manage external identities.

Access management in Azure is powered by role-based access control (RBAC), enabling fine-grained permissions based on job roles or responsibilities. Meanwhile, Azure's security services, such as Microsoft Defender for Cloud, help continuously monitor your environment, detect threats, and strengthen your security posture.

In this chapter, we'll start by learning the foundational security concepts that guide Azure's approach: Zero Trust and defense in depth. Once we understand these principles, we'll explore the key Azure services that implement identity, access, and security controls, including:

- Microsoft Entra ID and Microsoft Entra Domain Services
- Authentication in Azure
- Microsoft Entra External ID
- Microsoft Entra Conditional Access
- Azure RBAC
- Azure Key Vault
- Microsoft Defender for Cloud

Understanding the Zero Trust Security Model

The *Zero Trust security model* is a modern approach to cybersecurity that starts with a simple but powerful principle:

> Never trust; always verify.

In traditional security models, being inside the corporate network often meant automatic trust. Today, however, with remote work, mobile devices, and cloud apps being omnipresent in the environment, that model no longer holds up.

Zero Trust assumes that no device, user, or location is trusted by default, even if it's inside your organization's network.

Why Do We Need Zero Trust?

The modern workplace is borderless. People access corporate resources from:

- Cloud platforms
- Personal laptops and devices
- Public WiFi and home networks
- Workplaces that can be anywhere

Because of this, companies need stronger security that:

- Protects sensitive data wherever it resides
- Verifies every access request
- Continuously detects and responds to threats

Zero Trust is designed to meet these challenges.

The Core Principles of Zero Trust

Microsoft recommends building your security strategy around the three key principles shown in Table 12-1.

Table 12-1. The core principles of Zero Trust

Principle	What it means
Verify explicitly	Always check the identity and context of every request using: • User identity • Sign-in location • Device health • User role • Access history • Behavior
Use least-privilege access	Only give users the minimum permissions they need—and nothing more. To make this work, use tools like these: • Just-in-time access (temporary access) • Just-enough-access (only what's needed) • Conditional Access policies
Assume a breach has occurred	Act as if attackers are already in the network: • Monitor continuously for suspicious activity. • Use encryption. • Segment your environment to limit the blast radius of a potential attack.

Comparing Traditional Security and the Zero Trust Model

Table 12-2 lays out a comparison of the traditional security model and the Zero Trust model.

Table 12-2. Traditional security model versus Zero Trust model

Feature	Traditional security model	Zero Trust model
Trust	Trusted if inside the network	Nothing trusted by default
Access	Granted if inside the network	Based on identity, context, and risk
Devices	Primarily managed, corporate devices	Any approved and compliant device, verified first
Risk response	Reactive	Proactive and continuous monitoring

Real-World Scenario

Imagine the following scenario. A user working from home tries to access a sensitive app. Azure checks who the user is, what device they're using, and where they're signing in from. If anything indicates the sign-on is unusual or risky, the system might require MFA or even block access. If everything checks out, access is granted—but only to the app the user needs.

Zero Trust is a modern, flexible security approach that helps protect:

- Users
- Devices
- Applications
- Data

Zero Trust ensures that every access request is verified, access is limited, and threats are assumed, not ignored. With Zero Trust, security follows the user, no matter where they work or what device they use.

Defense-in-Depth Model

Defense in depth is a security strategy that protects data and systems through multiple layers of defense (see Figure 12-1). Unlike Zero Trust, which focuses on strict verification for every access request, defense in depth does not rely on a single security control (such as a firewall) but instead surrounds your data with several layers of protection, much like an onion, so that if one layer is compromised, others remain in place to safeguard your resources.

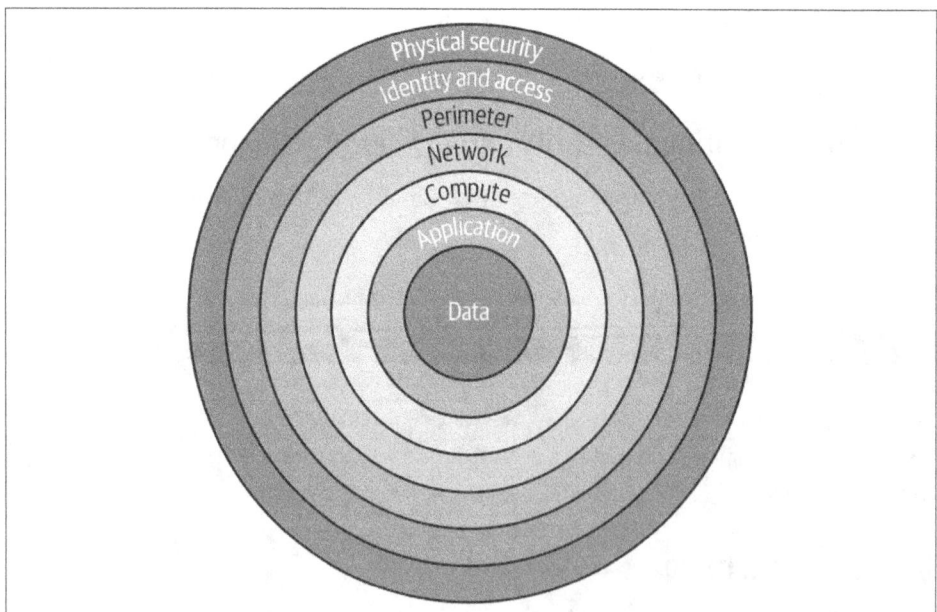

Figure 12-1. Defense-in-depth model

Modern Azure implementations of defense in depth include firewalls, network security groups, Microsoft Defender for Endpoint, Microsoft Sentinel for security information and event management (SIEM) and threat detection, encryption at rest and in transit, identity and access management via Microsoft Entra ID, and continuous monitoring. Taken together, these layers provide a comprehensive and resilient security posture.

> The goal of defense-in-depth is simple: stop attackers from reaching your valuable data.

Think of your data as the center of a target. Each surrounding security layer acts like a barrier, slowing down or stopping attacks and giving your security team time to detect and respond. The more layers in place, the greater the protection against a full-scale breach. Each layer contributes its own unique defense, as described in Table 12-3.

Table 12-3. Layers of defense in depth

Layer	What it protects	How it protects
Physical security	Data center buildings and hardware	• Microsoft uses security badges, biometric scanners, surveillance cameras, and guards. • Managed by Microsoft for Azure regions.
Identity and access	Who can log in and what they can do	• Uses MFA, SSO, and Azure RBAC. • Logs sign-ins and admin actions for auditing.
Perimeter	The outer edge of your network	• Uses DDoS protection to stop massive attacks. • Uses firewalls to block or alert on malicious traffic.
Network	How resources communicate inside your cloud	• Uses rules to allow only necessary communication. • Applies NSGs and subnet rules. • Enforces "deny by default" and allows only needed traffic.
Compute	Virtual machines and cloud resources	• Applies VM security. • Uses endpoint protection. • Keeps systems updated and protected with antivirus software. • Limits admin privileges to reduce risks.
Application	Your apps and their code	• Ensures that your software is built securely. • Scans for vulnerabilities. • Stores secrets (like passwords and keys) safely and enforces secure deployment pipelines. • Uses application firewalls.
Data	Your business and customer data	• Encrypts data at rest and in transit. • Encrypts sensitive data and restricts who can access it. • Follows data compliance and privacy rules.

Defense in depth is about using many layers of protection instead of relying on just one. With Azure, you have built-in tools at every layer, empowering you to build a resilient, modern security posture that adapts to evolving threats. No matter where an attacker starts, there's always another layer of defense waiting.

In the next section, you'll learn about the Microsoft Entra ID.

Microsoft Entra ID

Microsoft Entra ID is Microsoft's cloud-based identity and access management service. It helps users securely sign in and access Microsoft cloud services (like Microsoft 365 and Azure) as well as other applications your organization may use or build.

If your organization already uses Active Directory (AD) on Windows Server for on-premises identity management, Microsoft Entra ID works as the cloud-based counterpart. While AD is managed locally, Microsoft Entra ID is hosted and managed by Microsoft, providing global availability and built-in security features like suspicious sign-in detection.

What Does Microsoft Entra ID Offer?

Here are the key features of Microsoft Entra ID:

Authentication
Provides secure sign-in with support for MFA, smart lockout, self-service password reset, and custom password policies.

SSO
Enables signing in once to access many apps, reducing the number of passwords users need to remember.

Application management
Controls access to cloud and on-premises apps using features like application proxy and the My Apps portal.

Device management
Allows the registration and management of devices with Microsoft Intune and the ability to apply Conditional Access policies based on device compliance.

Why Use Microsoft Entra ID?

Microsoft Entra ID provides a centralized identity platform that helps organizations manage access securely and efficiently:

- End users can sign in safely, reset passwords, and manage their own accounts, reducing IT overhead.
- Cloud service subscribers, such as Microsoft 365, Azure, and Dynamics 365 users, already rely on Entra ID for seamless authentication across services.

- Developers benefit because they can integrate authentication features, such as SSO and social or personal account logins, directly into their applications, enabling secure access for employees, partners, or customers without building custom authentication systems.
- IT administrators can centrally manage who has access to apps and resources, enforce policies, and maintain security across the organization.

All this makes Entra ID more than just a standard unique identifier (UID) system. It provides scalable, secure identity management across multiple applications and scenarios.

Microsoft Entra Connect Sync: Connecting On-Premises Active Directory to Azure

If your organization uses an on-premises AD, there's no need to manage separate identity systems in the cloud. With Microsoft Entra Connect Sync, you can synchronize user identities between your on-premises AD and Microsoft Entra ID. This hybrid setup enables seamless SSO and consistent password policies across both environments, streamlining identity management and enhancing security.

Microsoft Entra Domain Services

For organizations with traditional, domain-based applications that are moving to the cloud, *Microsoft Entra Domain Services* offers a managed solution. It provides key domain features without the need to deploy or manage domain controllers yourself. These include:

Domain join
　　Enables VMs and servers in Azure to join the managed domain, allowing centralized management and authentication like on-premises Active Directory.

Group policy
　　Allows administrators to apply policies to users and computers for security, configuration, and compliance across the domain.

Lightweight Directory Access Protocol (LDAP) support
　　Provides standard directory access protocols so legacy applications can query and authenticate against the managed domain.

Kerberos and NT LAN Manager (NTLM) authentication
　　Ensures secure authentication for applications and services that rely on these traditional protocols.

This service is especially useful for lifting and shifting legacy applications that don't support modern authentication methods.

Domain controllers are servers that handle authentication, authorization, and directory services for the domain.

Here's how it works. When you create a Microsoft Entra Domain Services instance, Azure automatically deploys a pair of managed domain controllers in your chosen region. These domain controllers are fully managed by Microsoft with no patching, configuration, or maintenance required. *One-way synchronization* from Microsoft Entra ID ensures that cloud-based identities stay current. In hybrid environments, Microsoft Entra Connect sync synchronizes identities from your on-prem AD to Microsoft Entra ID, which then updates Entra Domain Services.

This setup securely and efficiently bridges the gap between legacy systems and modern cloud infrastructure.

Comparing Microsoft Entra ID and Microsoft Entra Domain Services

Table 12-4 compares Microsoft Entra ID and Microsoft Entra Domain Services.

Table 12-4. Comparison of Microsoft Entra ID versus Microsoft Entra Domain Services

Feature	Microsoft Entra ID	Microsoft Entra Domain Services
Type	Identity and access management (IAM)	Managed domain services
Works with cloud apps	Yes	No (for traditional apps only)
Supports modern SSO and MFA	Yes	No (Kerberos-based SSO only)
Domain join support	No	Yes
LDAP, Kerberos, NTLM	No	Yes
Managed by Microsoft	Yes	Yes

Authentication in Azure

Authentication is the process of verifying identity, or proving that you are who you say you are. Think of authentication as being like what happens when you show your ID at airport security and the security officer confirms your identity so that you're allowed to proceed.

In Azure, authentication ensures that only legitimate users, devices, or services can access resources. Azure offers several authentication methods, each designed to balance security and convenience in different ways. In this section, we'll explore three key methods:

- Single sign-on (SSO)
- Multifactor Authentication (MFA)
- Passwordless authentication

Single Sign-On

Single sign-on (SSO) lets users sign in just once and then access multiple applications and services, without needing to sign in again for each one. It has the following benefits:

- Simplified password management since users need to remember just one set of credentials
- Reduced help desk calls for password resets
- Centralized access control for IT administrators
- Easier deactivation of accounts when users leave the organization

The security of SSO depends on the strength of the initial sign-in method. Microsoft and security best practices recommend combining SSO with MFA. We'll cover MFA next!

Multifactor Authentication

Multifactor authentication (MFA) adds a second layer of protection beyond just a username and a password. MFA requires users to verify their identity using two or more of the following factors:

- Something you know (e.g., password or PIN)
- Something you have (e.g., smartphone, security key, or security token)
- Something you are (e.g., fingerprint or facial recognition)

This dramatically improves security. Even if the password is compromised, access is still denied unless the user can supply the second factor.

With Microsoft Entra MFA, users can authenticate using:

- The Microsoft Authenticator app (push notifications, biometrics, or PIN)
- Phone calls to a registered number
- Text messages (SMS) with verification codes

Microsoft recommends using the Microsoft Authenticator app or passwordless authentication (which we'll cover next) over SMS and phone calls, as they're more secure.

Passwordless Authentication

Passwordless authentication eliminates the need for passwords entirely, replacing them with secure, phishing-resistant alternatives. It improves user experience and enhances protection against credential-based attacks.

Microsoft Entra ID supports three primary passwordless options:

Windows Hello for Business
> This security feature, which is built into Windows 10 and above, uses facial recognition, fingerprint, or a PIN tied to a specific device. It's a strong, phishing-resistant authentication method, and its built-in SSO gives easy access to company apps and resources on Windows 10+ devices.

Microsoft Authenticator app
> This app turns your smartphone into a passwordless sign-in tool. The user gets a push notification and then approves the sign-in with biometrics or a device PIN. It works across platforms, including Azure portal, Microsoft 365, and custom apps.

FIDO2 (Fast IDentity Online) security keys
> This phishing-resistant, highly secure method involves physical authentication devices (e.g., USB, Bluetooth, NFC) that verify identity without passwords. FIDO2 (*https://oreil.ly/WJPqu*) is ideal for high-security environments, frontline workers, or shared workstations, and it's supported by major browsers and operating systems.

Let's go into a bit more depth on FIDO2 security keys. These provide strong phishing-resistant authentication by using public key cryptography instead of passwords. Here's how it works:

Key pair generation
> When you register a FIDO2 key with a service, the device generates a public-private key pair. The public key is stored by the service, and the private key stays securely on the hardware key.

Authentication
> When you log in, the service sends a challenge that the private key must sign. The private key never leaves the device, so attackers can't steal it even if the service is compromised.

Domain verification
    The key is tied to the specific website or domain you registered with. If a phishing site tries to trick you, the key will refuse to authenticate because the domain doesn't match the one it's registered with.

No shared secrets
    Unlike passwords, there's no secret for attackers to intercept or reuse. Even if someone tries a man-in-the-middle attack, the private key can't be phished.

The result is that users can authenticate securely without fear of phishing, because the key only works with the legitimate service it was registered to.

Microsoft recommends moving toward passwordless strategies to reduce phishing risks, credential theft, and password fatigue.

Comparison of Authentication Methods at a Glance

Table 12-5 succinctly compares the authentication methods we've looked at so far.

Table 12-5. Comparison of authentication methods

Method	Description	Security level	Convenience level
Password only	Basic username and password	Low	High
SSO	One sign-in grants access to many apps	Medium	High
MFA	Adds a second layer, like a code or fingerprint	High	Medium
Passwordless	Uses biometrics, phone, or hardware keys	High	High

By using these modern authentication methods, Azure helps secure user identities while improving the overall authentication experience.

Microsoft Entra External ID

In today's connected world, businesses frequently collaborate with people outside their organization (partners, vendors, contractors, or customers) who are referred to as *external identities*.

Microsoft Entra External ID (formerly known as Azure AD B2B and B2C) allows organizations to securely collaborate with these external users while keeping internal resources protected and under centralized control.

Key Benefits of Microsoft Entra External ID

A key advantage, especially for business-to-consumer (B2C) scenarios, is that your application can leverage a trusted, enterprise-grade identity provider rather than relying on a homegrown authentication system. This reduces security risks, ensures compliance with best practices, and simplifies identity management for developers.

External users don't need to create new accounts. They can sign in using existing identities, such as:

- A Microsoft 365 work or school account
- A government or enterprise identity
- A social account like Google or Facebook (when using Entra B2C)

The external identities remain managed by their home organization, while you control what resources and permissions they have in your environment.

The main features of Microsoft Entra External ID

This listing outlines the main features of this authentication system:

B2B collaboration
    It allows you to invite external users to your organization as guest users, who can be assigned roles and permissions just like internal users.

B2B direct connect
    It enables seamless, two-way collaboration between Microsoft Entra organizations, especially in apps like Microsoft Teams shared channels. These users don't show up in your directory but can be managed within Teams. Although collaboration occurs in Teams, trust relationships are managed via cross-tenant access settings in Entra ID.

Azure AD B2C (B2C)
    Microsoft's legacy solution for customer identity and access management, this is designed for public-facing applications. It allows consumers to sign in using social identities (such as Facebook or Google) or local accounts, and it's ideal for developers who manage customer-facing apps and custom authentication flows.

Keeping external access secure

Security remains a top priority when giving access to guests. Microsoft Entra ID includes built-in tools to help you manage and monitor external users:

- Access reviews let you regularly check whether guest users still need access.
- Admins or designated reviewers can approve, modify, or remove access based on current needs.
- You can enforce Conditional Access policies and MFA for guest users, just like internal ones.

This approach keeps your directory lean and your data protected.

A Real-World Scenario

Imagine that your organization is collaborating with a third-party design agency. You want them to:

- View specific files in SharePoint
- Join project meetings in Microsoft Teams
- Access a shared Power BI report

Using Microsoft Entra External ID:

1. You invite their users as guests.
2. They log in using their existing corporate credentials.
3. You assign permissions to only the resources they need (e.g., access to a specific SharePoint site, Teams channel, or application).
4. Periodically, you conduct an access review and remove users who no longer require access.

There are no new accounts to set up and no password management headaches. You just enjoy secure, seamless collaboration.

Microsoft Entra Conditional Access

Conditional Access, a feature of Microsoft Entra ID, is a tool that helps organizations control how users access apps and data based on real-time conditions like user identity, location, device, user role, and risk level. Conditional Access also integrates with Microsoft Entra ID Protection, enabling advanced, risk-based policies that adapt dynamically to threats detected in real time.

Think of Conditional Access as being a digital bouncer who checks who you are, where you're coming from, and what you're using. It then decides if you get in, need extra checks, or get blocked.

How It Works

When someone attempts to sign in to an application or service, Conditional Access evaluates a set of *signals* (conditions), such as:

- Who is signing in (e.g., administrator versus regular user)?
- Where are they (e.g., trusted location versus unfamiliar country)?
- What device are they using (e.g., compliant corporate laptop versus personal phone)?
- What app or resource are they trying to access?
- Is a sign-in risk detected by Microsoft Entra's identity protection services?

Based on these signals, Conditional Access makes a decision:

- To allow access
- To require additional verification (like MFA)
- To block access

The goal is to provide just the right amount of security (not too much friction for safe scenarios but tighter control when risk is higher).

A Real-World Example

Let's say four different employees are logging into Microsoft Teams, as shown in Table 12-6.

Table 12-6. Conditional Access handling four different logins

Situation	User sign-in context	Policy result	Explanation/Notes
Signing in from corporate office on a compliant corporate device	Trusted network, company-managed laptop	✓ Access granted	User has baseline MFA enforced; no additional steps needed because device and location are trusted.
Signing in from a personal phone in another country	Untrusted device and location	MFA required	Conditional Access triggers a step-up verification. User completes MFA (SMS, Authenticator app, or FIDO2 key) before access is granted.
Signing in from a flagged high-risk location	Suspicious or flagged IP / risky sign-in detected by ID Protection	✗ Access blocked	Sign-in blocked automatically. User must contact IT to review, verify identity, or perform remediation (e.g., reset credentials). Policy can also be configured for limited access or step-up verification instead of full block if organization allows.
Signing in from corporate laptop at a trusted location but account flagged as high-risk	Compliant device, office network, but IDProtection detects potential compromise	MFA or ✗ Access blocked depending on policy	Admin can configure Conditional Access to either require additional verification or block entirely until risk is resolved.

Common Use Cases for Conditional Access

The following are common Conditional Access use cases:

Require MFA only when needed
    Require MFA based on risk signals (such as device compliance, user role, and sign-in risk), rather than relying solely on location.

Restrict app access
    Allow only approved apps like Outlook to access email and block others.

Enforce device compliance
    Limit access to devices that meet your organization's security standards.

Block risky sign-ins
    Deny access from suspicious countries, anonymous IPs, or unfamiliar devices.

Why Conditional Access Matters

Conditional Access helps your organization:

- Keep users productive by allowing seamless access in low-risk situations
- Improve security by increasing verification only when necessary
- Implement Zero Trust principles: never trust, always verify

As you can see, Conditional Access is like a smart security gatekeeper. It checks who is coming in, from where, and how, and it decides what level of access (if any) to allow. It's a flexible, context-aware solution that helps protect your organization without getting in the way of productivity.

Azure Role-Based Access Control

Azure RBAC allows you to manage who has access to what in your Azure environment. Instead of giving everyone full control, RBAC helps you follow the *principle of least privilege* (giving users only the access they need to do their jobs).

As discussed in Chapter 8, Azure organizes resources hierarchically into management groups, subscriptions, resource groups, and individual resources (see Figure 12-2). Azure RBAC permissions can be assigned at any of these scope levels, allowing for fine-grained access control that aligns with organizational policies and security requirements.

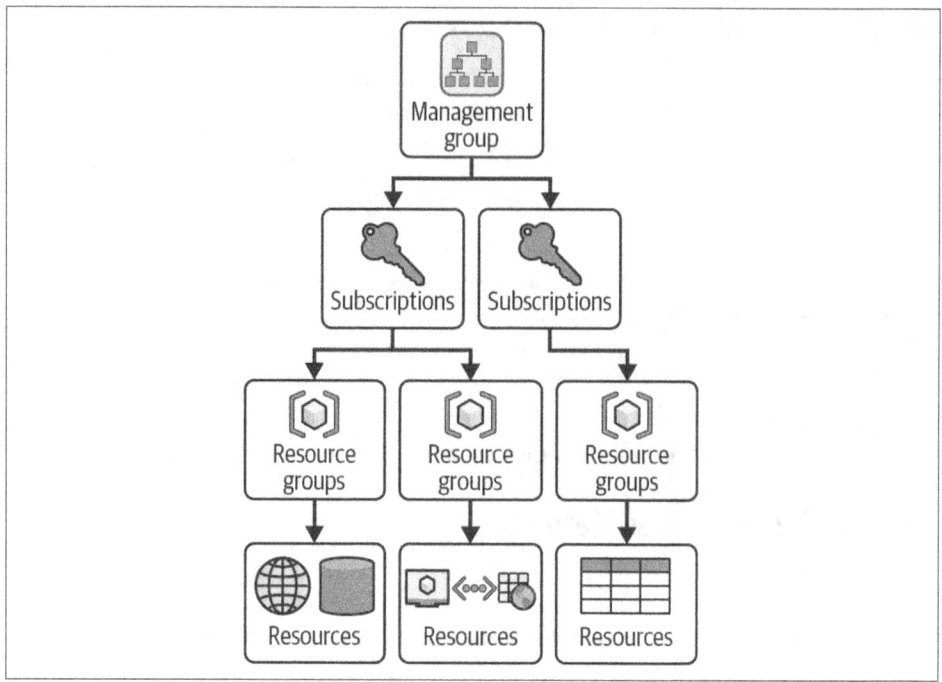

Figure 12-2. The RBAC scope levels

For scenarios that require just-in-time, temporary elevated access, Microsoft Entra Privileged Identity Management (PIM) complements RBAC. While RBAC defines the baseline permissions a user has, PIM allows administrators to grant time-limited, on-demand roles with approval workflows and activity auditing, enhancing security for sensitive operations.

Why Use RBAC?

Imagine that you have a team with different responsibilities:

- Developers only need access to deploy code to a storage account.
- Data analysts should be able to view reports in a database but not modify anything.
- IT administrators need full control over the network infrastructure.

With RBAC, you can tailor access precisely so everyone can do their job without putting other resources at risk.

How Does RBAC Work?

RBAC uses three main components:

Roles
A role is a set of permissions (like "read," "write," "delete"). Azure comes with built-in roles like:

- *Owner*: Full access to everything
- *Contributor*: Can make changes, but not manage access
- *Reader*: View-only access

You can also create custom roles for fine-grained control.

Role assignments
You assign roles to users, groups, or service principals (apps).

Scopes
The access applies to:

- *Management group*: A collection of subscriptions
- *Subscription*: A full Azure account
- *Resource group*: A container for multiple resources
- *Individual resource*: Like a specific VM or database

RBAC is hierarchical. Permissions assigned at a higher scope automatically apply to all resources within lower scopes.

Real-World RBAC Scenarios

To understand how RBAC works in practice, consider a few real-world scenarios.

- Suppose you assign the Owner role at the subscription level: this gives the user full control over all resources in that subscription (including VMs, databases, networks, and storage) and everything under that subscription.
- If you assign the Reader role at the resource group level, the user can view all resources within that group (such as VMs, databases, or app services) but can't make any changes.
- Finally, assigning the Contributor role to a specific storage account allows the user to manage that storage account (e.g., upload or delete blobs, change settings) but they can't modify resources outside that storage account.

These examples illustrate how RBAC limits or expands access depending on both the role and the scope, and although storage is used here for illustration, RBAC applies broadly across all Azure resources.

How Is RBAC Applied?

RBAC permissions are enforced through Azure Resource Manager (ARM), the service that handles requests in Azure.

You'll learn more about Azure CLI, PowerShell, Bicep, ARM templates, and Terraform in Chapter 15.

If you use . . .

- Azure portal
- Azure CLI or PowerShell
- Bicep, ARM templates, or Terraform

. . . your actions go through ARM, and RBAC checks whether you're allowed to perform that action.

RBAC controls access to *management actions*, not what's inside an app or database. For example, it can allow you to manage a database but not control what queries users can run inside that database.

Key Points to Remember

Here are some things to remember when you're using RBAC:

- Assign the minimum access required for each role.
- Use *built-in roles* when possible; define *custom roles* only when needed:
  - For example, if you want to grant a user a read-only role, you can grant this user the built-in "reader" role without creating a custom role. However, if a user needs to read from Azure Storage and manage Azure VMs, but no single built-in role provides that exact combination, you can create a custom role that includes both permissions.
- Access at higher scopes is inherited by all lower levels.
- RBAC works with Azure Resource Manager to enforce permissions.

Azure Key Vault

Azure Key Vault is a cloud service that securely stores and manages sensitive information (such as encryption keys, certificates, secrets, and passwords). Storing these secrets in configuration files or application code increases the risk of exposure. By centralizing sensitive information in Azure Key Vault, organizations reduce the risk of credential leaks and maintain stronger control over how security assets are used.

What Does Azure Key Vault Do?

Azure Key Vault is part of Azure's identity, access, and security ecosystem. It follows industry-standard security models and integrates seamlessly with Microsoft Entra ID for authentication, and supports authorization using Azure RBAC (recommended) or legacy Key Vault access policies. Azure Key Vault also supports automated secret and key rotation, ensuring that only approved users, applications, and services can access sensitive assets. Together, these capabilities help enforce modern security best practices while reducing operational complexity.

Azure Key Vault has a number of core capabilities:

Secrets management
Securely stores sensitive values such as passwords, API keys, and connection strings. Applications can retrieve these secrets at runtime without exposing them in code.

Key management
Manages encryption keys used by applications and Azure services. Supports hardware-backed keys using hardware security modules (HSMs) for high assurance.

Certificate management
Stores and manages TLS/SSL certificates. Integrates with certificate authorities to automate certificate renewal.

Access control and auditing
Uses Microsoft Entra ID and RBAC to control who or what (apps, VMs, services) can access the vault. Provides logs for auditing and compliance.

Automated rotation
Supports automatic key and secret rotation to reduce exposure and strengthen security posture.

Why Use Azure Key Vault?

Azure Key Vault simplifies and strengthens how organizations handle sensitive credentials in the following ways:

- It keeps secrets out of application code so developers no longer need to embed passwords or keys inside scripts or configuration files.
- It improves compliance by enabling consistent security practices across the organization, including encryption key policies and auditing.
- It centralizes and standardizes security asset management; with one service to store, rotate, and protect sensitive information, IT teams gain improved control and visibility.
- It supports secure integration with Azure services, and many Azure services (e.g., VMs, AKS, and Azure App Service) can pull secrets directly from Azure Key Vault.
- It reduces the risk of credential theft because secrets are encrypted, monitored, and can be retrieved only by authorized identities.

How Applications Access Secrets

Applications access Azure Key Vault using managed identities, eliminating the need for password-based authentication. Using managed identities, an app can request a secret or key directly from Key Vault and use it at runtime without ever handling a stored credential.

This follows the principles of:

Least privilege access
    Only permitted apps/users can read specific secrets.

Zero Trust
    Every request is authenticated and authorized.

Defense in depth
    Secrets are stored centrally with hardware-level protections.

Real-World Scenario

Consider a situation in which an application running in Azure App Service needs to connect to a database. Instead of placing the database password in configuration files:

- The password is stored securely in Azure Key Vault.
- The App Service has a managed identity with "Get Secret" permission.
- At runtime, the application retrieves the password securely from the vault.
- If the password needs to change, it's updated in the Key Vault, not in the application code.

This ensures that the application always uses the latest secret without requiring developers to redeploy code or risk exposing credentials.

Microsoft Defender for Cloud

Microsoft Defender for Cloud is a unified security tool designed to help organizations assess, protect, and monitor their security posture across Azure, on-premises environments, and multi-cloud platforms like AWS and GCP.

Why Use Microsoft Defender for Cloud?

Microsoft Defender for Cloud will help your organizations assess their security posture and identify vulnerabilities. It does this by:

- Continuously scanning their environment (e.g., VMs, containers, and databases) for vulnerabilities.
- Providing a *Secure Score*, which is a visual representation of their overall security posture:
    - A higher score (closer to 100%) indicates strong adherence to Microsoft security best practices (though it does not guarantee the absence of risk).
    - A lower score signals areas of vulnerability and opportunities for improvement.
- Giving them a prioritized list of recommendations to improve their security.

It also assists organizations with securing their resources by:

- Applying best practices and policies
- Using built-in security policies based on the Azure Security Benchmark
- Automatically evaluating new resources as they're deployed
- Working with Azure Policy to enforce compliance at scale (across subscriptions, management groups, or tenants)

Finally, Microsoft Defender for Cloud will defend against threats by issuing real-time alerts and providing automated protection:

- Detecting suspicious activities and generating detailed security alerts
- Sending security alerts when suspicious activity is detected
- Including in the alerts key details, remediation steps, and automation options (like triggering Logic Apps)

- Using advanced threat protection for VMs, SQL, containers, web apps, and networks
- Making available features like just-in-time VM access and application control that help block unauthorized behavior

Key Components of Microsoft Defender for Cloud

Here are the key components of Microsoft Defender for Cloud:

Cloud security posture management (CSPM)
    Provides agentless security monitoring for misconfigurations and compliance gaps across Azure, AWS, GCP, and hybrid environments.

Cloud workload protection platform (CWPP)
    Offers real-time threat protection for workloads including VMs, containers, and databases.

How Microsoft Defender for Cloud Protects Different Environments

Microsoft Defender for Cloud (*https://oreil.ly/YI1Ah*) protects *Azure-native services* by:

- Deeply integrating with Azure services like App Services, Azure SQL, Azure Storage, and more
- Offering advanced protections like anomaly detection, sensitive data discovery, and data threat protection

It protects hybrid and multi-cloud environments by:

- Extending Defender to on-premises servers and workloads using Azure Arc
- Protecting AWS and GCP resources with agentless CSPM

Microsoft Defender for Cloud provides a centralized view of security, actionable recommendations, and automated protections. By improving their Secure Score and following its guidance, organizations can strengthen defenses across all cloud and hybrid environments.

Summary

In this chapter, we explored Azure's identity and security services, focusing on Microsoft Entra ID for managing authentication and access, including SSO, MFA, passwordless options, and external identity collaboration. We examined key access control strategies such as Conditional Access policies, RBAC, Azure Key Vault, the Zero Trust model, and defense in depth to enforce least-privilege access and layered protection. Finally, we introduced Microsoft Defender for Cloud, which provides unified security management to help organizations monitor, assess, and protect their cloud and hybrid environments.

In the next chapter, you'll learn about cost management in Azure.

Chapter 12 Quiz

To check your answers, please refer to the "Chapter 12 Answer Key" on page 306.

1. Your security team is evaluating whether to adopt passwordless authentication using technologies like biometrics and FIDO2 keys. Your manager insists that passwordless authentication is less secure than methods that use traditional passwords.

    Is this statement true or false?

    A. True

    B. False

2. Management at your organization has heard a little about the Zero Trust model and is considering whether to implement it. The CEO asks you to summarize the core principle of the Zero Trust model.

    How do you respond?

    A. Trust all users by default.

    B. Verify explicitly and assume breach.

    C. Use passwords for all authentication.

    D. Rely on perimeter security.

3. You need to explain to your team how the defense-in-depth model protects against threats at multiple levels.

    Why does defense in depth recommend using multiple security controls instead of relying on a single solution?

    A. To increase operational costs and complexity

    B. Because a single security control can fail or be bypassed

    C. To eliminate the need for user security training

    D. Because firewalls alone can prevent all attacks

PART III
Azure Management and Governance

In the third part of this study guide, you'll explore Azure's management and governance capabilities, equipping you with the tools to control costs, ensure compliance, deploy resources efficiently, and maintain visibility across your cloud environment—essential skills for the AZ-900 Azure Fundamentals exam. Mastering these will help you understand how to operate Azure responsibly, securely, and at scale.

- Chapter 13, "Cost Management in Azure"
- Chapter 14, "Azure Governance and Compliance"
- Chapter 15, "Managing and Deploying Azure Resources"
- Chapter 16, "Azure Monitoring Tools"

CHAPTER 13
Cost Management in Azure

In the previous chapter, we explored the core principles that protect your Azure environment through identity, access, and security. Now, we turn our attention to another essential aspect of cloud governance: cost management.

Think of using Azure as like having household utilities (electricity, water, and gas) that are all billed on a pay-as-you-go model. It's flexible and convenient, but if you leave the lights on all the time or let the water run, unchecked usage can lead to unexpectedly high bills!

Now imagine that your home is equipped with smart meters with usage alerts and budget controls. You can see exactly how much each appliance costs to operate, set monthly limits, and receive notifications when you're approaching your budget limit. This empowers you to make smarter decisions (lower the thermostat, run the dishwasher at off-peak times, or take shorter showers) to stay within budget.

Azure offers the same kind of visibility and control for your cloud spending. With the right tools, you can monitor usage, forecast costs, and fine-tune your resources to prevent budget overruns. As your cloud environment scales, cost management becomes just as important as securing your infrastructure.

Cost optimization in Azure is a shared responsibility. While finance and IT admins often lead the effort, developers, DevOps engineers, and operations teams all play a role in controlling resource usage, rightsizing services, and implementing automation to reduce waste.

Cost Management provides a comprehensive suite of tools that support these collaborative efforts and help you estimate, track, and optimize your cloud spending. Whether you're deploying new services or analyzing ongoing consumption, these tools empower you to make informed and cost-effective decisions.

In this chapter, we'll deep dive into the core concepts, tools, and strategies of Azure Cost Management to help you prepare for the AZ-900 Azure Fundamentals exam.

You'll learn how to:

- Estimate costs before deployment with the Azure pricing calculator
- Track spending across subscriptions using Cost Management + Billing
- Set up budgets and alerts to avoid unexpected charges
- Use resource tags to categorize and allocate costs efficiently

Make sure to read through to the end of this chapter, where we reveal the top 10 tips to help you save money on Azure and get the most value from your cloud investment.

Let's get started and take control of your cloud costs with confidence!

Cost Management in Azure

As organizations scale their cloud usage, managing costs becomes just as critical as securing their resources. In a dynamic environment where resources can be provisioned in a matter of minutes, costs can quickly spiral out of control without proper visibility and control.

To effectively manage spending in Azure, we need a suite of tools that helps you monitor, control, and optimize your cloud spending. Whether you're estimating costs before deploying resources or tracking real-time usage across subscriptions, Azure gives you the insight needed to stay within budget and make informed decisions.

In this section, you'll learn how Azure enables cost transparency through calculators, budgets, alerts, tagging strategies, and more to ensure that your cloud investments stay aligned with your business goals.

From CapEx to OpEx: A Shift in Cost Models

Migrating to Azure changes how organizations fund IT. Traditional on-premises infrastructure requires large, up-front investments in hardware known as *capital expenditures (CapEx)*.

In contrast, Azure operates on an *operational expenditure (OpEx)* model, where you pay for the resources you consume such as compute, networking, and storage. This consumption-based approach provides the flexibility to scale workloads on demand, making it a key driver for cloud adoption and enabling organizations to align costs directly with usage.

Factors That Influence Azure Costs

A common question is "How much will Azure cost?"

The answer depends on several key factors, highlighted as follows.

Resource type and size

Azure pricing depends on the types of resources you provision, how they're configured, and where they're deployed.

While VMs and storage are commonly referenced examples, Azure offers a wide range of resources, including databases, networking, AI services, containers, and more, each with its own metrics that influence cost. When any resource is provisioned, Azure tracks usage through meters, collecting data that's converted into billing information based on actual consumption.

For example:

Azure Virtual Machine
　　Costs vary based on OS licensing, number of vCPUs, attached storage, etc.

Azure Storage
　　Cost depends on storage type (e.g., Blob, Disk, etc.), performance tier, redundancy level, access tier, and region.

When a resource is provisioned, Azure tracks resource usage through meters. Usage data is then turned into billing information.

Consumption and usage patterns

Azure operates on a pay-as-you-go pricing model, which means you only pay for what you actually use during each billing cycle. Your usage patterns play a key role in determining your overall costs.

Common cost drivers to keep in mind include:

Idle resources
　　Running VMs or databases that are not actively used can lead to unnecessary charges.

Peak demand
　　Spikes in usage often require additional resources to be provisioned. This will increase your costs.

Data movement
　　Transferring data across regions, or out of Azure, often incurs additional charges.

Geographic region

Azure resources must be deployed in specific regions. Here are some facts about the relationship between Azure costs and regions:

- Regional pricing can vary due to factors such as regional energy costs, labor, and taxes.
- Network traffic costs can depend on geography.
- Intra-region traffic (within the same region) is cheaper than inter-region or global traffic.
- Outbound data transfers (e.g., from Europe to Asia) cost more than internal transfers.
- Azure groups regions into bandwidth pricing zones that determine outbound data transfer costs. Inbound data transfer is generally free.
- Inbound data is generally free, while outbound data incurs zone-based charges.

Subscription type

Your Azure subscription type affects both access to services and billing options. Table 13-1 shows the most common Azure subscription types.

Table 13-1. Common Azure subscription types

Subscription type	Description	Usage example
Free trial	Provides a $200 credit for 30 days and access to a limited set of free services for 12 months. Requires a credit card for identity verification. Note: During the free trial, you're limited by the $200 credit and free-tier usage. To go beyond, you must switch to a pay-as-you-go subscription, after which standard charges apply.	Individuals exploring Azure for the first time or learning about cloud technologies
Pay-as-you-go	Standard subscription has you pay monthly for what you use with no up-front commitment or long-term contract.	Startups or small businesses scaling usage gradually with no long-term resource commitments
Microsoft Customer Agreement (MCA)	This newer agreement type simplifies billing and combines multiple Azure subscriptions. It's suitable for both individual and organizational use.	Enterprises consolidating billing for multiple departments or projects
Microsoft Enterprise Agreement (EA)	Designed for large organizations committing to substantial cloud usage. Offers custom pricing for a long-term financial commitment.	Large corporations with predictable, high-volume Azure consumption across regions and teams
Microsoft AI Cloud Partner Program	Offers free Azure credits to Microsoft partners. Includes Action Pack and competency-based benefits.	IT consultants or Microsoft partners building or demoing solutions for clients

Subscription type	Description	Usage example
Visual Studio subscription	Provides monthly Azure credits to subscribers of Visual Studio. Credits vary by subscription tier (e.g., Professional, Enterprise).	Developers testing and developing applications in a non-production environment
Azure for Students (*https://oreil.ly/ 3L2aP*)	Offers free access to Azure tools and services with no credit card required. Includes $100 one-time total credit and free services for 12 months.	University students learning cloud computing or building academic projects
Azure Sponsorship	A promotional subscription comes with a limited budget provided by Microsoft (e.g., for hackathons, research, or startups).	Research teams or nonprofit organizations using Azure under grant or sponsorship programs
Cloud Solution Provider (CSP)	Managed and billed by a Microsoft partner. Customers work directly with a partner for provisioning, billing, and support.	Small and medium businesses (SMBs) receiving Azure services through a trusted Microsoft reseller or IT provider
Azure for Students Starter	Similar to the Students offer but offers fewer services.	Younger students or those ineligible for the full Azure for Students program
Azure Government	Tailored for US federal, state, local, and tribal governments. Meets strict compliance and regulatory requirements.	Government agencies deploying cloud infrastructure with security and compliance needs
Azure for Nonprofits	Offers discounted or free Azure services to eligible nonprofit organizations.	Non-governmental organizations (NGOs) building internal systems or donor-facing applications

In the next section, we'll explore useful Azure tools that can help you plan effectively to stay within budget and maximize your return on investment.

Tools to Help Estimate and Manage Azure Costs

Azure provides several powerful tools to help you plan, estimate, track, optimize, and manage your cloud spending. Whether your organization is evaluating a migration or managing an existing cloud footprint, these capabilities support financial accountability and informed decision-making.

The primary tools to help estimate and manage Azure costs are:

- Azure Migrate: Assessment & Business Case
- Azure pricing calculator
- Azure Advisor
- Cost Management + Billing

Let's look at each in detail.

Azure Migrate: Assessment & Business Case

The legacy Total Cost of Ownership (TCO) Calculator is now obsolete. *Azure Migrate* replaces it with a more powerful, automated approach for modeling costs and calculating the true total cost of ownership.

In this section, you'll learn about the latest Microsoft guidance, including the shift away from the legacy TCO calculator. Today, the Azure Migrate Assessment and Business Case capabilities provide a more comprehensive, accurate method for comparing on-premises infrastructure to Azure.

Azure Migrate provides two features for financial analysis:

- Azure Migrate: Assessment
- Azure Migrate: Business Case

Azure Migrate: Assessment

For organizations planning to move on-premises workloads to Azure, the first step (especially from a financial perspective) is to understand the cost impact of migration.

Azure Migrate: Assessment provides an automated, data-driven way to build an accurate cost model by helping you:

- Estimate projected Azure costs for your existing on-premises servers based on real usage patterns rather than static assumptions.
- Perform rightsizing of resources by analyzing CPU, memory, disk, and performance trends to determine the most cost-effective Azure VM sizes, Azure SQL SKUs, or Azure VMware Solution node counts.
- Evaluate migration readiness for servers, databases, and web applications to avoid unexpected remediation costs.
- Analyze application and network dependencies so you can plan a reliable migration without incurring additional expenses from overlooked systems or misaligned cutovers.

In essence, *Azure Migrate: Assessment* gives organizations the visibility needed to build accurate Azure cost projections and optimize sizing decisions to ensure that migration planning is both technically sound and financially optimized.

Azure Migrate: Business Case

After completing the technical assessment, *Azure Migrate: Business Case* translates those findings into a detailed, multi-year financial model. Its purpose is to help organizations clearly understand the true cost impact of migration and build an evidence-based business justification.

Azure Migrate: Business Case provides projections that include:

- Current on-premises costs, including both operational expenses (OpEx) and capital investments (CapEx).
- Expected Azure consumption and licensing costs, modeled using rightsizing insights from the assessment.
- Facility and infrastructure overhead, such as power, cooling, physical datacenter space, and hardware refresh cycles.
- IT labor, support, and maintenance costs, compared against Azure-managed services.
- Financial impact of shifting from CapEx to an OpEx-based cloud model.
- Cash flow projections and long-term savings, showing how costs evolve over time.
- Break-even analysis, identifying the point at which Azure becomes more cost-efficient than on-premises.
- Optimized Azure resource sizing to ensure that the cost model reflects real usage rather than overprovisioned estimates.

This comprehensive financial approach reflects Microsoft's current guidance: a modern Total Cost of Ownership model must account for all meaningful cost categories to accurately quantify the financial benefits of migrating to Azure.

To learn more, please visit the Azure Migrate website (*https://oreil.ly/JiDVm*).

Azure Pricing Calculator

Use this tool, shown in Figure 13-1, to estimate the cost of specific Azure services based on your selections. You can configure subscriptions, services, regions, billing models, dev/test pricing, and support options to see how your choices affect the total cost. It's especially helpful for budget planning.

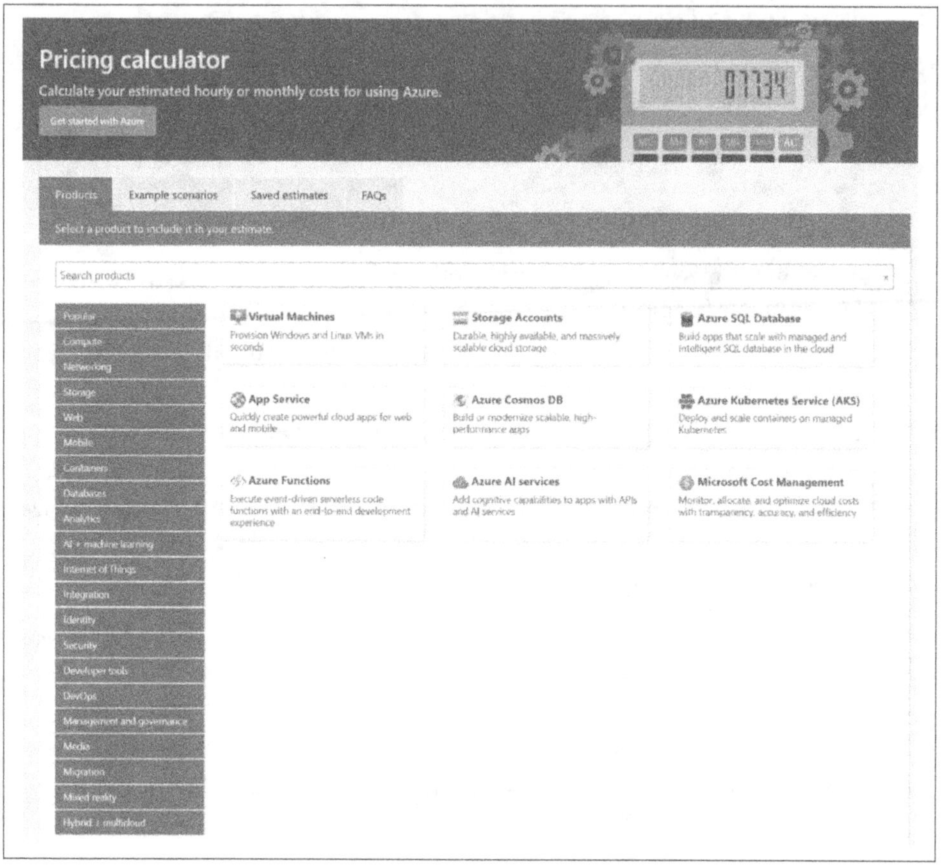

Figure 13-1. Azure pricing calculator

With the pricing calculator, you can:

- Get pricing for individual services like VMs, storage, or databases
- Build a complete solution to estimate total monthly or yearly costs
- Use example scenarios to explore typical Azure deployments

 The pricing calculator only provides estimates. Intended for planning and informational purposes, it doesn't actually provision any resources.

You can tailor your estimates by adjusting settings such as:

- Storage type, access tiers, and redundancy
- Regions and expected usage
- Associated networking and compute resources

You can check it out at the pricing calculator website (*https://oreil.ly/EsQnt*).

Azure Advisor

After your Azure resources are deployed and provisioned, you can use Azure Advisor in the Azure portal (*https://portal.azure.com*) to analyze your environment and provide tailored cost-optimization recommendations. It helps identify underutilized resources and offers recommendations to reduce waste and improve efficiency. Figure 13-2 gives an example view of Azure Advisor.

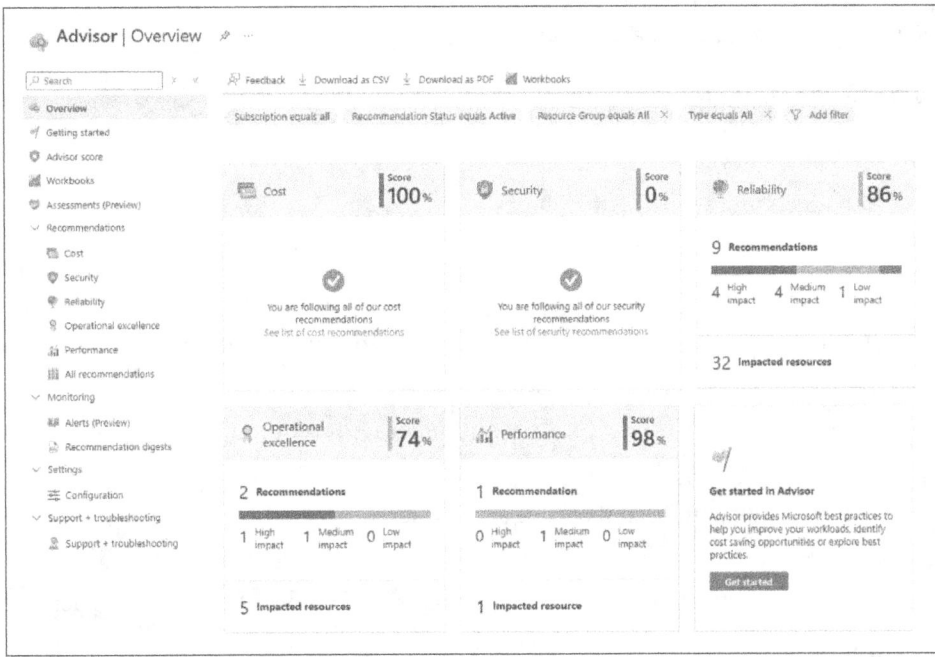

Figure 13-2. Azure Advisor

Cost Management + Billing

Cost Management + Billing (see Figure 13-3) helps you monitor, control, and optimize your cloud spending to avoid spending surprises.

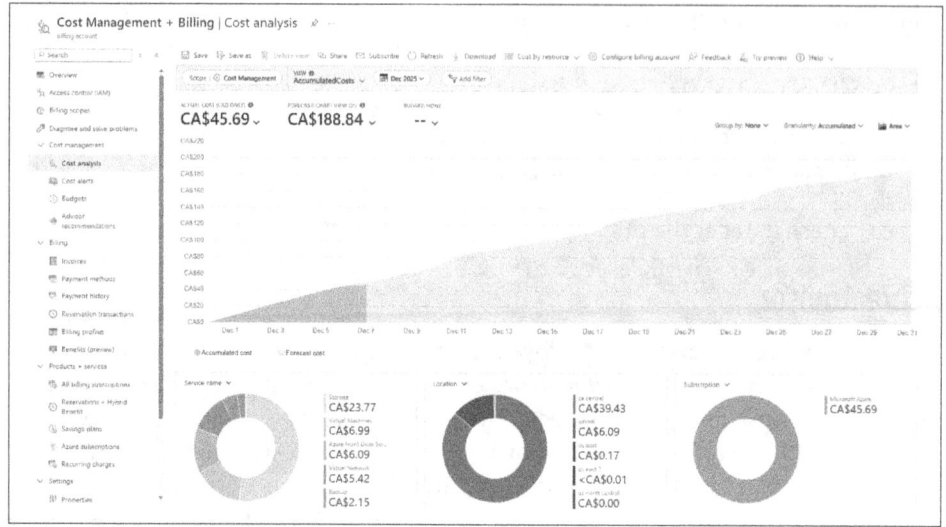

Figure 13-3. Cost Management + Billing

With Cost Management, you can:

- Track and analyze resource costs
- Set budgets and spending thresholds
- Create alerts to monitor usage and prevent overspending

These features help ensure financial accountability and proactive cost control across your Azure environment. These are the key features of Cost Management + Billing:

Cost analysis
  Visualize spending by service, subscription, or resource group over time.

Budgets
  Define spending limits and receive alerts when nearing thresholds.

Recommendations
  Identify cost-saving opportunities (e.g., rightsize VMs, buy Reserved Instances).

Forecasting
  Predict future costs based on current usage patterns.

Exportable reports
  Download data in CSV or Excel format for sharing and deeper analysis.

Cost analysis is a particularly powerful feature of Cost Management that gives you visual insights into your spending. It allows you to:

- Break down costs by billing cycle, region, resource, and more
- View costs aggregated across your organization
- Identify trends and forecast future expenses (monthly, quarterly, or annually)

These insights facilitate better financial planning and decision making.

Creating cost alerts

Cost Management allows you to create cost alerts to stay informed and in control of your spending. All active alerts are viewable in a centralized dashboard. There are three primary alert types: budget alerts, credit alerts, and spending quota alerts.

Budget alerts notify you when your cost or usage reaches a defined threshold:

- They're triggered when spending or usage meets a predefined threshold.
- They're configurable in the Azure portal or via the Azure Consumption API.
- Alerts appear in the dashboard and are emailed to designated recipients.
- Optionally, you can automate responses (e.g., scale down or shut off resources).

For EA customers and Azure Sponsorship subscriptions, Azure provides *credit alerts*. These notify you when your monetary commitment (Azure credit) is nearly or fully consumed:

- Alerts are automatically triggered at 90% and 100% of credit usage.
- Notifications appear in Cost Alerts and are emailed to account owners.

Spending quota alerts notify department owners when spending reaches a defined percentage of their allocated quota so they can manage their budgets proactively:

- Alerts are configured through the EA portal
- They're typically triggered at thresholds like 50% or 75%.

Using budgets to set spending limits

Budgets allow you to set spending limits for Azure at various scopes, including:

- Subscription
- Resource group
- Service type
- Custom filters

When actual costs or usage reach the defined budget threshold:

- A budget alert is triggered.
- Notifications are sent via email (if configured).

For advanced scenarios, you can link budgets to automation workflows that adjust or halt services automatically once thresholds are reached.

Best practices for using Cost Management + Billing

Here are some best practices for using Cost Management + Billing:

- Set budgets early to avoid overspending surprises.
- Review recommendations regularly to identify cost-saving opportunities.
- Use filters (e.g., by resource group) to pinpoint costly areas.
- Share reports with teams to improve financial transparency.

By using Cost Management + Billing, you can gain deeper visibility into your cloud costs, reduce financial risk, and ensure that your Azure environment stays both effective and cost-efficient.

Bringing It All Together

The following steps outline how and where to use Azure's cost management tools throughout the cloud adoption lifecycle to plan, deploy, and optimize workloads effectively:

1. *Discovery and baseline*

    Start with *Azure Migrate: Assessment* to discover on-premises servers, databases, storage, and application dependencies. Use this tool to capture real usage patterns and understand current costs, including hardware, licensing, labor, and datacenter operations. This establishes the financial baseline for comparison.

2. *Translation to Azure*

    Continue by using *Azure Migrate: Assessment* to map on-premises workloads to Azure equivalents. The tool provides automated rightsizing recommendations and generates cost projections for Azure VMs, storage, networking, and platform services. This stage helps you understand what your environment will cost once migrated.

3. *Business case and decision making*

    Use *Azure Migrate: Business Case* to build a financial justification for migration. This tool compares on-premises costs with projected Azure costs, models multi-year savings, evaluates the transition from CapEx to OpEx, and highlights efficiency gains from retiring legacy infrastructure. You can use this information to support funding requests and executive decision making.

4. *Deployment planning*

   Use the *Azure pricing calculator* to design your target Azure architecture and estimate the cost of each Azure service you plan to deploy. This tool is ideal for modeling multiple deployment scenarios, testing different regions, choosing support plans, and exploring pricing options such as dev/test rates or reserved instances.

5. *Deployment and migration*

   During migration, refer back to *Azure Migrate* for guidance on rightsized resources and dependency groupings. Although not a cost tool at this stage, Azure Migrate ensures that you deploy the correct resources so your projected costs remain accurate.

6. *Ongoing optimization*

   After workloads are running in Azure, use *Azure Advisor* and *Cost Management + Billing* to continually optimize cost and performance.

   - *Azure Advisor* identifies idle or underutilized resources and provides recommendations such as rightsizing and purchasing Reserved Instances or Azure Savings Plans for eligible workloads.
   - *Cost Management + Billing* provides dashboards, budgets, alerts, cost allocation, forecasting, and anomaly detection to keep long-term spending under control.

By applying these tools strategically across the lifecycle, organizations can maintain cost visibility, control, and efficiency from planning through ongoing operations.

In the next section, you'll learn how Azure tags can help with cost management.

Organizing Resources with Azure Tags

To effectively manage your Azure environment while controlling costs, enforcing security, and meeting compliance requirements, it's essential to keep your Azure resources well organized. Azure provides several built-in features to help you structure and manage your environment:

Subscriptions
   Segment and manage collections of related resources, often by department, environment, or project.

Resource groups
   Organize resources that share a common lifecycle or function, making it easier to deploy, monitor, and manage them together.

Tags
> Attach custom metadata to resources for improved classification, cost management, automation, and reporting.

Note that subscriptions and resource groups are described in Chapter 8. In this section, we'll focus on how tags can bring structure and clarity to your Azure environment, helping you manage resources more efficiently.

What Are Tags?

Tags are metadata labels in the form of name-value pairs (e.g., Environment=QA or Environment=Prod) that you can assign to Azure resources. These tags help you categorize, manage, and track your assets more effectively. With tags, you can:

- Logically group Azure resources by attributes such as project, department, or owner.
- Filter and organize resources for dashboards, automation scripts, or governance reports.
- Track and allocate cloud spending more accurately, since tags are queryable in cost analysis reports.
- Enforce consistent governance through policy-based tagging.

By applying consistent tagging strategies, you gain better visibility and control over your entire Azure landscape. Table 13-2 shows some of the benefits of using tags.

Table 13-2. Benefits of using tags

Category	How tags help
Resource management	Group resources by workload, environment, owner, or department for easier identification and control.
Cost management and optimization	Track and allocate spending, generate cost reports, and forecast usage trends.
Operations management	Tag resources by SLA or criticality to support operational planning and reliability.
Security	Classify resources by data sensitivity (e.g., confidential, public) to align with data protection policies.
Governance and compliance	Enforce standards like ISO 27001 by requiring tags such as "Owner" or "Department."
Automation and workload management	Automate deployment and maintenance tasks based on tag values using Azure DevOps and other tools.

Managing Tags in Azure

Let's think about tags in the context of a real-world scenario. Imagine a company with multiple projects running in Azure. Each project has resources like virtual machines, storage accounts, and databases. To track costs and responsibilities, the company wants to tag resources by "Project=AI_Chatbot," "Environment=Prod," and "Owner=Jack." This helps teams see which resources belong to which project and who is responsible for them.

You can add, update, or remove tags using a variety of tools:

- Azure portal
- Azure CLI
- PowerShell
- ARM templates, Bicep, and Terraform
- REST API

To enforce consistent tagging across your environment, use Azure Policy, a governance tool that allows you to define and enforce rules for your Azure resources. With Azure Policy, you can:

- Require specific tags when new resources are created
- Automatically add missing tags or correct tag values
- Define and enforce custom tagging rules at the resource, resource group, or subscription level

You'll learn more about Azure Policy in Chapter 14.

Tags are not inherited from resource groups to resources inside them. For example, if you tag a resource group with "Environment=Prod," the VMs and storage accounts inside it won't automatically inherit that tag. This gives you flexibility to assign more granular tags (such as "Owner=Bob" or "CostCenter=1234") to individual resources as required.

Using tags effectively enhances visibility, accountability, and governance. This helps you stay in control as your Azure footprint scales.

We're almost at the end of this chapter. As promised, it's time to reveal our top 10 tips for saving money with Azure.

Top 10 Tips for Saving Money with Azure

Azure costs typically rise as the number and size of resources you consume grow. Here are 10 practical ways to optimize your Azure spending.

Tip #1: Rightsize your resources.

- Regularly review VMs, databases, and other services.
- Scale down overprovisioned resources or shut down idle/underutilized instances.
- Look to tools like Azure Advisor and Cost Management + Billing for recommendations for scaling down or shutting off underutilized instances, helping to balance performance and cost.

Tip #2: Use Azure Reserved Instances.

- Azure Reserved Instances allow you to commit to one-year or three-year terms for predictable workloads like VMs, databases, and storage.
- You can save up to 72% (or more with Azure Hybrid Benefit) compared to pay-as-you-go pricing.
- If your usage exceeds the reserved capacity, the extra consumption is billed at regular pay-as-you-go rates, providing a balance of cost savings and flexibility.

Tip #3: Leverage Azure Hybrid Benefit.

- If you have existing on-premises Windows Server or SQL Server licenses with Software Assurance, you can apply them to Azure VMs or SQL services, reducing costs significantly.
- This will lower the cost of running VMs and SQL services in Azure.

Tip #4: Use the Cost Management + Billing tool.

- Track spending, set budgets, and analyze usage trends.
- Set up alerts to stay informed and avoid unexpected charges.
- You can generate reports by resource, subscription, or tag to see exactly where costs are coming from.

Tip #5: Schedule auto-shutdown for VMs.

- Automate start/stop schedules for development, testing, or other non-production environments to avoid unnecessary runtime charges.
- Use Azure Automation or VM auto-shutdown policies to save on runtime costs without affecting availability.

Tip #6: Optimize storage costs.

- Move infrequently accessed data to lower-cost tiers such as Cool, Cold, or Archive.

- Delete unused disks, snapshots, and backups.
- Use Azure Storage metrics and cost analysis reports to identify candidates for optimization.

Tip #7: Run interruptible or fault-tolerant workloads on Azure Spot VMs.

- Azure Spot VMs offer deep discounts for workloads that can tolerate interruptions.
- Spot VMs are ideal for batch processing, dev/test environments, and stateless applications.

Tip #8: Consolidate workloads.

- Host multiple applications on fewer compute instances using Azure App Service or AKS.
- Consolidation improves resource utilization and reduces overhead.

Tip #9: Deploy Azure resources in cost-effective regions.

- Azure pricing varies by region, but you'll need to choose a region that meets both cost and compliance needs.
- Tools like the Azure pricing calculator can help you compare regional costs, but consider performance and user proximity before choosing a lower-cost region.

Tip #10: Audit and clean up unused resources regularly.

- To avoid unnecessary charges, remove resources and their dependencies that are no longer in use.
- Regularly audit your environment to ensure that only needed resources remain active.
- Use tags, resource groups, Azure Advisor, and Cost Management reports to identify underutilized resources and maintain an efficient environment.

Summary

In this chapter, you learned how to plan, estimate, monitor, and optimize Azure costs using tools like Azure Migrate, the pricing calculator, Azure Advisor, and Cost Management + Billing. You also explored tagging, budgets, alerts, and practical cost-saving strategies to help prevent overspending and improve financial visibility. These skills not only support your AZ-900 exam preparation but also ensure that your cloud investments stay aligned with business goals.

In the next chapter, we'll shift focus to another crucial area of cloud management: governance and compliance.

Chapter 13 Quiz

To check your answers, please refer to the "Chapter 13 Answer Key" on page 306.

1. Your team is planning to deploy multiple Azure resources for a new application and needs to estimate monthly operating costs before deployment. You want to compare different configuration sizes and pricing models to forecast spending.

   Which tool should you use?

   A. Azure Advisor

   B. Azure pricing calculator

   C. Azure Monitor

   D. Cost Management

2. Your finance team is reviewing cloud cost drivers and wants to understand what variables directly affect Azure pricing as they prepare budget controls.

   Which one of the following items does NOT directly affect Azure pricing?

   A. Resource type and size

   B. Geographic region

   C. Number of users

   D. Usage patterns

3. Your organization is experiencing higher-than-expected Azure charges and wants to identify unused or underutilized resources (e.g., VMs running at 5% CPU). You need a tool that provides actionable cost-saving recommendations.

   Which tool should you use?

   A. Azure pricing calculator

   B. Azure Monitor

   C. Cost Management

   D. Azure Advisor

CHAPTER 14
Azure Governance and Compliance

In the previous chapter, we explored Azure cost management, learning how to monitor, control, and optimize cloud spending. However, managing costs is only one part of responsible cloud usage. To operate securely, reliably, and in line with organizational or regulatory standards, you also need *governance*.

Azure provides a set of tools and controls that help organizations with all aspects of governance: enforcing standards, maintaining compliance, and protecting critical resources. It ensures that resources are deployed correctly, securely, and consistently.

In this chapter, we'll explore key governance and compliance tools in Azure, each of which serves a unique role in building a well-managed cloud environment:

- Microsoft Purview
- Azure Policy
- Resource locks
- Microsoft Service Trust Portal

By the end of this chapter, you'll understand how Azure's governance tools work together to help you create an environment that's secure, compliant, and resilient.

Let's get started.

Microsoft Purview: Unified Data Governance

As organizations generate more data across diverse systems (for example, on-premises, multi-cloud, and SaaS), it becomes increasingly difficult to answer critical questions like:

- Where is our sensitive data?
- Who can access our data?
- Are we meeting regulatory and privacy requirements for our data?

Microsoft Purview addresses these challenges by providing a unified solution for data governance, security, and regulatory compliance. It enables organizations to discover and classify data, understand how data moves, and support compliance efforts across data estates including Azure, AWS, GCP, on-premises environments, and Microsoft 365.

The Microsoft Purview Portal

The *Microsoft Purview portal* (*https://purview.microsoft.com*) delivers a centralized experience for managing data governance tasks (see Figure 14-1).

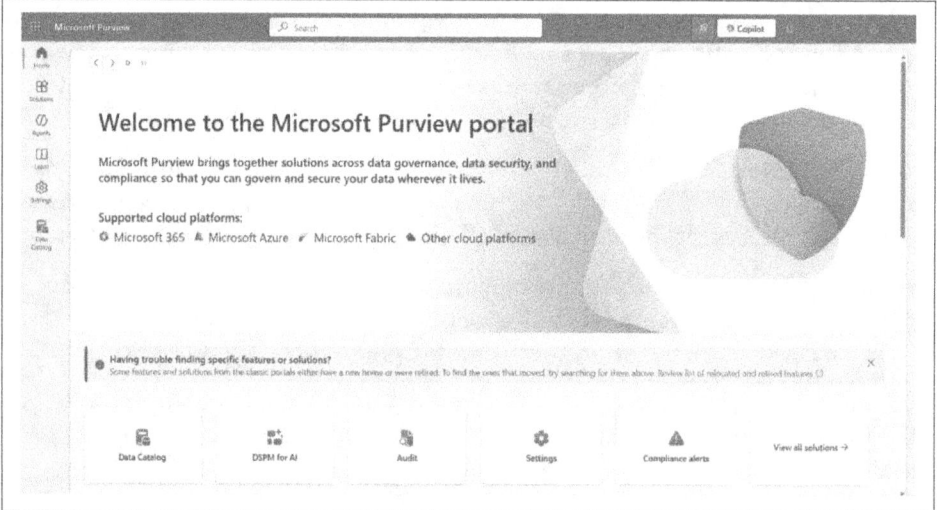

Figure 14-1. The Microsoft Purview portal

The portal brings together all of Microsoft Purview's core functionalities in one place:

Data governance
　　Discover, classify, and catalog data across your environment.

Data security
　　Apply sensitivity labels, manage access, and protect sensitive information.

Risk and compliance
　　Monitor data activity, detect risks, and enforce compliance policies.

What Microsoft Purview Enables

Microsoft Purview provides a comprehensive approach to data governance by:

- *Protecting sensitive data* across cloud services, on-premises systems, and Microsoft 365 apps like Teams, Exchange, and OneDrive
- *Identifying and mitigating data risks* by applying policies that support privacy and regulatory standards
- *Enabling secure, responsible data use* through automated discovery, classification, and access controls
- *Gaining complete visibility into your data estate* with a centralized, always-updated data map

Key Functional Areas of Microsoft Purview

Following are Microsoft Purview's key features:

Data Map
  Scans and catalogs data across Azure, on-premises systems, and third-party clouds like AWS. Enables data classification by using built-in or custom labels to classify sensitive data such as personally identifiable information (PII) or financial records.

Data Catalog
  Allows users to search, explore, and understand data assets through rich metadata. Enables tracing of data lineage to understand how data moves and transforms across systems.

Data access insights
  Provides visibility into how sensitive data is accessed and used through audit logs, activity monitoring, and data classification insights, primarily within Microsoft 365 and other supported services integrated with Microsoft Purview.

Compliance reporting
  Generates audit-ready reports and dashboards to support regulatory requirements.

Deep Integration with Microsoft 365 Compliance

Microsoft Purview is closely integrated with Microsoft 365 compliance tools to extend governance across:

- Teams
- Exchange
- OneDrive

Capabilities include:

- Applying sensitivity labels to documents and emails
- Monitoring data usage across endpoints
- Enforcing compliance policies across collaboration tools

This integration ensures consistent protection of sensitive data wherever the user collaborates.

Common Use Cases of Microsoft Purview

These are the common use cases of Microsoft Purview:

Regulatory compliance

- Automatically identify and label PII, financial, or health data.
- Generate audit-ready reports for standards like GDPR and HIPAA.
- Enforce data retention or access policies based on data sensitivity.

Data discovery and lineage

- Help analysts find trusted, approved datasets.
- Understand how data has been transformed from its source.
- Identify the downstream impact of schema changes.

Centralized governance

- Create a single source of truth for data assets.
- Control access to data securely and at scale.
- Empower teams to share and reuse data responsibly.

A Real-World Example: Healthcare

A healthcare organization stores patient data across Azure SQL, Amazon S3, and Excel files in OneDrive. Using Microsoft Purview, it can:

- Discover and classify records containing personal health information (PHI)
- Apply access controls to protect sensitive patient data

- Produce compliance dashboards for HIPAA reporting
- Visualize how patient data flows between systems to mitigate operational risk

Integration with the Microsoft Data Ecosystem

Microsoft Purview works seamlessly with other Azure and Microsoft services:

Azure Synapse Analytics
　　Track data lineage and flows in analytical pipelines.

Microsoft Defender for Cloud
　　Surface security alerts for sensitive data.

Azure Policy
　　Apply governance rules based on sensitivity classification.

Microsoft Purview
　　Unify data governance across email, documents, and apps.

Azure Policy: Enforce Organizational Standards

In fast-paced cloud environments, multiple teams often deploy resources independently, which can lead to inconsistent configurations, security vulnerabilities, and rising costs. Without clear governance, environments quickly become difficult to manage.

Azure Policy is Microsoft's built-in governance service designed to bring order and consistency by automatically enforcing rules across your Azure environment.

What Is Azure Policy?

Azure Policy acts as a set of automated, organization-wide rules that help ensure that every resource is deployed and configured according to your standards. It allows you to:

- *Block noncompliant deployments* (e.g., prevent resources from being created in unapproved regions)
- *Enforce configuration settings* (e.g., require encryption or mandatory tags)
- *Audit existing resources* for adherence to standards (e.g., identify resources that are missing mandatory settings)
- *Autoremediate* certain noncompliant resources (e.g., add missing tags or apply required security configurations automatically)

Azure Policy helps to reduce human error, eliminate drift, and simplify regulatory compliance.

Why Azure Policy Matters

Azure Policy is an essential governance tool because it:

- Enforces security best practices without relying solely on manual checks
- Maintains operational consistency across teams and subscriptions
- Reduces human error and configuration drift
- Simplifies compliance reporting and regulatory alignment

By using Azure Policy strategically, you ensure that your resources are deployed correctly, configured securely, and aligned with your business requirements without needing to perform constant hands-on oversight.

Common Use Cases of Azure Policy

Following are the common use cases for Azure Policy:

Enforcement of tagging
　　It blocks deployments that lack the required tags (e.g., "CostCenter" or "Owner").

Restricting locations
　　It allows resource creation only in approved regions (e.g., "Canada Central").

Limiting resource types
　　It prevents the use of unapproved services or expensive SKUs.

Enforcement of encryption
　　It requires storage accounts to use encryption at rest.

Auditing insecure settings
　　It flags resources without HTTPS, firewall rules, or other best practices.

Key Components of Azure Policy

Here are the key components of Azure Policy:

Policy definition
　　A specific rule or condition (e.g., "Require tags on all resources")

Policy assignment
　　The application of a policy to a scope like a subscription or resource group

Initiative
　　A collection of related policies (e.g., a set for ISO 27001 compliance)

Compliance state
　　A report showing which resources meet or violate assigned policies

Built-In Policies

Azure offers hundreds of built-in policies covering common scenarios such as:

Security enforcement
　Policies can require the encryption of storage accounts, enforcement of HTTPS-only traffic, blocking of public network access, or use only of approved images by VMs. This helps to maintain strong security baselines without reliance on manual configuration.

Location restrictions
　You can limit where resources are deployed (e.g., allowing resources only in Canada Central or East US). Organizations use these restrictions to meet compliance or data residency requirements (e.g., in the healthcare and finance industries) or to standardize deployments.

Tagging requirements
　Policies can require tags such as "Environment," "CostCenter," or "Owner." Tags improve cost allocation, reporting, automation, and governance. In addition, Cost Management can filter and group costs by tags, giving you precise insights into which team or project is spending what.

Cost controls
　These policies help prevent unexpected spending (e.g., by restricting VM sizes to cost-efficient tiers, preventing premium storage in dev/test environments, or blocking expensive SKUs). Note that Azure Policy does not shut off resources when budgets are exceeded; instead, it proactively prevents noncompliant or costly resources from being deployed in the first place.

Custom Policies

If built-in policies don't meet your needs, you can create custom policies using JSON. For example, if your organization requires every resource to have "Environment" and "Owner" tags, you can assign a policy that automatically adds missing tags or denies deployment until tags are included.

Monitoring and Remediation

The *Azure Policy compliance dashboard* provides a central view of:

- The percentage of compliant versus noncompliant resources
- The most frequently violated policies
- Recommended and automated remediation actions

For example, if developers frequently forget to add tags when provisioning new resources, you can assign a policy that denies deployments unless specific tags are present. This enforces governance automatically at deployment time.

Policy Effects: What Happens When a Rule Is Triggered?

For each policy, Azure Policy uses an *effect* to determine what happens when a resource violates the rule:

Deny
    Blocks the deployment or update

Audit
    Flags the resource as noncompliant but allows deployment

Append
    Adds missing configuration settings (e.g., tags)

DeployIfNotExists
    Automatically deploys a required resource if it's missing

AuditIfNotExists
    Flags a resource if a related resource is missing (e.g., Network Security Group for a subnet)

Next up, we'll explore resource locks, which provide another layer of protection by preventing accidental changes or deletions to critical resources.

Resource Locks: Protecting Critical Resources

The flexibility of Azure allows teams to rapidly create and delete resources. However, the ease of creating and deleting resources also introduces risks. A single mistaken click or script could accidentally delete a critical production virtual machine, a critical database, or an essential network gateway. Such mistakes can lead to downtime, data loss, and costly business disruptions.

This is where resource locks come in.

What Are Resource Locks?

Resource locks provide an additional layer of protection by preventing accidental changes or deletions. Applied on top of RBAC, resource locks can ensure that even users with permissions can't modify or remove critical resources without deliberate action.

You can apply a resource lock at multiple levels:

- Individual resources
- Entire resource groups
- Across a subscription

Two Types of Resource Locks

See Table 14-1 for information about the two types of resource locks.

Table 14-1. Comparison of two types of resource locks

Lock type	Description	Read	Update	Delete
Delete	Allows reading and updating, but disallows deletion	Yes	Yes	No
ReadOnly	Allows read-only access to the resource, but disallows updates or deletions	Yes	No	No

Where to Use Resource Locks

Apply resource locks where accidental modification or deletion could have serious consequences. Common scenarios include:

- Production VMs
- Mission-critical databases
- Core networking components (e.g., VNets or gateways)
- Shared resource groups used by multiple teams

Real-Life Example: Protecting a Production VM

Imagine you have a production VM named Prod-VM-01. When you apply a delete lock to that VM:

- The VM is protected from accidental deletion.
- A developer with contributor access can't delete the VM.
- Only users with roles that include lock management permissions (such as Owner or User Access Administrator) can remove the lock.

How to Apply a Resource Lock

You can apply a lock using:

- Azure portal (via the Locks blade on the resource or resource group)
- Azure CLI
- Azure PowerShell
- ARM templates or Bicep (for deployment-time governance)

Here's an example of creating a `CanNotDelete` resource-level lock on a VNet resource using the Azure CLI:

```
az lock create --name lockName --resource-group group
--lock-type CanNotDelete --resource-type Microsoft.Network/virtualNetworks
--resource myVNet
```

The same command in Azure PowerShell looks like this:

```
New-AzResourceLock -LockName "lockName" `
-LockLevel "CanNotDelete" `
-ResourceGroupName "group" `
-ResourceName "myVNet" `
-ResourceType "Microsoft.Network/virtualNetworks"
```

Comparing Resource Locks and Azure Policy

Resource locks and Azure Policy have different purposes:

Resource lock
　　Prevents accidental deletion or modification.

Azure Policy
　　Enforces rules on what and how resources can be deployed.

Although both resource locks and Azure Policy support governance, they serve different purposes. Resource locks protect resources at the management layer by preventing deletion or modification, while Azure Policy controls *configurations and deployments*. They are most effective when used together.

Best Practices and Limitations

Here are some best practices for applying resource locks:

- Apply delete locks to protect all production resource groups from accidental deletion.
- Use ReadOnly locks cautiously, as they block all updates.
- Combine resource locks with RBAC for layered access control.
- Document the usage of locks so that teams understand the locks' purpose and scope.

Here are some things to keep in mind about the limitations of resource locks:

- Resource locks do not prevent billing or quota consumption.
- They do not encrypt or protect data. They prevent only changes and deletions.
- Locks can be removed by users with high-level roles (e.g., owner).

Service Trust Portal: Compliance Transparency

When using cloud services, organizations need to ensure that their providers meet high standards for security, privacy, and compliance. Whether you're a small business or a global enterprise, you must be confident that your cloud provider complies with regulatory requirements and follows trusted security practices.

This is where the Service Trust Portal comes in.

What Is the Service Trust Portal?

The *Service Trust Portal* (*https://oreil.ly/k2skM*) is a centralized, web-based platform that provides access to Microsoft's compliance, security, and privacy resources across services like Azure, Microsoft 365, and Dynamics 365 (see Figure 14-2).

The portal helps organizations:

- Review Microsoft's audit reports, certifications, and regulatory assessments
- Understand how Microsoft manages security, privacy, and compliance
- Access resources and links to tools such as Microsoft Purview Compliance Manager to help track and manage their own compliance efforts

The Service Trust Portal is a one-stop hub for customers seeking to validate Microsoft's cloud practices and align them with their own regulatory obligations

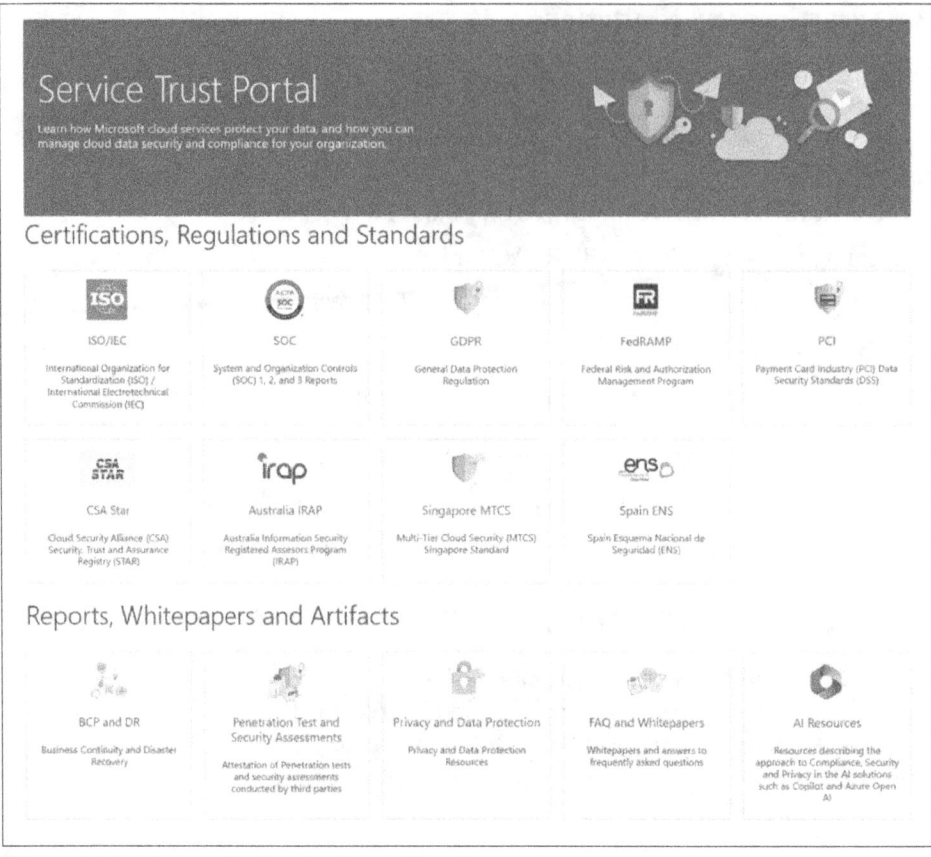

Figure 14-2. Microsoft's Service Trust Portal

Key Features of the Service Trust Portal

This listing describes Service Trust Portal's key features:

Audit reports
    Download third-party audit results such as these and others:

- System and Organization Controls (SOC) 1, 2, and 3 reports
- International Organization for Standardization (ISO) reports
- Federal Risk and Authorization Management Program (FedRAMP) reports

Microsoft Purview Compliance Manager
    Use this Microsoft tool for assistance with managing your own regulatory compliance posture, complete with templates and actionable insights.

Data Protection Resources repository
    Find needed information in this searchable repository of white papers, FAQs, and implementation guides about Microsoft's approach to security, privacy, and compliance.

Regulatory compliance information
    Find details on how Microsoft supports major compliance frameworks like GDPR, HIPAA, and National Institute of Standards and Technology (NIST).

Real-World Example: Preparing for a GDPR Audit

If your organization is preparing for a GDPR audit, you can use the Service Trust Portal to:

- Download the Azure GDPR Implementation Guide
- Access Microsoft's Data Protection Addendum (DPA)
- Review ISO 27001 and SOC 2 audit reports
- Use Compliance Manager to track GDPR-related tasks and control implementation

This helps demonstrate your organization's alignment with regulatory expectations when using Microsoft cloud services.

How Do These Azure Governance Tools Work Together?

Each governance tool we've discussed serves a specific purpose, but their real strength lies in how they work together. When strategically combined, these tools provide layered, end-to-end governance that helps organizations secure resources, meet compliance requirements, and scale operations with confidence.

Let's look at how these four key tools and services complement one another in a practical scenario.

Imagine your organization is preparing to launch a new application in Azure. Here's how these tools might be used together:

Enforce standards
    Use Azure Policy to apply rules that enforce tagging, restrict regions, and require encryption. Azure policies ensure that resources are deployed consistently across environments.

Protect critical infrastructure
    Apply resource locks (e.g., a delete lock) to prevent accidental deletion or changes to essential production resources.

Govern sensitive data
   Use Microsoft Purview to automatically discover and classify sensitive data across Azure and hybrid systems, enabling visibility into where data resides and how it's handled to support both security and compliance.

Demonstrate compliance
   Access the Service Trust Portal to download Microsoft's audit reports, certifications (e.g., SOC, ISO, GDPR), and documentation. These resources help satisfy internal reviews and external regulatory requirements.

By combining these tools, organizations can ensure that:

- Resource standards are enforced automatically
- Production systems are protected from accidental disruption
- Sensitive data is managed and monitored
- Compliance requirements are supported with verifiable documentation

Summary

In this chapter, you learned how Azure's governance tools (such as Azure Policy, Microsoft Purview, resource locks, and the Service Trust Portal) work together to maintain control, consistency, and compliance across cloud environments. These services help enforce configuration standards, protect critical resources from accidental changes, and provide visibility into sensitive data and Microsoft's compliance commitments. Together, they form a layered governance strategy that keeps your Azure environment secure, well organized, and aligned with regulatory and organizational requirements.

In the next chapter, we'll move from governance strategy to operational execution as we explore how to manage and deploy Azure resources effectively.

Chapter 14 Quiz

To check your answers, please refer to the "Chapter 14 Answer Key" on page 307.

1. Your organization must ensure that all deployed resources follow strict company rules, such as those enforcing specific naming conventions, restricting storage types, and requiring encryption by default. You intend to recommend Azure Policy to meet this requirement.

    Which of the following best describes the primary purpose of Azure Policy?

    A. Enforcing rules and ensuring resource compliance

    B. Controlling who can access Azure resources

    C. Monitoring billing information in Azure

    D. Providing firewall rules for Azure services

2. Your international organization stores data across multiple platforms, including Azure SQL Database, on-premises Microsoft SQL Server, Amazon S3, and Microsoft 365. Due to strict data privacy laws, the compliance team must be able to locate, classify, label, and monitor sensitive data across all environments from a centralized governance dashboard.

    Which Azure service should you recommend to meet this requirement?

    A. Azure Advisor

    B. Azure Monitor

    C. Microsoft Purview

    D. Azure Policy

3. Your production team is concerned that a critical production Virtual Machine could be accidentally deleted or modified by mistake during maintenance or troubleshooting, causing major business disruption. You need to implement a solution to protect against accidental changes or deletion of resources regardless of RBAC permissions.

    What should you use?

    A. Azure Policy

    B. Azure tags

    C. Azure Front Door

    D. Resource locks

CHAPTER 15
Managing and Deploying Azure Resources

In the previous chapter, we explored Azure governance and compliance. In this chapter, we'll walk through the essential tools and features used to deploy and manage resources in Azure.

Here's what you'll learn about:

Azure portal
　　The browser-based control center for managing everything visually

Azure Cloud Shell
　　A browser-accessible command-line environment with built-in tools

Azure CLI and Azure PowerShell
　　The differences between CLI and PowerShell

Infrastructure as code (IaC)
　　Why it's essential for consistency, automation, and scaling

Azure Resource Manager (ARM)
　　The backbone of Azure's deployment engine

Deployment templates using ARM Templates and Bicep
　　How to choose the one that will be better for your workflow (we'll also talk about Terraform)

Azure Arc
　　A tool that extends Azure's management plane to your on-premises or multi-cloud environments

By the end of this chapter, you'll not only be familiar with the tools Azure offers for managing and deploying resources, but you'll understand which one is right for each job and how they all work together.

Let's get started.

Azure Portal

In Chapter 6, we began to explore the Azure portal. In this chapter, we'll discuss its key features, best uses of the Azure portal, and when to use the Azure portal (and when not to).

As you'll recall, the Azure portal (see Figure 15-1) is Microsoft's browser-based graphical user interface (GUI) for managing and interacting with Azure resources and services.

With just a web browser and an Azure account, you can use the Azure portal to manage your entire Azure environment, from spinning up virtual machines to configuring firewalls, setting budgets, or viewing compliance reports.

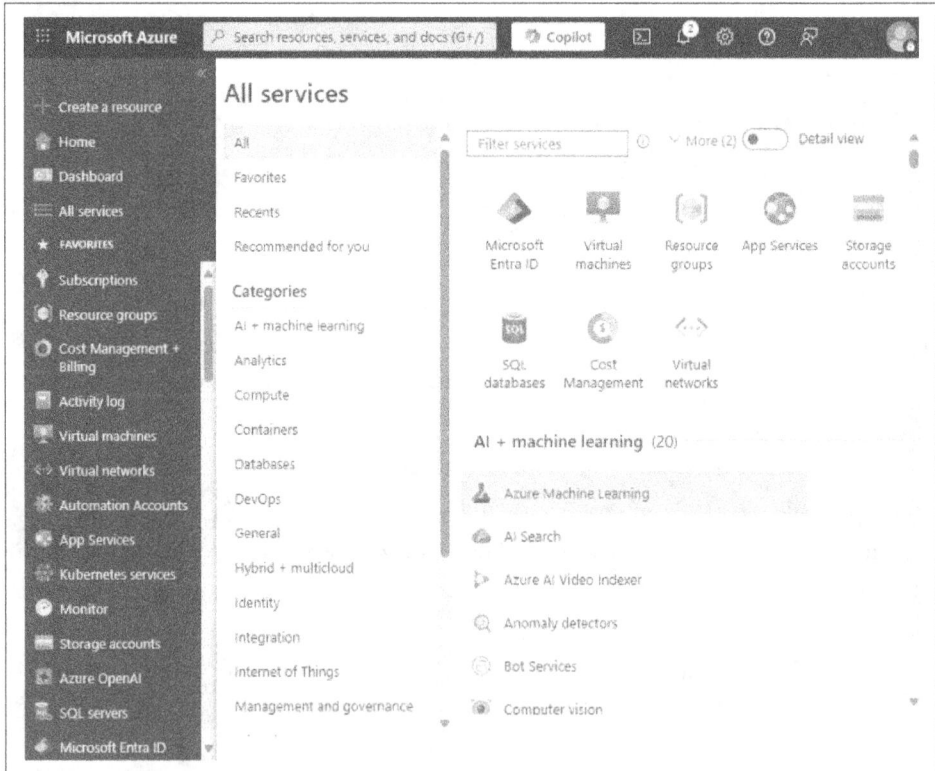

Figure 15-1. The Azure portal

Key Features of the Azure Portal

Here's what you can do using the Azure portal:

Create, configure, and manage resources

- Provision VMs, databases, storage accounts, or networks.
- Organize resources using resource groups and tags.
- Manage configurations with a few clicks.

Monitor performance and set alerts

- Track performance metrics like CPU usage, disk I/O, and network activity.
- Set alerts to notify you when thresholds are exceeded.

Build custom dashboards

- Create custom dashboards using drag-and-drop widgets to visualize key data and monitor critical systems in real time.

Search and filter resources

- Use the global search bar to quickly find resources, subscriptions, or services across your entire Azure environment.

What Are the Best Uses of the Azure Portal?

The Azure portal is ideal for:

Beginners
   It's a great place to learn Azure services with a visual, interactive experience.

One-time changes
   You can quickly update settings or deploy a test service without writing code.

Monitoring and troubleshooting
   You can use built-in tools like Network Watcher, Log Analytics, and cost analysis dashboards to keep everything under control.

Key Benefits of Azure Portal

These are the key benefits of Azure portal:

No coding required
   Managing everything with clicks instead of code

User-friendly
   Clean design, intuitive navigation, built-in help and wizards

Integrated
  Ability to work with all Azure services and tools in one central location

Customizable
  Dashboards, favorites, and pinned tiles that allow you to personalize your portal

Always up-to-date
  Continuously improved by Microsoft with new features

Common Tasks in the Azure Portal

Let's walk through some of the most common (and useful) actions you can perform in the portal in Table 15-1.

Table 15-1. Common tasks in the Azure portal

Task	Description	Example
Provision resources	Create new cloud services to support your workloads.	You can spin up a VM, deploy an Azure SQL Database, or create a storage account.
Configure settings	Modify properties of your resources or organize them for better management.	You can easily change VM size, update network security group rules, or apply tags to group costs.
Monitor usage	Keep an eye on the performance, health, and cost of your resources.	Every resource in Azure produces metrics and logs. You can: • Set up alerts when a VM has high CPU usage • Track your subscription's monthly spending • View audit logs to see who did what and when You can even visualize this info using charts and dashboards tailored to your team's needs.
Automate workflows	Set up rules, scripts, or workflows that run in response to events.	In addition to manual actions, you can automate and create workflows like: • Automatically backing up databases • Starting VMs at 9 a.m. and stopping them at 6 p.m. • Notifying your team on Microsoft Teams when a deployment fails

When to Use the Azure Portal (and When Not To)

While the Azure portal is powerful and convenient, it's not always the best option for large-scale or repeatable tasks. For example, if you need to deploy 50 virtual machines, applying the same configuration over and over in the Azure portal can be time-consuming and error-prone.

Later in this chapter, we'll introduce you to tools that can be suitable for large-scale and repeatable tasks, including Azure CLI, PowerShell, and infrastructure as code.

The Azure portal shines when:

- You're new to Azure and learning how things work
- You want to test or experiment with new services
- You're making one-time changes or adjustments
- You need to visually inspect the state of your resources
- You want to configure something once in the Azure portal and then export it as an ARM template to reuse, customize, or scale later

However, as your infrastructure grows, clicking through the UI becomes tedious and error-prone. For repeatable, scalable, and version-controlled deployments, you'll want to shift to automation with tools like the Azure CLI, Azure PowerShell, and Bicep. We'll cover these later in this chapter. Stay tuned!

In the next section, we'll cover the Azure Cloud Shell.

Azure Cloud Shell

Azure Cloud Shell is a browser-based, interactive command-line environment. It's built right into the Azure portal. Once you're logged into the Azure portal, you can use Azure Cloud Shell instantly without installing anything on your local machine.

You simply open your browser, log in to the Azure portal, and click the **Cloud Shell icon** (see Figure 15-2) in the top menu bar.

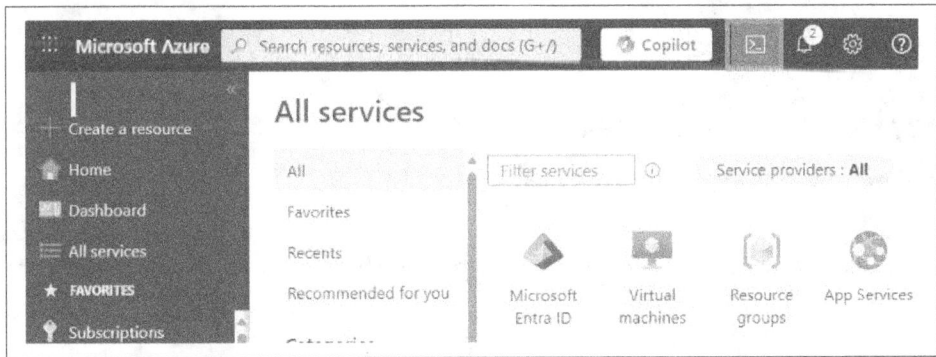

Figure 15-2. Launching Azure Cloud Shell by clicking on the Cloud Shell icon

Since it runs entirely in the cloud, Cloud Shell is accessible from virtually any device (including your laptop, tablet, and even your smartphone). Figure 15-3 shows how the Cloud Shell looks in the Microsoft Edge browser.

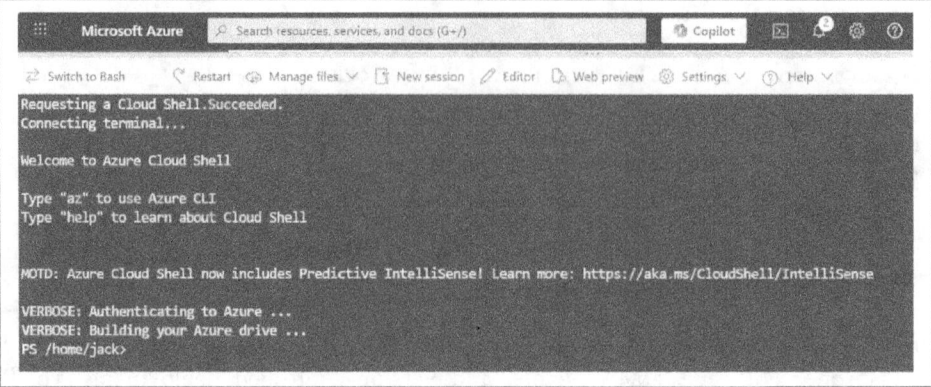

Figure 15-3. A successful launch of the Azure Cloud Shell!

Why Use Cloud Shell?

Cloud Shell lets you run Azure CLI and Azure PowerShell commands directly from your browser without installing additional software. You'll learn more about Azure CLI and Azure PowerShell later in this chapter.

Cloud Shell is all about convenience. It's especially helpful when:

- You're switching between managing resources in the portal and using command-line tools.
- You want to avoid installing and updating Azure CLI or Azure PowerShell locally.
- You're working from a device where installing tools isn't possible (like a shared or locked-down machine).

Key Features of Cloud Shell

Following are the key features of Cloud Shell:

Persistent storage
 Mounts a storage account with an Azure Files share, so your files and scripts are saved between sessions.

Preinstalled tools
 Comes with popular tools like Azure CLI, Azure PowerShell, Git, Terraform, and text editors such as Visual Studio Code (browser-based version), Vim, and GNU nano.

Bash or PowerShell choice
 Allows you to choose between a Linux-style environment (Bash) or a Windows-style environment (PowerShell), depending on your preference.

Cloud-based
   Requires no setup or configuration on your local machine.

Integrated with the portal
   Lets you easily switch between clicking in the Azure portal UI and running command-line tasks in the Cloud Shell.

Cloud Shell is perfect for quick tasks, scripting on the fly, or managing resources when you're away from your primary development environment. It brings the power of the CLI without the hassle of setup.

In the next section, we'll look at the Azure command-line interface.

Azure CLI

The *Azure command-line interface (Azure CLI)* is a cross-platform tool that lets you create, configure, and automate Azure resources using text-based commands. You can install Azure CLI locally on Windows, macOS, and Linux. As mentioned in the previous section, you can run the same commands in Azure Cloud Shell without installing anything. However, one of the advantages of installing Azure CLI locally is that you can write and run scripts locally from your laptop and do local automation, as long as you have network connectivity to Azure.

Instead of clicking around in the Azure portal, with the Azure CLI, you can describe what you want in concise, scriptable language. It's built with automation in mind, making it perfect for developers, DevOps engineers, and cloud admins who want to get things done fast and repeatably.

Use the Azure portal to interactively explore and learn but use Azure CLI to automate via command line.

Why Use Azure CLI?

Azure CLI is built for automation and efficiency. It's ideal when you want to:

- Quickly spin up or delete resources via command line
- Automate deployments using scripts
- Integrate with CI/CD tools (like GitHub Actions or Azure DevOps)
- Get fast answers regarding the state of your environment (e.g., "List all VMs that are currently running in my Azure subscription")

Example: Creating a Resource Group Using Azure CLI

Here's an Azure CLI command to create a resource group called `MyResourceGroup` in the East US region:

```
az group create --name MyResourceGroup --location eastus
```

Let's break it down:

- `az` calls the Azure CLI.
- `group create` is the specific command to create a new resource group.
- `--name` designates the name of the resource group you want to create. In our example, we want the name to be `MyResourceGroup`.
- `--location` designates the Azure region where you want the group deployed. In our example, we want the region to be `eastus`.

Where You Can Run Azure CLI

Here's how you can use Azure CL on different platforms:

Azure Cloud Shell
  No installation needed—just open it in the browser.

Windows/macOS/Linux
  Install it via command-line package managers (e.g., brew, apt, choco).

VS Code
  Run commands directly in the integrated terminal with Azure CLI installed.

CI/CD pipelines
  Add Azure CLI tasks in tools like GitHub Actions or Azure DevOps.

Azure CLI Versus Azure Portal

Table 15-2 compares Azure portal and Azure CLI.

Table 15-2. A comparison between Azure portal and Azure CLI

Azure portal	Azure CLI
Point-and-click	Command based
Visual and beginner friendly	Efficient and scriptable
Good for manual changes	Repeatable and version controlled
Slower for bulk tasks	Faster for batch operations

Exam Tip

For AZ-900, you don't need to memorize CLI commands, but you do need to understand that Azure CLI is a fast, efficient alternative to the Azure portal, built for users who prefer code over clicks.

Next, we'll look at Azure PowerShell. It's a favorite among Windows admins and IT professionals who want to bring their PowerShell skills to the cloud.

Azure PowerShell

Azure PowerShell is a set of PowerShell cmdlets (commands) specifically built to manage Azure resources. These cmdlets interact with the Azure REST API behind the scenes to perform tasks like provisioning, configuring, and managing cloud services. It's part of the broader PowerShell ecosystem, which makes it ideal for IT professionals who already use PowerShell to manage Windows environments.

Azure PowerShell is incredibly powerful when used in scripts. You can loop through VMs, apply conditional logic, and chain cmdlets together in complex automation workflows.

Azure PowerShell can be used for quick, one-off changes. It can also be combined into full scripts that automate complex tasks, such as:

- Deploying an entire infrastructure with a large number of components
- Creating repeatable, automated workflows by capturing commands in scripts
- Setting up, decommissioning, or maintaining single or multiple connected resources

Example: Creating a Resource Group Using Azure PowerShell

Here's how you create a resource group using Azure PowerShell:

```
New-AzResourceGroup -Name "MyResourceGroup" -Location "EastUS"
```

Let's break it down:

- `New-AzResourceGroup` is the cmdlet to create a new resource group.
- `-Name` – specifies the name of the resource group. In our example, we want the name to be `MyResourceGroup`.

- `-Location` specifies the Azure region to deploy the group in. In our example, we want the region to be `EastUS`.

As you can see, Azure PowerShell is quite readable and scriptable.

Why Use Azure PowerShell?

Azure PowerShell is ideal when you need to:

- Leverage existing PowerShell knowledge to manage the cloud
- Automate the setup and teardown of environments
- Manage both Azure and on-premises Windows resources in hybrid setups

Where Can You Use Azure PowerShell?

Just like Azure CLI, Azure PowerShell runs in a variety of environments:

Azure Cloud Shell
: No install needed—it runs directly in the browser.

Windows terminal
: Install the Azure PowerShell module using PowerShellGet or a package manager.

Visual Studio Code
: Use the integrated terminal with the PowerShell extension.

CI/CD pipelines
: Run PowerShell scripts in Azure DevOps, GitHub Actions, or other automation tools.

Azure CLI Versus Azure PowerShell

Table 15-3 compares Azure CLI and Azure PowerShell.

Table 15-3. Azure CLI versus Azure PowerShell

Feature	Azure CLI	Azure PowerShell
Syntax style	Unix-like (bash-style commands)	Verb-noun format (PowerShell-style cmdlets)
Typical user	Developers, DevOps, Linux/macOS users	Windows admins, IT professionals
Platform support	Cross-platform (Windows, macOS, Linux, Cloud Shell)	Cross-platform, but feels native on Windows
Learning curve	Easier for those with scripting or bash experience	Easier for those with PowerShell/Windows experience
Output format	JSON, table, TSV (tab-separated values)	Rich .NET objects (easy to manipulate in scripts)
Script file types	.sh, .bash	.ps1

Feature	Azure CLI	Azure PowerShell
Integration	Azure DevOps, GitHub Actions, CI/CD pipelines	Azure Automation, hybrid management scenarios
Use case examples	Quick VM deployment, DevTest scripting, pipeline automation	Complex enterprise workflows, RBAC automation, hybrid management

Which Tool Should You Use?

Table 15-4 is a quick guide to help you decide which Azure tool is best for your scenario.

Table 15-4. Azure tool choices

Scenario	Best choice
You're a developer working on a CI/CD pipeline.	Azure CLI
You're a Windows admin managing Azure and on-premises servers.	Azure PowerShell
You need to write portable scripts for Linux/macOS.	Azure CLI
You want to automate RBAC or resource policies.	Azure PowerShell
You prefer clean, concise commands.	Azure CLI
You need rich scripting capabilities with loops and conditions.	Azure PowerShell

Azure CLI and Azure PowerShell are both excellent command-line tools for managing your cloud environment. Your choice depends on what feels more natural to you:

- Use Azure CLI if you come from a dev or Linux background.
- Use Azure PowerShell if you're a seasoned Windows admin.

Next, we'll explore infrastructure as code, the next level of resource deployment that takes automation to new heights.

Infrastructure as Code

Infrastructure as code (IaC) is the practice of defining your infrastructure using code instead of manually configuring it through a user interface like the Azure portal. You write this infrastructure definition in JSON, YAML, or domain-specific languages (DSL) such as Bicep or Terraform. Azure will execute the provisioning for you based on your IaC definitions. Instead of clicking through UI menus to create a virtual machine, a network, or a storage account, you write a file that says, "This is what I need," and Azure makes it happen!

IaC has become the standard for managing modern cloud environments, especially in enterprise and DevOps settings.

Why IaC Matters

Here's why IaC is important:

Consistency
　Every deployment is identical—no more missed steps or forgotten settings.

Repeatability
　Reuse the same code to build dev, test, and production environments.

Version control
　Store infrastructure code in Git, track changes, and roll back as needed.

Automation
　Deploy infrastructure using scripts or pipelines, with no manual clicks required.

Documentation
　The code is self-documenting so anyone can read it and understand what's deployed.

IaC Approaches: Declarative Versus Imperative

Table 15-5 describes the two main approaches to IaC.

Table 15-5. Declarative versus imperative approaches to IaC

Approach	Description	Tools
Declarative	You describe what the desired end state should be, and the system figures out how to get there. *Example*: "I want a VM in the East US region with this name and size."	• ARM templates • Bicep • Terraform
Imperative	You describe how to do each step in order to get to the desired state. *Example*: "First create a resource group. Then create a VM. Then set its size…"	• Azure CLI • Azure PowerShell

Azure emphasizes the declarative style, which makes it ideal for automation and predictable deployments.

In the following sections, we'll take a deeper dive into Azure Resource Manager (ARM), ARM templates, Bicep, and Terraform.

Exam Tip

On the AZ-900 exam, you won't need to write IaC code, but you should understand what it is, what it does, and why it matters.

Azure Resource Manager

Azure Resource Manager (ARM) is Azure's deployment and management engine. It provides a consistent management layer that allows you to create, update, and delete resources in your Azure account. Whether you're using the portal, CLI, PowerShell, SDKs, or REST APIs—every action goes through ARM.

When a request is made, ARM handles authentication and authorization, then forwards the request to the appropriate Azure service. Because all tools interact with Azure through ARM's unified API, you get consistent behavior and results across every interface.

Key benefits of Azure Resource Manager

With ARM, you can:

- Manage infrastructure using declarative templates (JSON) rather than by writing scripts.
- Deploy, manage, and monitor resources as a group instead of handling them one by one.
- Ensure consistency across environments by redeploying the same template during development and production stages.
- Define dependencies between resources to control deployment order.
- Enforce access control with built-in RBAC.
- Tag resources for better organization and logical grouping within your subscription.
- Track and analyze costs by grouping resources with shared tags, improving billing transparency.

ARM templates

ARM templates are files written in JSON that describe the infrastructure and configuration of your Azure environment.

Think of an ARM template as a detailed instruction manual or recipe that tells Azure exactly what resources to create, their properties, and how they relate to one another.

ARM templates are powerful and fully supported. However, they tend to be verbose and harder to manage manually.

Here are the benefits of ARM templates:

- Native to Azure
- Very detailed and flexible
- Fully supported by Azure

And here are their limitations:

- Verbose and difficult to read
- Tricky to edit manually (e.g., small mistakes like missing commas can cause deployment failures)

Let's take a look at an ARM template written in JSON. This defines a storage account named `mystorageacct` in the `eastus` region, using the `StorageV2` kind with a `Standard_LRS` SKU.

```
{
  "type": "Microsoft.Storage/storageAccounts",
  "apiVersion": "2025-06-01",
  "name": "mystorageacct",
  "location": "eastus",
  "sku": { "name": "Standard_LRS" },
  "kind": "StorageV2",
  "properties": {}
}
```

ARM templates are the core declarative IaC mechanism native to Azure, providing a powerful, scriptable way to define your infrastructure. While they can be verbose and intimidating at first, they offer unparalleled control and integration with Azure services.

To improve on ARM Templates, Microsoft introduced Bicep, which we'll take a look at next.

Bicep

Bicep is a DSL created by Microsoft specifically for writing Azure IaC. It offers all the power of ARM templates but removes the tedious and error-prone parts of JSON syntax.

The key features of Bicep are:

- It's a declarative language designed to simplify Azure deployments.
- It compiles down into ARM template JSON behind the scenes, so Azure still understands it natively.

- You write fewer lines of code, with much better readability.
- It supports all Azure resources and is constantly updated with new features.

Bicep offers a number of advantages over ARM templates:

- Cleaner, more readable syntax
- Easier to read and maintain
- Still native to Azure
- Fully supported by Azure
- Better error messages and validation during authoring

However, it does have some disadvantages:

- It's usable with Azure only.
- It requires learning a new syntax (but is beginner friendly).

Let's look at an example Bicep template. This creates a storage account named `mystorageacct` in the `eastus` region with the `StorageV2` kind and a `Standard_LRS` SKU:

```
resource storage 'Microsoft.Storage/storageAccounts@2025-06-01' = {
  name: 'mystorageacct'
  location: 'eastus'
  sku: {
    name: 'Standard_LRS'
  }
  kind: 'StorageV2'
}
```

Bicep has all the power of ARM templates but makes writing and managing them much easier and less frustrating.

Terraform

HashiCorp Terraform is a popular open source IaC tool that works across Azure, AWS, GCP, and more. It's ideal if your organization is multi-cloud or already uses DevOps pipelines.

There are several advantages to using Terraform:

- Works across all major cloud providers
- Enjoys strong community and tooling support
- Is ideal for DevOps integration

When choosing Terraform, consider the following trade-offs:

- Requires installing and maintaining the Terraform CLI (locally or in CI/CD)
- Uses a state file to track and manage resources (stored locally or in a remote backend)
- Provides a cloud-agnostic approach, but may require more setup than Azure-native tools (ARM Template/Bicep) for Azure-only environments

Let's look at some example Terraform code. This creates an Azure storage account named `mystorageacct` in the `MyResourceGroup` resource group, located in `eastus`, with a `Standard` tier and locally redundant storage (LRS):

```
resource "azurerm_storage_account" "example" {
  name                     = "mystorageacct"
  resource_group_name      = "MyResourceGroup"
  location                 = "eastus"
  account_tier             = "Standard"
  account_replication_type = "LRS"
}
```

IaC Tool Comparison

Table 15-6 compares the four IaC tools we've discussed in this chapter.

Table 15-6. IaC tool comparison

Feature	ARM templates	Bicep	Terraform	Azure CLI / Azure PowerShell
Language	JSON	Bicep (DSL)	HCL	Bash/PowerShell
Azure native	Yes	Yes	No (HashiCorp)	Yes
Multi-cloud	No	No	Yes	No
Requires a state file	No	No	Yes	No
Readability	Low	High	Mostly	Mostly
Style	Declarative	Declarative	Declarative	Imperative
Best for	Complex and Azure-only applications	General Azure and IaC applications	Cross-cloud automation	Quick jobs and scripting

In summary, IaC helps you shift from manual configuration ("click-ops") to consistent, scalable cloud infrastructure. As a general rule of thumb:

- Use Bicep for clean, Azure-native infrastructure code.
- Use Terraform for multi-cloud deployments or advanced DevOps.

- Use CLI or PowerShell for quick scripting and procedural tasks.

Ultimately, the choice of tools depends on your team's skill set, preference, and requirements.

In the final section of this chapter, we'll look at Azure Arc.

Managing Hybrid and Multi-Cloud Environments Using Azure Arc

As mentioned in Chapter 5, *Azure Arc* is Microsoft's solution for managing hybrid and multi-cloud environments. It extends Azure's governance, security, and monitoring capabilities to infrastructure and services running outside of Azure, whether in on-premises data centers, other public clouds like AWS or Google Cloud, or edge locations such as retail stores, factories, or IoT deployments. By projecting these external resources into ARM, Azure Arc enables you to manage them using familiar tools like the Azure portal, Azure CLI, and Azure Policy.

Most organizations today operate in a hybrid environment that spans on-premises, multiple public clouds, and edge locations. Azure Arc plays a critical role in unifying operations across these diverse environments by providing consistent management, centralized security, and streamlined governance, no matter where your resources reside.

Here's what you can do with Azure Arc:

Manage anywhere
    Bring together on-premises servers, VMs, Kubernetes clusters, and databases from any environment for centralized Azure management.

Unify operations
    Apply Azure policies, RBAC, and tags across your hybrid and multi-cloud resources.

Monitor everything
    Use Azure Monitor to collect and analyze logs and metrics across environments.

Strengthen security
    Extend Microsoft Defender for Cloud to protect non-Azure workloads.

Deploy Azure services beyond Azure
    Deploy services like Azure SQL Managed Instance and Azure Cosmos DB for PostgreSQL on supported Arc-enabled infrastructure.

Bridge ITOps and DevOps
    Support traditional management models while enabling DevOps workflows.

Configure custom locations
  Use Arc-enabled Kubernetes clusters as deployment targets for added flexibility.

Let's consider a real-life example of using Azure Arc. Consider a manufacturing company with the following workloads:

- Legacy applications running on on-premises servers
- Microservices deployed in AWS-hosted Kubernetes clusters
- IoT workloads processed on edge devices in factories

With Azure Arc, the company can apply consistent security and compliance policies across all environments, monitor all systems from a single Azure dashboard, and use Azure Update Manager to patch remote machines. Thus, Azure Arc streamlines operations and improves the organization's security posture.

Azure Arc extends Azure's powerful management capabilities beyond its native boundaries, allowing you to manage hybrid and multi-cloud environments as one cohesive system.

To wrap up this chapter, we'll share some best practices for managing and deploying Azure resources effectively.

Best Practices for Managing and Deploying Azure Resources

Now that you're familiar with the tools and features Azure provides, it's time to adopt best practices that will help you manage cloud resources more efficiently, consistently, and securely. Start with the Azure portal but move toward automation and IaC:

Why?
  The Azure portal is perfect for getting started and understanding your environment. It's visual, intuitive, and great for quick changes. However, manual clicks can lead to errors and inconsistent environments.

Best practice
  Use the Azure portal to explore and learn, but move toward IaC with tools like Bicep or ARM templates to automate deployments, reduce errors, and ensure repeatability.

Choose Bicep for clean and simple IaC:

Why?
  While ARM templates are powerful, they can be verbose and hard to manage. Bicep simplifies template authoring with a cleaner, more readable syntax that compiles down to ARM JSON.

Best practice
> Use Bicep for new deployments to write clearer code, reduce bugs, and streamline your infrastructure workflow.

Store your IaC templates in version control:

Why?
> Storing your ARM templates or Bicep files in version control (like GitHub or Azure Repos) helps you track changes, collaborate with your team, and roll back if something goes wrong.

Best practice
> Treat your infrastructure code just like application code: commit often, use branching strategies, and perform code reviews before deployments.

Test in development and staging before production deployments:

Why?
> Deploying directly to production is risky. Testing your templates in lower environments helps identify issues early and ensures reliable deployments.

Best practice
> Set up separate resource groups or subscriptions for development, staging, and production. Validate your infrastructure in each stage before promoting it to production.

Use Azure Cloud Shell for portability and convenience:

Why?
> Cloud Shell gives you a ready-to-use, browser-accessible command-line environment preconfigured with Azure CLI, PowerShell, and other useful tools.

Best practice
> Use Cloud Shell to avoid environment setup hassles. It's perfect when working from different devices or locations.

Apply consistent naming and tagging:

Why?
> As your cloud footprint grows, keeping things organized becomes critical. A standardized approach to naming and tagging helps with visibility, cost management, automation, and compliance.

Best practice
> Define and enforce naming conventions and tagging policies using Azure Policy and include them in your Bicep or ARM templates.

Summary

This chapter introduced key tools and features Azure offers to manage and deploy resources efficiently, from the visual Azure portal to automation-friendly tools like Azure CLI and PowerShell. We covered IaC options, including ARM templates, Bicep, and Terraform, which enable consistent, repeatable deployments, as well as Azure Arc for managing non-Azure resources. These tools provide a foundation for beginners and pros to deploy, manage, and scale resources securely and consistently.

In the next chapter, we'll look at monitoring tools in Azure.

Chapter 15 Quiz

To check your answers, please refer to the "Chapter 15 Answer Key" on page 307.

1. Your organization has resources in Azure, in AWS, and on-premises.

    Which Azure tool would you use to manage all these resources from a single interface?

    A. Azure Monitor

    B. Azure Arc

    C. Bicep

    D. Azure Resource Manager

2. You need to create a new virtual machine in Azure.

    Which tool would you use to automate this process using code?

    A. Azure portal

    B. Azure Arc

    C. ARM templates or Bicep

    D. Azure Monitor

3. Your team is collaborating on IaC and needs to edit and version-control ARM templates for Azure deployments.

    Which file format will these templates use?

    A. YAML

    B. CSV

    C. XML

    D. JSON

CHAPTER 16
Azure Monitoring Tools

In the previous chapter, you learned how to manage and deploy Azure resources. In this chapter, we'll turn our attention to the Azure monitoring tools that will help you maintain a healthy, secure, and optimized cloud environment.

Think of monitoring tools as being similar to the dashboard of a car, which continuously informs you of the vehicle's fuel level, battery status, engine health, and tire pressure. In the same way, Azure provides a set of robust monitoring and advisory tools that alert you to potential issues and offer actionable recommendations to keep your cloud environment running smoothly and efficiently.

In this chapter, we'll explore three key Azure monitoring tools:

- Azure Advisor
- Azure Service Health
- Azure Monitor (including Log Analytics, Azure Monitor alerts, and Application Insights)

By the end of this chapter, you'll understand how these tools work together to give you full visibility into and control over your Azure environment.

Let's begin!

What Is Azure Advisor?

Having Azure Advisor is like having a personal fitness coach for your cloud environment. Just as a coach evaluates your diet, workouts, and sleep habits to suggest improvements, *Azure Advisor*, shown in Figure 16-1, analyzes your Azure environment and provides recommendations to help you optimize across five key categories:

- Cost
- Security
- Reliability
- Operational excellence
- Performance

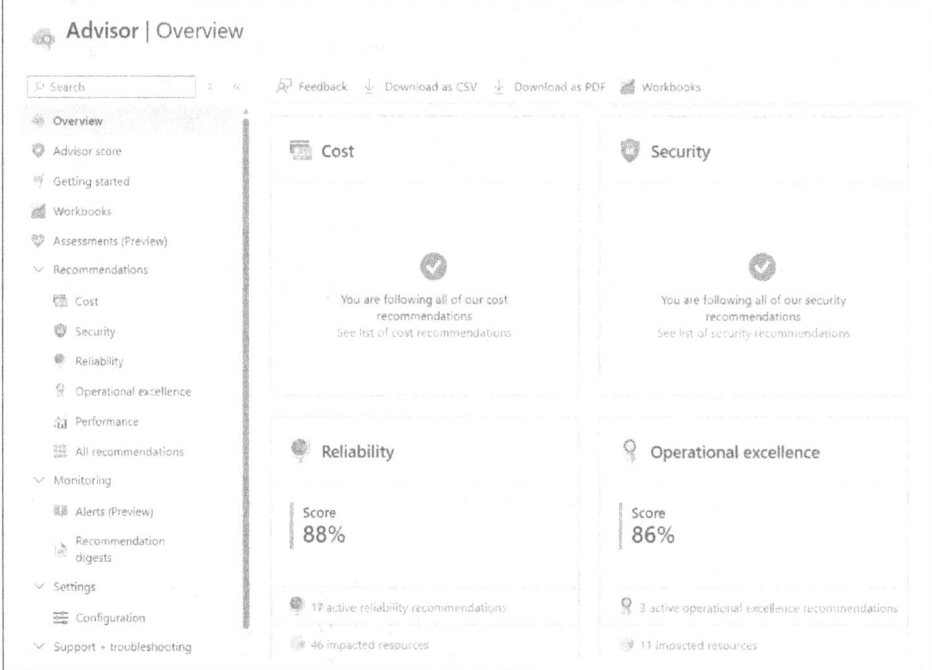

Figure 16-1. Azure Advisor

 Azure Advisor provides best practice recommendations across cost, security, reliability, operational excellence, and performance. However, it doesn't automatically apply any changes to your environment.

Administrators are responsible for reviewing and implementing Azure Advisor's recommendations through their own operational processes or automation workflows.

Let's look at what Azure Advisor evaluates in each of these categories in Table 16-1.

Table 16-1. What Azure Advisor evaluates

Category	What Azure Advisor evaluates	Example recommendation
Cost	Identifies underutilized resources	"Your virtual machine is running at only 5% CPU, so consider resizing to save money."
Security	Integrates with Microsoft Defender for Cloud	"Enable MFA to strengthen account security."
Reliability	Ensures availability and redundancy	"Add a backup region for your Azure storage account for disaster recovery."
Operational excellence	Improves governance and resource management	"Apply tags to resources for better cost tracking and organization."
Performance	Analyzes workload efficiency	"Enable caching for faster response times."

What Is Azure Service Health?

Having Azure Service Health is like getting real-time traffic alerts on your GPS.

If there's congestion, an accident, or roadwork ahead, your GPS warns you and may even suggest alternate routes. Similarly, Azure Service Health (Figure 16-2) keeps you informed about Azure incidents, planned maintenance, and health advisories so you can minimize disruption and keep workloads running smoothly.

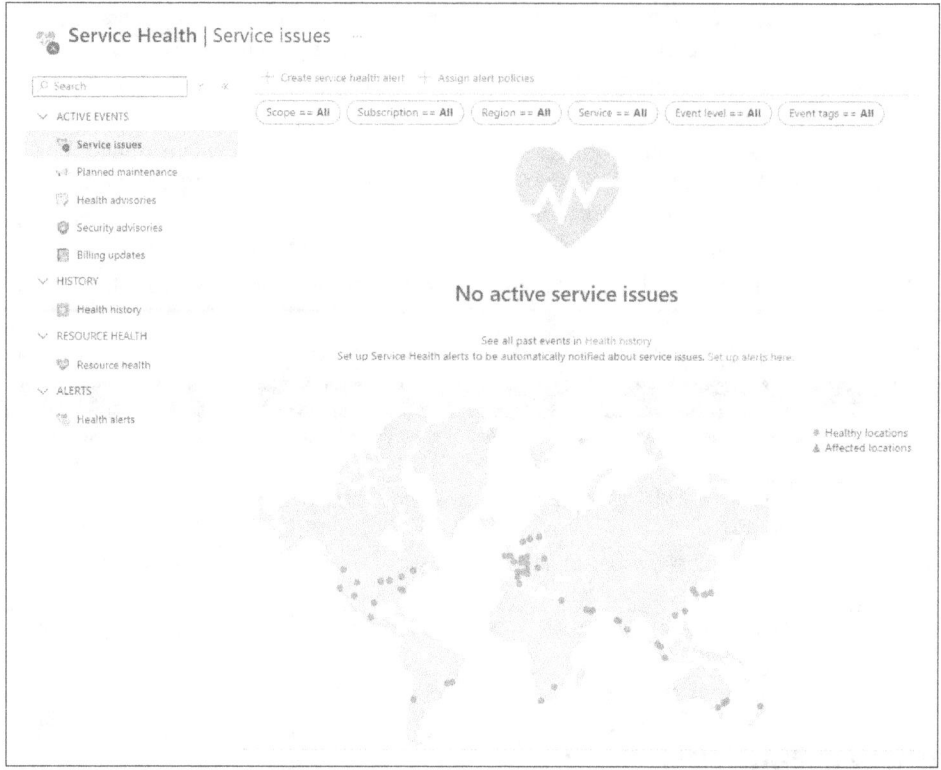

Figure 16-2. Azure Service Health

Azure Service Health provides both global visibility and personalized insights. It covers the overall Azure ecosystem as well as the health of your specific resources. To do this, it integrates three components, as shown in Table 16-2.

Table 16-2. Comparison of the Azure status page, Service Health, and Resource Health

Component	Purpose	Example scenario
Azure status	Shows the health status of all Azure services across regions globally; ideal for tracking widespread outages	"The Azure Storage service is down in the East US region."
Service Health	Delivers relevant, timely updates about outages, planned maintenance, and relevant health advisories that focus on the Azure services and regions you actually use	"Your Azure SQL Database service in Canada Central is experiencing issues."
Resource Health	Offers granular insights into the status of individual resources, such as a virtual machine or an app instance, helping you diagnose current issues and understand the historical health of your resources	"Your specific VM is down due to a platform issue."

What Is Azure Monitor?

Having Azure Monitor is like having a smart home-monitoring system for your cloud.

Just as a smart home system tracks energy usage, temperature, and security cameras and even alerts you when something unusual happens, *Azure Monitor* (Figure 16-3) tracks the health and performance of your applications, infrastructure, and services.

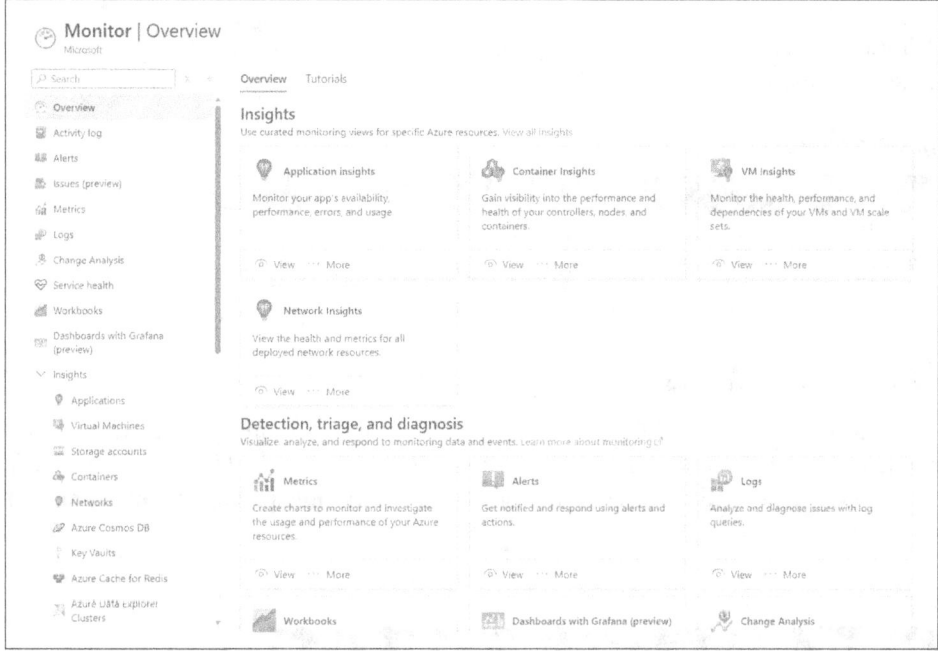

Figure 16-3. Azure Monitor

It's important to note that Azure Monitor isn't a single tool. It's a suite of integrated services that supports both IaaS and PaaS monitoring:

Azure Log Analytics
　　Centralizes and analyzes logs from multiple sources.

Azure Monitor alerts
　　Sends notifications or triggers actions based on defined thresholds.

Azure Monitor Application Insights
　　Monitors live applications (server-side and client-side), user behavior, dependencies, and performance.

Let's take a closer look at each of these services.

Azure Log Analytics

Azure Log Analytics acts like the central control panel where all monitoring data comes together. It gathers and analyzes information from multiple sources, such as:

- Virtual machines
- Applications
- Network resources

Admins can use Kusto Query Language (KQL) to dig deeper into logs and gain actionable insights, as shown in Table 16-3.

Table 16-3. Azure Log Analytics features

Feature	Description	Example
Data collection	Gathers logs and metrics	CPU usage logs from VMs
KQL queries	Query data for deep insights	"Show failed login attempts in the last 24 hours."
Dashboards	Visualize metrics and trends	Display of VM performance trends over time

Azure Monitor Alerts

Azure Monitor alerts act like motion detectors or smoke alarms for your cloud environment. *Azure Monitor alerts* watch for unusual activities and immediately notify you or even take automated actions when certain thresholds are breached, as shown in Table 16-4.

Table 16-4. Azure Monitor alerts

Type of alert	Description	Example scenario
Metric alert	Based on numerical data	"CPU > 90% for 10 minutes."
Log alert	Based on query results	"More than 3 failed logins in an hour."
Activity log alert	Based on changes in resources	"A VM was deleted."

Azure Monitor alerts can be configured to send emails or SMS messages or trigger automated actions (for example, scaling a VM).

Application Insights

Application Insights is a detailed diagnostic tool for your applications that can tell you if one is consuming too many resources or is not working as expected.

Application Insights focuses on monitoring live applications to:

- Detect performance anomalies

- Provide analytics tools to help developers diagnose issues
- Help improve application performance

Table 16-5 lists and gives examples of some features of Application Insights.

Table 16-5. Application Insights

Feature	Purpose	Example
Availability tests	Simulates user requests to check uptime	Pings your app every 5 minutes
Performance metrics	Tracks response times and dependencies	Identifies slow database queries
Failure analysis	Captures errors and exceptions	Pinpoints where app crashes occur
User analytics	Tracks user behavior	Identifies which pages are most visited

Table 16-6 is a handy comparison chart of Azure monitoring tools.

Table 16-6. Comparison of Azure monitoring tools

Tool	Focus area	Best used for
Azure Advisor	Personalized recommendations	Optimization (cost, security, performance)
Azure Service Health	Service outages and health notifications	Awareness of platform-level issues
Azure Monitor	Resource monitoring and telemetry	Collecting and analyzing logs, metrics
Log Analytics	Log collection and queries	Investigating issues deeply
Monitor alerts	Real-time notifications	Quick response to issues
Application Insights	App monitoring and user analytics	Improving application reliability and user experience (UX)

Summary

In this chapter, we explored the key monitoring and advisory tools available in Azure and how they complement each other to ensure that your cloud environment remains healthy, secure, reliable, and optimized:

Azure Advisor
> Provides personalized recommendations for cost, security, reliability, performance, and operational excellence.

Azure Service Health
> Keeps you informed of global and subscription-specific outages, maintenance, and resource health.

Azure Monitor
> Collects and analyzes telemetry across your environment, using these tools:
> - Log Analytics for deep investigation
> - Azure Monitor alerts for real-time notifications

- Application Insights for application performance and user behavior

Together, these monitoring tools provide end-to-end visibility and control so that you're not just reacting to issues but proactively improving performance, reliability, and user experience.

Chapter 16 Quiz

To check your answers, please refer to the "Chapter 16 Answer Key" on page 308.

1. Your company reports that a production Azure VM is unreachable, and users cannot access the application hosted on it. You need to quickly determine whether the issue is related to the VM itself (e.g., platform failure, unexpected shutdown, maintenance, etc.).

    Which Azure service should you check first?

    A. Azure Status

    B. Service Health

    C. Resource Health

    D. Log Analytics

2. Your development team is preparing a new web application for release and needs to analyze performance, identify code-level errors, and understand user interaction patterns to improve UX before going live.

    Which tool would meet this requirement?

    A. Azure Advisor

    B. Log Analytics

    C. Azure Service Health

    D. Application Insights

3. You are investigating a security incident and need to perform deep log queries using Kusto Query Language to analyze telemetry across multiple Azure services.

    Which service should you use?

    A. Azure Log Analytics

    B. Application Insights

    C. Azure Monitor alerts

    D. Azure Advisor

Wrap-Up

Congratulations! Take a moment to celebrate. You've completed the *Azure Fundamentals (AZ-900) Study Guide*. You've built a strong foundation in Azure, and every concept you've learned brings you one step closer to success on the exam. If any topics feel unclear, feel free to revisit those chapters.

As you prepare to take the AZ-900 Microsoft Azure Fundamentals exam, let's review the three core learning paths and their essential concepts. This recap will reinforce your understanding, boost your confidence, and equip you to tackle the exam with clarity and assurance.

Path 1: Cloud Concepts

This foundational path introduces the principles of cloud computing:

Basic cloud computing principles
　　What the cloud is and the shared responsibility model

Deployment models
　　Public, private, hybrid, and multi-cloud

The benefits of using cloud services
　　High availability, scalability, reliability, predictability, security, governance, and manageability

Cloud service types
　　IaaS, PaaS, and SaaS—and when using each is advantageous

Key Takeaway

From this path, you should be able to describe the advantages of cloud models and how they differ from traditional on-premises solutions. This is the foundation of Azure knowledge.

Path 2: Azure Architecture and Services

This path dives into Azure-specific infrastructure and services:

Core architectural components of Azure
  Including Azure physical infrastructure, regions, availability zones, resource groups, and fault tolerance

Compute and networking services
  Azure Virtual Machine, VM Scale Set, App Service, Functions, Virtual Network, VPN Gateway, DNS, and ExpressRoute

Storage services
  Storage accounts, types (blobs, files, queues, tables), tiers, redundancy, data migration, and tools like AzCopy or Storage Explorer

Azure Identity, access, and security
  Microsoft Entra ID, RBAC, Conditional Access, external identities, Zero Trust, defense in depth, and Microsoft Defender for Cloud

Key Takeaway

You should now understand Azure's structure and how its compute, storage, networking, and security services interconnect, as well as how to manage them effectively.

Path 3: Management and Governance

This final path brings operational control and compliance into focus:

Cost management
  How to monitor, budget, and optimize spending in Azure

Azure governance and compliance
  Policy enforcement, organizational compliance, and access control across subscriptions

Managing and deploying Azure resources
  Including Azure Resource Manager, templates, deployment tools, and managing both cloud and on-premises resources

Monitoring tools
  Azure Monitor, alerts, and insights to track performance and ensure reliability

Key Takeaway

In path 3, you learned that effective cost monitoring, governance, resource deployment, and health monitoring are essential to managing Azure securely and efficiently.

Bringing It All Together

Your learning journey has followed a logical progression:

1. *Cloud fundamentals*
   You learned why the cloud matters and its core models and benefits.

2. *Azure architecture and services*
   You explored how Azure organizes infrastructure and delivers services like compute, storage, networking, and identity.

3. *Management and governance*
   You mastered operational practices, including cost management, governance, deployment, and monitoring.

Final Checklist: Your AZ-900 Readiness

You're ready to take the exam when you can:

- Explain cloud models: public, private, hybrid, multi-cloud
- Explain service types: IaaS, PaaS, SaaS
- Describe Azure infrastructure, resource organization, and global reliability features
- Outline core Azure services: compute, networking, storage, identity, and security
- Detail the cost management, governance, deployment strategies, and monitoring mechanisms in Azure

Exam Blueprint Alignment

According to Microsoft, the weightings for the AZ-900 exam are approximately:

- Cloud concepts: 25%–30%
- Azure architecture and services: 35%–40%
- Management and governance: 30%–35%

This balance underscores the importance of mastering all three areas for success on AZ-900.

To learn more about the AZ-900 Azure Fundamentals exam, please visit the official Microsoft certification site (*https://oreil.ly/BjSzd*).

Good Luck!

This wraps up our Azure Fundamentals journey. Thank you for taking the time to explore these concepts and tools with me. With the knowledge you've gained, you're well prepared to tackle the AZ-900 exam with confidence.

Good luck, and may your path to Azure certification be smooth and successful!

APPENDIX A
Practice Exam

To check your answers, please refer to the "Practice Exam Answer Key" on page 309.

1. Your company plans to deploy a new web application. Management does not want to purchase or maintain physical servers, nor do they want to hire a system administrator to manage the operating system. The development team should focus only on developing and deploying web application code.

   Which cloud service type is most appropriate?

   A. IaaS

   B. PaaS

   C. SaaS

   D. IaaS, PaaS, and SaaS are equally appropriate for this situation.

2. Your company's on-premises email server is reaching the end of its useful life. Management wants a fully managed solution where the vendor is responsible for the infrastructure, maintenance, updating, and security of the email service.

   Which cloud service model best meets this requirement?

   A. IaaS

   B. PaaS

   C. SaaS

   D. IaaS, PaaS, and SaaS are equally appropriate for this situation.

3. Your company needs a highly customizable environment to run legacy applications that require a specific, unsupported version of an operating system.

   Which cloud service type gives you the most control over the OS?

A. IaaS

   B. PaaS

   C. SaaS

   D. IaaS, PaaS, and SaaS are very similar with respect to OS control.

4. Your company experiences a massive, but predictable, surge in traffic to its ecommerce website for two weeks during the holiday season.

   Which core cloud benefit allows you to temporarily add resources to handle the load and then remove resources afterward to minimize cost?

   A. High availability

   B. Scalability

   C. Disaster recovery

   D. Fault tolerance

5. Your company cannot host its data in a multitenant environment due to strict regulatory requirements. You need to have a cloud environment dedicated solely to your organization.

   Which cloud deployment model should you consider?

   A. Public cloud

   B. Private cloud

   C. Hybrid cloud

   D. Multi-cloud

6. Your company wants to keep its sensitive customer data on-premises for compliance but would like to use cloud AI and analytics services to process that data.

   Which cloud deployment model would connect your on-premises infrastructure to the cloud to achieve this?

   A. Public cloud

   B. Private cloud

   C. Hybrid cloud

   D. Multi-cloud

7. You are explaining the shared responsibility model for an IaaS deployment to your team. One team member asks: "Who is responsible for the physical hosts and the physical network?"

   What is your answer?

   A. The customer

   B. The cloud service provider

C. Both the customer and the cloud service provider

   D. A third-party vendor

8. A development team is creating a function that automatically processes an image whenever it is uploaded to an Azure Storage account. The team wants to focus only on the code and avoid managing any servers or infrastructure.

   This is an example of which cloud computing concept?

   A. Serverless

   B. Virtualization

   C. High availability

   D. Containerization

9. Which of the following best describes the consumption-based pricing model used in cloud computing?

   A. Up-front capital expenditure

   B. Pay-as-you-go pricing with no up-front costs

   C. Long-term licensing agreements

   D. Fixed monthly costs regardless of usage

10. To ensure the highest level of resilience and protect virtual machines from a datacenter-wide failure, which Azure feature should you use?

    A. Single Azure region

    B. Availability set

    C. Availability zones

    D. Resource group

11. An Azure resource group is best described as:

    A. A geographical grouping of Azure datacenters

    B. A directory for user identities and applications

    C. A boundary for applying compliance policies

    D. A logical container for resources that share the same lifecycle.

12. Your company has multiple departments, each using its own Azure subscription for billing. You need to enforce consistent governance rules (such as allowed regions) across all subscriptions.

    Which Azure component should you use?

    A. Resource group

    B. Management group

C. Availability zone

D. Subscription

13. You need a private, dedicated network connection from your on-premises datacenter to Azure to avoid sending traffic over the public internet.

    Which Azure networking service should you use?

    A. Azure VPN Gateway

    B. Azure ExpressRoute

    C. Azure Virtual Network peering

    D. Azure Load Balancer

14. You want a fully managed storage solution in Azure that allows multiple users or applications to access data using SMB or NFS protocols.

    Which Azure Storage service should you use?

    A. Azure Files

    B. Azure Blob Storage

    C. Azure Tables

    D. Azure Queues

15. You need to move 100 TB of data from your on-premises server to Azure, but your internet connection is slow and unreliable.

    Which Azure service is the most efficient for this migration?

    A. AzCopy over the internet

    B. Azure Storage Explorer

    C. Azure Data Box

    D. Azure File Sync

16. You want a centralized identity and access management service to control sign-in and access to Azure resources. Which Azure service should you use?

    A. Azure role-based access control

    B. Microsoft Entra ID

    C. Azure Policy

    D. Azure Key Vault

17. You want to allow a user to manage storage accounts in an Azure subscription but restrict the user from modifying virtual machines or networks.

    Which Azure security feature should you use?

A. Azure role-based access control (RBAC)

B. Multifactor authentication

C. Conditional Access

D. Privileged Identity Management

18. Your security team mandates that any user accessing the Azure portal from an untrusted network location must be required to perform multifactor authentication.

    Which Microsoft Entra ID feature can enforce this rule?

    A. Single sign-on

    B. Conditional Access

    C. Privileged Identity Management

    D. Identity protection

19. You want to implement a security approach that never trusts any request automatically, always assumes breach, and verifies every access attempt.

    Which security model does this describe?

    A. Defense-in-depth

    B. Zero Trust

    C. Shared responsibility model

    D. Least privilege

20. You want a service that provides unified security management and advanced threat protection for workloads running in Azure and on-premises.

    Which Azure service should you use?

    A. Azure Sentinel

    B. Microsoft Defender for Cloud

    C. Azure DDoS Protection

    D. Azure Firewall

21. An Azure region pair is primarily used for:

    A. Replicating data for redundancy and disaster recovery

    B. Grouping resources for billing

    C. Providing the lowest latency for users

    D. Isolating resources for compliance

22. You need to host a stateless API that experiences unpredictable, sporadic bursts of traffic.

    Which compute option will be most cost-effective?

    A. Azure Virtual Machine (always running)

    B. Azure App Service Plan (always on)

    C. Azure Functions (consumption plan)

    D. Azure Kubernetes Service

23. You want to store data in Azure so that it is replicated synchronously across three availability zones in the primary region, protecting it from zone-level failures.

    Which Azure storage redundancy option should you use?

    A. Locally redundant storage

    B. Zone-redundant storage

    C. Geo-redundant storage

    D. Geo-zone-redundant storage

24. You want to create a private network in Azure where you can define subnets, IP address ranges, and network security policies.

    Which Azure service should you deploy?

    A. Azure Load Balancer

    B. Azure Route Table

    C. Azure DNS zone

    D. Azure Virtual Network

25. You want to allow two Azure virtual networks to communicate directly with each other through the Azure backbone network, as if they were a single network.

    Which Azure service should you use?

    A. VNet peering

    B. VPN gateway

    C. ExpressRoute

    D. Network security group

26. What is the primary purpose of the defense-in-depth security model?

    A. To assume breach and verify every request

    B. To provide a single, powerful security perimeter

    C. To use multiple, layered security controls

    D. To enforce the principle of least privilege

27. Which factor is often overlooked as a potential cost of using Azure because it is free within a region but incurs a charge when data travels between regions?

   A. Compute cost

   B. Storage cost

   C. Bandwidth (egress) cost

   D. Support plan cost

28. You want to estimate the potential cost savings of moving an organization's on-premises workloads to Azure over three years.

   Which tool is best suited for this?

   A. Azure pricing calculator

   B. Azure Migrate: Assessment

   C. Cost Management

   D. Azure Advisor

29. You need to quickly generate an estimate for the monthly cost of running 10 D2s v3 virtual machines in the West US region.

   Which tool should you use?

   A. Azure Advisor

   B. Azure pricing calculator

   C. Azure Service Health

   D. Azure Cost Management

30. Your company has resources for development, testing, and production environments all in one subscription. You need to track costs separately for each environment for internal chargeback.

   What is the best way to organize these costs?

   A. Create separate resource groups for each environment.

   B. Deploy each environment to a different Azure region.

   C. Use separate subscriptions for each environment.

   D. Apply tags like "Environment: Production" to resources.

31. You want to manage governance and compliance for servers and Kubernetes clusters that are running outside of Azure, such as on-premises or in another cloud like AWS.

   Which Azure service should you use?

   A. Azure Policy

   B. Azure Arc

C. Microsoft Entra ID

D. Azure Monitor

32. You want to define and deploy Azure infrastructure and resources programmatically instead of manually configuring resources through the Azure portal.

    Which practice does this describe?

    A. Continuous integration

    B. Infrastructure as code

    C. Agile development

    D. Continuous deployment

33. You want to receive personalized, actionable recommendations to help optimize your Azure resources for high availability, security, performance, and cost.

    Which Azure service should you use?

    A. Azure Monitor

    B. Azure Advisor

    C. Azure Service Health

    D. Microsoft Defender for Cloud

34. You want to check whether Azure is experiencing a platform-wide outage that could be affecting your Azure Virtual Machine.

    Which Azure service should you use?

    A. Azure Monitor

    B. Azure Advisor

    C. Azure Service Health

    D. Azure Resource Health

35. What is the primary benefit of using an Azure Resource Manager template over manually creating resources in the portal?

    A. Consistency and repeatability

    B. Lower cost

    C. Higher performance

    D. Built-in security compliance

36. You want to run complex queries against log data collected from various Azure resources, such as virtual machines, activity logs, and diagnostics.

    Which Azure Monitor feature should you use?

A. Application Insights

B. Log Analytics

C. Azure dashboards

D. Azure Workbooks

37. You want to receive an email alert whenever the CPU usage of a critical Azure Virtual Machine exceeds 95% for 5 minutes.

    Which Azure service should you configure?

    A. Azure Service Health

    B. Azure Monitor alert

    C. Azure Advisor

    D. Azure Resource Graph

38. You want to manage Azure resources using bash or Azure PowerShell commands directly from your browser, without installing anything locally.

    Which tool should you use?

    A. Azure Portal

    B. Azure Arc

    C. Azure Resource Manager

    D. Azure Cloud Shell

39. You want to view detailed usage reports and trends for your Azure spending to monitor and analyze costs over time.

    Which Azure tool should you use?

    A. Pricing calculator

    B. Azure Migrate: Assessment

    C. Cost Management + Billing

    D. Azure Advisor

40. You want to ensure that all new Azure resources are deployed only to the West US or East US regions to meet data residency requirements.

    What is the most efficient way to enforce this?

    A. Use an Azure Policy that defines the allowed regions.

    B. Manually check each new deployment.

    C. Use a resource lock on all other regions.

    D. Create an Azure Monitor alert to notify administrators when resources are deployed to unapproved regions.

APPENDIX B
Answer Keys

Chapter 1 Answer Key

1. **C:** Cloud computing allows effortless, on-demand scaling, enabling users to increase or decrease compute resources without the need for physical hardware changes. This rapid and flexible approach is possible because the cloud provider manages the underlying infrastructure, handling all upgrades and maintenance. In contrast, scaling in a traditional on-premises environment requires the time-consuming process of manually purchasing, installing, and configuring additional servers or resources.

2. **B:** Cloud computing provides organizations with scalable storage capacity, allowing them to adjust resources on demand without the need to install or maintain physical hardware. This flexibility is a core advantage of cloud platforms, which offer virtually unlimited and dynamically provisioned storage. In contrast, capacity in a traditional on-premises environment is constrained by physical hardware, often resulting in fixed storage limits that require manual and time-consuming increases. Additionally, cloud platforms provide a wide range of storage types, such as Blob, File, Queue, and Table storage, designed to meet diverse performance and availability needs.

3. **D:** The pay-as-you-go model is one of the most significant cost advantages of cloud computing. Organizations pay only for the resources they actually consume, removing the need for large up-front hardware investments common in traditional on-premises environments. This model also reduces ongoing operational expenses because the cloud provider manages the underlying infrastructure, handling hardware upkeep and eliminating the need for internal teams to maintain physical infrastructure.

Chapter 2 Answer Key

1. D: Scalability in Azure is the key to handling dynamic and unpredictable customer demand, such as traffic surges during seasonal spikes. Azure can automatically increase or decrease resources, allowing an ecommerce platform to remain responsive without manual intervention. This capability, driven by dynamic resource adjustment, is a core advantage of cloud computing for managing fluctuating workloads.

2. A: High availability ensures that cloud services remain accessible and functional even during hardware failures or unexpected spikes in demand, minimizing downtime and disruptions. It achieves this by distributing workloads across multiple redundant systems. High availability is specifically focused on continuous accessibility and reliability, separate from concerns like data encryption (a security feature), automated software patching (operational maintenance), or guaranteed lower operational costs (the necessary redundancy may increase expenses).

3. B: Governance is essential for ensuring that organizations can implement rules and policies to maintain compliance, security, and organizational standards across their cloud environments. Its primary role is to enforce these policies and requirements. Governance is distinct from other capabilities like automatically backing up sensitive data (a feature of backup and recovery), controlling pricing or affordability, or dynamically scaling resources (a feature of scalability).

Chapter 3 Answer Key

1. B: Azure Virtual Machines represents IaaS, because Azure provides the underlying hardware while you manage the operating system, configurations, and applications. This aligns with the IaaS model, which offers maximum control over the virtualized environment. The other services fall under different cloud models: Microsoft 365 is SaaS, because it delivers fully managed productivity applications. Azure App Service is PaaS, because Azure manages the OS and runtime while you deploy your application code. Azure Functions is a serverless PaaS offering that abstracts infrastructure management entirely.

2. A: Full control over the operating system is not available in Azure App Service. Because this is a PaaS offering, Microsoft is responsible for managing the underlying OS, applying updates, and handling platform-level maintenance. As a customer, your control is limited to the application and its configuration, meaning you cannot log in to or customize the OS itself. However, you retain control over several key application capabilities. Automatic scaling is supported, allowing you to configure scale-out rules based on metrics or schedules. You also have full control over custom domain and SSL configuration, enabling you to map custom domains and upload SSL certificates. Furthermore, Azure App Service allows you

to configure CD to integrate with GitHub, Azure DevOps, Bitbucket, and other supported CI/CD tooling.

3. C: SaaS is the ideal choice as it provides ready-to-use applications, such as collaboration tools, email systems, and document-sharing platforms, all fully managed by the cloud provider. In the SaaS model, the provider handles all infrastructure, platform, and software maintenance, allowing customers to focus solely on using the service. In contrast, IaaS would require you to install and configure the collaboration software yourself on virtualized infrastructure, and PaaS offers a managed environment for deploying your own custom applications, not prebuilt, ready-to-use tools.

Chapter 4 Answer Key

1. A: IaaS places the most operational responsibility on the customer, who must manage the operating system, middleware, applications, and many network configurations; in this model, the provider only manages the physical hardware. PaaS offloads the management of the OS, middleware, and runtime to the provider, leaving customers responsible mainly for application code. SaaS places almost all responsibilities on the provider, with the customer only managing user access and data within the application.

2. B: Microsoft, as the cloud service provider, is entirely responsible for maintaining physical servers, storage systems, networking equipment, power, cooling, and the overall datacenter infrastructure. This eliminates the need for customers to handle physical hardware they manage only virtual and logical resources.

3. C: SaaS delivers a fully managed application where the provider handles updates, infrastructure, security, and platform components, leaving the customer responsible only for user access and data. In contrast, PaaS reduces the customer's operational burden by managing the OS and middleware, but the customer still manages and maintains the application itself. IaaS places the most responsibility on the customer, as the customer must manage the operating system, middleware, applications, and many configuration tasks.

Chapter 5 Answer Key

1. C: In this scenario, the hybrid cloud model is the most effective solution. It enables the hospital to keep sensitive patient data on-premises, satisfying regulatory compliance requirements, while simultaneously leveraging Azure's public cloud capabilities for analytics and AI workloads. A private cloud would not be sufficient as it would keep all operations on-premises, preventing the hospital from easily using Azure's advanced services. Conversely, a public cloud is inappropriate because moving all patient data to a fully public environment could violate

regulatory requirements. Finally, a multi-cloud model is not the right choice because it involves using multiple public cloud providers and does not address the fundamental requirement to retain data control by integrating on-premises systems.

2. A: Private cloud is the most suitable model because it is built on dedicated infrastructure controlled by the organization. It therefore offers maximum control over security, compliance, and customization, albeit with higher cost and operational responsibility. In contrast, a public cloud provides limited control over the underlying infrastructure, as it operates on shared, multi-tenant systems. A hybrid cloud offers a blend of environments but does not guarantee the full exclusivity or complete control over all components that the company requires. Similarly, a multi-cloud approach, which involves multiple public cloud providers, does not provide the dedicated, highly controlled environment necessary to comply with strict data privacy regulations.

3. B: For this company, the public cloud model is the most appropriate choice. It is specifically designed for elastic scaling and does not require customers to manage the underlying infrastructure. In contrast, a private cloud offers greater control but requires additional planning and infrastructure for scaling. A hybrid cloud can add complexity to operations and does not provide the same level of immediate scalability as purely public cloud services. While a multi-cloud setup can offer benefits like redundancy or cost optimization, it typically increases operational overhead and does not inherently speed up deployment or scaling for high-traffic periods.

Chapter 6 Answer Key

1. C: The Azure portal provides a graphical, web-based interface that allows users to manage, configure, and monitor Azure resources without needing to install any software or write code. In contrast, Azure CLI and Azure PowerShell are command-line tools that require knowledge of commands and scripting, making them unsuitable for users seeking a purely graphical interface. ARM templates enable IaC deployments but require coding in JSON syntax.

2. C: The free trial subscription is ideal for new users preparing for the AZ-900 exam, as it provides $200 in credits for the first 30 days and access to a limited set of free services for a year, allowing experimentation without up-front costs. In contrast, the pay-as-you-go plan requires immediate payment for usage and does not include free credits. The EA is tailored for large organizations with volume licensing and is generally not suitable for individual exam preparation. Lastly, Azure for Students requires the user to verify active enrollment at an eligible academic institution. Since Peter is no longer a student, he would not qualify for this subscription type.

3. B: Microsoft Entra focuses on managing users, identities, and access permissions across Azure and other integrated applications. This makes it distinct from other Azure functions: web traffic management is handled by services like Azure Front Door or Traffic Manager, VM management falls under Azure Compute, and storage management is provided by Azure Storage services.

Chapter 7 Answer Key

1. A: Availability zones are physically separate datacenters within a single region, specifically designed to isolate failures and maintain high availability in the event of a single datacenter outage. An Azure region, while a broader geographic area containing multiple datacenters, does not guarantee this level of isolation at the individual datacenter level. A region pair, which links two regions for geo-redundancy and disaster recovery, is intended for region-wide outages rather than local high availability. Lastly, a sovereign region provides isolated cloud instances for strict regulatory and compliance requirements, such as government workloads, and its primary purpose is not high availability at the datacenter level.

2. C: Region pairs are strategically linked regions within the same geography that provide geo-redundancy and prioritized recovery, making them suitable for failover during region-wide outages. An availability zone provides resiliency only within a single region and cannot handle a full regional failure. An Azure region refers to a single geographic area and does not inherently provide failover capabilities across regions. A sovereign region is designed for regulatory and compliance requirements and does not automatically support cross-region failover for standard workloads.

3. D: Sovereign regions are isolated Azure instances specifically designed to meet strict compliance and regulatory requirements, as they ensure physical and operational separation for sensitive workloads. An availability zone provides resiliency within a single region but does not address compliance or sovereignty requirements. An Azure region is a standard region that does not meet specialized government standards. A region pair provides disaster recovery and failover between regions but does not inherently satisfy regulatory or data sovereignty needs.

Chapter 8 Answer Key

1. B: When you delete a resource group in Azure, not only the resource group but also all of its contained resources are automatically removed. This behavior is by design so that no orphaned resources remain to consume costs.

2. C: Azure subscriptions provide boundaries for billing and access control, serving as logical units for organizing resource groups and resources. They enable

detailed cost tracking and the application of policies and permissions at a broad level. While they are a key part of the organizational hierarchy, their purpose is not to organize individual resources (which is the role of resource groups), manage specific services like VNets, or create nested resource groups (as subscriptions themselves are not a nestable element).

3. C: Management groups are the only element in the Azure hierarchy that can be nested; they allow you to create a structured governance model up to six levels deep. This feature is crucial for applying policies and permissions consistently across a large organization. In contrast, both resource groups and subscriptions are intentionally flat structures, meaning you cannot nest a resource group within another resource group or a subscription within another subscription.

Chapter 9 Answer Key

1. C: Azure VMs provide full control over the operating system, installed software, and all configuration settings, making them an ideal solution for running legacy applications or workloads that require deep customization and complete administrative access. This contrasts with services like AKS, which orchestrates containers rather than full operating systems; Azure App Service, which abstracts the underlying platform and limits system file modification; and Azure Functions, which is designed for ephemeral, event-driven workloads and is not suited for persistent applications requiring OS-level access.

2. C: Azure Container Apps stands out as a fully managed, serverless container platform specifically designed for event-driven microservices. It offers built-in features like autoscaling, traffic splitting, and application lifecycle management without the need to manage infrastructure or complex orchestrators. This approach provides a significant advantage over other options. For instance, Azure VMs require taking on the manual overhead of managing the operating system and infrastructure. Azure Container Instances, while allowing containers to run without infrastructure management, does not include robust, built-in features for microservice scaling, traffic splitting, or application lifecycle management. Similarly, AKS, while a powerful orchestration solution, requires specialized Kubernetes management, introducing an operational complexity that does not align with a fully managed serverless requirement.

3. D: Azure VMSS are an ideal choice for applications with dynamic workloads, as they are designed to automatically scale multiple identical VM instances based on demand. Availability sets focus on improving VM uptime and availability within a single datacenter, without providing automatic scaling. Azure Firewall is a security service used for network protection and does not scale compute resources. AKS is a platform used to orchestrate and scale containerized workloads, not to scale identical VM instances.

Chapter 10 Answer Key

1. B: Azure VNets are fundamentally designed to enable secure communication. They provide isolated, private networks that allow Azure resources to communicate securely with each other, connect with on-premises networks, and interface with the internet when properly configured.

2. A: Azure ExpressRoute provides a dedicated, private connection between on-premises networks and Azure. It bypasses the public internet, offering higher performance, reliability, and security for hybrid connectivity.

3. C: Azure VPN Gateway is primarily used to connect on-premises networks to Azure over an encrypted tunnel. It establishes secure communication between your local networks and Azure VNets using site-to-site or point-to-site VPN tunnels.

Chapter 11 Answer Key

1. B: Azure Blob Storage is designed to store massive amounts of unstructured data, such as multimedia files, documents, logs, and backups. It also offers durability, scalability, global access, and cost optimization through tiering. Other services within Azure Storage serve other purposes. Azure Table Storage is a NoSQL key-value store intended for structured, non-relational data, not for large media files. Azure Queue Storage functions as a messaging service for asynchronous communication and decoupling application components. Lastly, Azure File Storage provides SMB-based file shares suitable for lift-and-shift workloads, but it is primarily optimized for shared file access, not for massive, large-scale unstructured objects like videos and images.

2. C: Data stored in the Cool tier of Azure Blob Storage must remain for a minimum of 30 days to avoid early deletion fees. In comparison, the Archive tier has a minimum retention period of 180 days.

3. B: LRS maintains three copies of data within a single datacenter, providing a basic level of redundancy at the lowest cost. ZRS replicates data across multiple availability zones within the same region, offering higher availability and resilience against datacenter-level failures. For cross-region disaster recovery, GRS replicates data to a secondary, geographically distant region. RA-GRS offers the same geo-redundancy as GRS but also provides read access to the secondary region, generally resulting in higher costs than LRS or ZRS.

Chapter 12 Answer Key

1. B: Passwordless authentication is generally more secure than using traditional passwords. It eliminates common risks such as phishing, credential stuffing, weak passwords, and password reuse by relying on strong authentication mechanisms like biometrics, hardware keys, or device-bound certificates. Since traditional passwords are one of the most frequently exploited attack surfaces, security is significantly improved when they are replaced with these robust, passwordless methods.

2. B: The Zero Trust security model is built on the principle of continuous verification: it demands that user identity, device health, and session risk be explicitly checked for every access request. This model rejects the traditional assumption of inherent trust for any user, even those within the network. Furthermore, Zero Trust operates with the mindset that safety lies in assuming that a breach has already happened. Under this assumption, it requires continuous monitoring and segmentation to limit potential attack impact. It recognizes that relying solely on passwords for authentication is insufficient, and perimeter-only defenses are inadequate because modern threats can easily bypass network firewalls through stolen credentials or remote access.

3. B: The purpose of the defense-in-depth security strategy is to mitigate the risk that any single control, such as a firewall or antivirus, might fail or be circumvented. By using multiple, independent layers of protection, the strategy ensures that if one layer is compromised, others remain in place to continue safeguarding resources and data.

Chapter 13 Answer Key

1. B: The Azure pricing calculator is the appropriate tool for estimating and modeling the cost of Azure resources before deployment. It allows you to forecast spending by adjusting parameters such as resource type, size, region, redundancy options, and usage patterns. This tool is distinct from others in the cost management suite. Azure Advisor provides tailored recommendations for cost optimization only *after* resources have been deployed, making it unsuitable for predeployment estimation. Azure Monitor is used for collecting, analyzing, and acting on telemetry data from Azure resources, not for estimating costs. Cost Management is used to monitor and analyze actual spending *after* deployment and does not provide predeployment cost projections.

2. C: Azure pricing is fundamentally based on resource consumption, not the number of users. Costs are directly influenced by factors such as the type and size of the provisioned resources, as larger or premium resources incur higher charges. Geographic region also plays a role, as prices can vary between regions due to

differences in infrastructure, energy costs, and taxes. Furthermore, actual usage patterns, including CPU, storage, and bandwidth consumption, directly affect the overall bill, as more intensive use increases costs.

3. D: Azure Advisor is the appropriate tool for this scenario, as it analyzes deployed resources and provides actionable recommendations for cost optimization. Its capabilities include suggesting actions like shutting down idle VMs, resizing underutilized resources, or recommending reserved instance purchases. This function distinguishes it from other tools: the Azure pricing calculator is used only to estimate costs before deployment and does not analyze live usage, Azure Monitor collects and visualizes telemetry data from resources but does not provide cost optimization recommendations, and Cost Management reports and tracks spending trends after deployment but does not generate the actionable, technical recommendations for resource optimization that Azure Advisor provides.

Chapter 14 Answer Key

1. A: Azure Policy is designed to define, enforce, and audit rules across Azure resources to ensure that deployments comport with organizational standards and resource compliance. It can proactively block noncompliant resources from being created. This service is distinct from others: access management is handled by Azure RBAC, cost tracking is managed through Cost Management, and network-level protection is provided by services like Azure Firewall or network security groups.

2. C: Microsoft Purview provides a centralized data governance solution that can discover, classify, label, and track sensitive data across Azure, on-premises, and multi-cloud platforms. It enables organizations to maintain compliance with privacy regulations while monitoring data usage and lineage.

3. D: Resource locks provide protection against accidental deletion or modification by applying `Delete` or `ReadOnly` locks at the resource or resource group level. This protection works even if a user has RBAC write permissions. Locks are specifically designed to prevent unintended changes to critical resources.

Chapter 15 Answer Key

1. B: Azure Arc provides a centralized management solution for hybrid and multi-cloud environments, enabling you to manage resources across Azure, AWS, and on-premises systems from a single interface. By comparison, Azure Monitor focuses on collecting logging, performance metrics, and alerts but does not provide governance or management for non-Azure resources. Bicep is an IaC tool

used for deploying native Azure resources, and ARM is Azure's core management engine solely for native Azure services.

2. C: For automating the creation of a new VM in Azure using code, ARM templates and Bicep are the appropriate tools. These are IaC solutions that enable you to define, automate, and consistently deploy Azure resources using declarative code. In contrast, the Azure portal is a graphical, manual interface that is not suitable for consistent, automated deployments at scale. Azure Arc's purpose is to manage hybrid and multi-cloud resources, not to deploy native Azure infrastructure, and Azure Monitor is designed for collecting logging, performance metrics, and alerts on resource performance.

3. D: ARM templates are fundamentally written in JSON. This structured, machine-readable format is the native way to declaratively define and deploy Azure infrastructure, allowing for consistent and automated deployments. Other configuration languages serve different purposes: YAML is commonly used for Azure DevOps pipelines and Kubernetes manifests, CSV is a flat-file format for tabular data, and XML is a legacy configuration format. These alternatives are not the underlying basis for ARM templates or Bicep deployments.

Chapter 16 Answer Key

1. C: Resource Health provides detailed information about the health of individual Azure resources. It can show whether a VM is healthy, unavailable due to platform issues, or affected by user actions. Azure Status only displays global service availability and not the status of specific resources. Service Health focuses on subscription- or region-wide issues and notifications, which might not pinpoint why a single VM is down. Log Analytics stores and queries logs, but it does not directly report the operational health of a specific resource.

2. D: Application Insights is the tool of choice for analyzing a new web application's performance, identifying code-level errors, and understanding user interaction patterns to improve the user experience. It provides detailed application performance monitoring, including telemetry, failure rates, latency breakdowns, dependency tracking, and usage analytics. In contrast, Azure Advisor focuses on providing recommendations for cost, performance, security, and reliability of the overall Azure environment, not detailed application telemetry. Log Analytics stores and queries logs but does not automatically collect the specific, detailed application-level performance data needed for this task. Finally, Azure Service Health monitors Azure service interruptions and incidents at the platform level and does not give insight into the performance of a specific application.

3. A: Azure Log Analytics is the appropriate service to use to investigate security incidents that require deep log queries using KQL across multiple Azure services, as it provides a centralized repository for logs from various sources. Application

Insights also utilizes KQL, but its focus is on application-specific telemetry and not broad, multi-resource log analysis at scale. Azure Monitor alerts are designed to give real-time notifications based on predefined rules and metrics, not for ad hoc queries. Finally, Azure Advisor provides recommendations for optimization and is not a tool for performing log analysis.

Practice Exam Answer Key

1. B: PaaS provides a fully managed environment where the cloud provider handles the operating system, middleware, and runtime, allowing the development team to focus entirely on writing and deploying web application code. Although IaaS eliminates the need to buy physical servers, the customer is still responsible for installing, configuring, and maintaining the operating system. SaaS refers to ready-to-use applications, such as Microsoft 365, and is not a suitable platform for developing and deploying custom web application code. It is not true that all three cloud services are equally suitable, because IaaS and SaaS do not satisfy the stated requirements.

2. C: SaaS provides a complete, fully managed software solution; the provider handles infrastructure, updates, and security, making it ideal for replacing an end-of-life email server. In contrast, IaaS requires the customer to install and maintain the email software. PaaS offers a development platform but not a ready-to-use email service. It is not true that all three cloud services are equally suitable because only SaaS delivers a complete, fully managed email application that meets all the stated needs.

3. A: IaaS offers full control over the operating system, allowing a company to install older or unsupported versions needed for legacy applications. PaaS removes OS-level control entirely, making it unsuitable for custom OS requirements. SaaS is a fully managed application service and gives no OS access. It is not true that all three cloud services are similar with respect to OS control, because only IaaS meets the stated requirement.

4. B: Scalability allows systems to dynamically add resources during peak demand and remove them when demand decreases, enabling the cost-efficient handling of seasonal workloads. This is distinct from high availability, which focuses on maintaining uptime, and disaster recovery, which deals with restoring services after catastrophic events. Fault tolerance ensures continuous operation during component failures but does not address the need for dynamic scaling in response to load fluctuations.

5. B: A private cloud provides a dedicated, single-tenant environment, which is necessary to meet the strict regulatory requirements that prohibit multitenant hosting. A public cloud is inherently multitenant and violates this regulatory requirement. A hybrid cloud blends both public and private clouds and cannot

guarantee the exclusive single-tenant hosting required. Multi-cloud, which involves multiple public cloud providers, also does not satisfy the dedicated, single-tenant data residency constraints.

6. C: Hybrid cloud integrates on-premises systems with cloud services, allowing the organization to keep sensitive data on-premises for compliance while still using cloud AI and analytics. Public cloud is not suitable as it would typically require moving sensitive data to a multitenant cloud environment. Private cloud keeps everything on-premises but does not provide access to external cloud-based AI and analytics tools. Multi-cloud involves multiple public cloud providers and does not meet the requirement for on-premises data residency.

7. B: Under the shared responsibility model, the provider always manages the underlying physical infrastructure. The customer is responsible for elements higher up the stack, such as the operating system, data, and applications. While overall responsibilities are shared in an IaaS deployment, the physical infrastructure remains solely with the provider and is not delegated to a third-party vendor.

8. A: Serverless computing (like Azure Functions) lets developers run code in response to events without the customer managing servers or infrastructure. Thus, serverless computing would meet the team's goal to focus only on the code. Virtualization, in contrast, requires the customer to manage virtual machines and infrastructure. High availability focuses on keeping systems running during failures; it is not a computing model for running event-driven code. Containerization packages applications but still requires managing the container environment, so it does not meet the requirement to avoid infrastructure management.

9. B: The consumption-based pricing model is a pay-as-you-go approach where customers pay only for the resources they use, with no up-front investment. In contrast, up-front capital expenditure is characteristic of traditional on-premises purchases. Long-term licensing agreements do not align with the model's focus on pay-as-you-go flexibility. Finally, fixed monthly costs are inconsistent with the consumption-based model, where costs fluctuate based on usage.

10. C: Availability zones are physically separate datacenters within an Azure region, providing strong protection against a datacenter-wide failure. A single Azure region does not guarantee this zone separation. An availability set only protects against hardware failures within a single datacenter (such as a rack failure) but not against the failure of an entire datacenter or zone. A resource group is simply a logical grouping construct and provides no resiliency or availability features.

11. D: An Azure resource group is best described as a logical container for resources that share the same lifecycle. Resource groups are primarily used to organize, deploy, manage, and delete related Azure resources as a unit. This is distinct from

a geographical grouping of datacenters (which describes Azure regions or geographies), a directory for user identities and applications (which describes Microsoft Entra ID), or a compliance boundary (while policies can be assigned to resource groups, this is not the core purpose of a resource group).

12. B: Management groups sit above subscriptions and allow policies, access controls, and governance rules to be applied consistently across all subscriptions within the hierarchy.

13. B: Azure ExpressRoute provides private, dedicated connectivity to Azure without using the public internet. Azure VPN Gateway encrypts traffic but still travels over the public internet. Azure VNet peering connects Azure virtual networks to each other, not to on-premises environments. Azure Load Balancer distributes traffic to backend resources but does not establish connectivity from on-premises networks.

14. A: Azure Files provides shared file storage accessible using SMB and NFS protocols, making it suitable for multiuser and multiapplication access. Azure Blob Storage, on the other hand, is for storing object data and does not support SMB or NFS. Azure Tables is a key-value NoSQL store, not a shared filesystem, and Azure Queues is used for message queuing rather than shared file access.

15. C: Azure Data Box provides a physical appliance for offline bulk data transfer, and this is the most efficient solution for moving 100 TB of data in order to avoid having to use a slow and unreliable internet connection. Services like AzCopy over the internet and Azure Storage Explorer depend heavily on network bandwidth, making them extremely time-consuming for such a large transfer. Azure File Sync is also unsuitable as it is designed for ongoing synchronization, not for a large, one-time data migration.

16. B: Microsoft Entra ID provides centralized identity management, authentication, and user access control for Azure and many other services. While Azure RBAC authorizes access, it relies on Entra ID to authenticate identities. Azure Policy governs resource configurations, not identity. Azure Key Vault stores secrets and certificates and does not manage user authentication.

17. A: Azure RBAC enables assigning fine-grained permissions. For example, you can assign the storage account contributor role, which grants access to manage storage accounts only and restricts the user from modifying virtual machines or networks. MFA secures sign-in but does not control authorization. Conditional Access controls when and how a user can sign in but not what they can manage. PIM manages privileged role activation rather than assigning specific resource-level permissions.

18. B: Conditional Access evaluates conditions such as location and triggers controls like requiring MFA, allowing for the enforcement of rules requiring additional authentication when a user accesses the Azure portal from an untrusted network

location. SSO enables streamlined sign-in but does not enforce conditional MFA. PIM manages privileged roles, not conditional MFA policies. Identity protection identifies risky sign-in behavior but is not the primary engine for location-based MFA policies.

19. B: Zero Trust is defined by the principle of never trusting any request automatically; always assuming a breach has occurred; and verifying every access attempt based on identity, device, and context. This approach differs from defense-in-depth, which focuses on layered security controls rather than continuous verification. The shared responsibility model outlines responsibilities between cloud providers and customers. The principle of least privilege limits access rights but does not define a full security model.

20. B: Microsoft Defender for Cloud provides cloud security posture management and workload protection for Azure, hybrid, and on-premises environments. Azure Sentinel is a SIEM for analytics and automation but is not a unified workload protection service. Azure DDoS Protection only mitigates denial-of-service attacks. Azure Firewall protects network traffic but does not provide full security posture management or workload threat protection.

21. A: Azure region pairs consist of two physically separated regions designed for synchronous and prioritized recovery during outages, making them ideal for durability and business continuity. Grouping resources for billing is handled through subscriptions and resource groups, not region pairs. Providing the lowest latency for users is not the purpose of region pairs; their purpose is resiliency. Isolating resources for compliance is the purpose of sovereign or specialized regions, not paired regions.

22. C: Azure Functions (consumption plan) is the most cost-effective option because it is serverless and scales to zero when idle, ensuring that you pay for execution time only during traffic bursts. In contrast, Azure VMs incur continuous cost even when idle. Azure App Service Plan has baseline charges regardless of activity. AKS requires paying for underlying VM node pools that must remain running.

23. B: ZRS synchronously replicates data across three availability zones in the same region, providing protection against zone-level failures. In contrast, LRS stores three copies within a single datacenter only. GRS replicates to a secondary region asynchronously and only uses LRS within the primary region. GZRS includes zone redundancy but adds cross-region replication, which is not required for protection within the primary region alone.

24. D: An Azure VNet provides the private IP space, subnets, and policy boundaries needed for custom network architecture. An Azure Load Balancer distributes traffic but does not define a network. An Azure DNS zone resolves names but

does not create private networking. An Azure Route Table only influences routing within a VNet and does not create the VNet itself.

25. A: VNet peering connects two Azure VNets with low-latency, high-bandwidth links over the Azure backbone, allowing them to communicate as if they were a single network. A VPN gateway is typically used for hybrid connectivity to on-premises environments and introduces unnecessary overhead for VNet-to-VNet connections. ExpressRoute connects on-premises networks to Azure, not virtual networks to each other. An NSG is used to enforce traffic filtering and does not establish connectivity between VNets.

26. C: Defense-in-depth relies on using multiple, layered security controls to protect against threats. With this approach, if one layer fails, others may still mitigate risk. To "assume breach and verify every request" is a statement of the Zero Trust principle. Defense in depth rejects the idea of a single, powerful security perimeter, and while the principle of least privilege is often a component of some broader security strategy, it is not the primary focus of the defense-in-depth model.

27. C: Bandwidth (egress) cost is often overlooked when using Azure because data moving out of a region incurs charges, including inter-region transfers, while intra-region transfers are typically free. Compute cost depends on resource size and runtime, not data movement. Storage cost is based on consumption and performance tier. Support plan cost is a fixed optional charge unrelated to data transfer.

28. B: Azure Migrate: Assessment provides detailed discovery, rightsizing recommendations, and multi year cost projections comparing your on-premises environment to Azure. It is the appropriate tool for estimating migration-related cost savings. The Azure pricing calculator estimates Azure costs only and does not compare them to on-premises spending. Azure Cost Management analyzes resources already deployed in Azure. Azure Advisor provides optimization guidance rather than premigration cost comparisons.

29. B: The Azure pricing calculator allows you to configure specific resource types and quantities to generate cost estimates before deployment. Other tools serve different purposes: Azure Advisor evaluates existing deployments, Azure Service Health reports service issues, and Azure Cost Management analyzes historical or current cloud spending.

30. D: Applying tags like "Environment: Production" to resources is the best way to organize these costs because Azure Cost Management can group and report costs by tag, enabling granular cost tracking within a single subscription. Creating separate resource groups for each environment is a less flexible option, as it limits you to one grouping dimension. Deploying each environment to a different Azure region complicates the architecture and is not the standard approach for

this kind of cost management. Using separate subscriptions is also more complex and generally unnecessary for simple internal chargeback.

31. B: Azure Arc brings on-premises and other cloud resources into Azure Resource Manager so that tools like Azure Policy and Microsoft Defender for Cloud can govern them. Azure Policy cannot directly manage external resources without Arc. Microsoft Entra ID handles identity, not governance. Azure Monitor collects logs and metrics but does not provide governance or compliance capabilities.

32. B: IaC uses machine-readable templates such as ARM, Bicep, or Terraform to provision infrastructure consistently. CI focuses on merging code frequently. Agile development is a methodology for iterative software development. CD automates the release of software changes, not infrastructure provisioning.

33. B: Azure Advisor analyzes resource configurations and usage patterns to provide personalized optimization recommendations across multiple categories, including high availability, security, performance, and cost. This differs from Azure Monitor, which collects telemetry but does not provide prescriptive advice. Azure Service Health reports service issues but does not make optimization recommendations. Meanwhile, Microsoft Defender for Cloud's recommendations focus solely on security, not on cost, performance, or reliability.

34. C: Azure Service Health reports active platform-wide issues, outages, and advisories that may affect your services. This differs from Azure Monitor, which is used to track the performance and logs of your own resources. Azure Advisor provides optimization recommendations, not outage information. Azure Resource Health reports the health state of a specific resource, not service-wide issues.

35. A: ARM templates allow you to deploy the same configuration across multiple environments with no manual variation, thereby achieving consistency and repeatability. Costs are not necessarily lower because they depend on the deployed resources, not the deployment method. Performance is not affected by the provisioning method. Security compliance is governed by Azure Policy, not ARM templates.

36. B: Log Analytics is the Azure Monitor feature that stores logs and enables complex querying using Kusto Query Language. Application Insights focuses on application telemetry and relies on Log Analytics for advanced queries. Azure dashboards visualize data but do not perform deep querying. Azure Workbooks create interactive reporting over data but still rely on Log Analytics as the query engine.

37. B: Azure Monitor alerts allow you to set thresholds on metrics like CPU usage for your resources and send notifications when those thresholds are exceeded. Azure Service Health covers platform-wide issues and outages, not resource-specific metrics. Azure Advisor provides optimization recommendations rather than

real-time alerts. Azure Resource Graph queries resource inventory and state but does not generate alerts.

38. D: Azure Cloud Shell provides a browser-based PowerShell and bash environment that is preconfigured for managing Azure resources. The Azure Portal is a GUI-based tool, not a command-line environment. Azure Arc extends Azure management to external environments but does not offer an interactive shell. ARM is a deployment and management framework, not an interactive command-line tool.

39. C: Cost Management + Billing provides data on usage, spending trends, and budgets for your Azure environment and conducts detailed cost analysis. The pricing calculator estimates costs before resources are deployed. Azure Migrate: Assessment provides detailed discovery, rightsizing recommendations, and multi-year cost projections comparing an on-premises environment to Azure; it does not provide historical data on Azure usage. Azure Advisor offers recommendations for cost optimization and other best practices but does not display detailed billing or usage information.

40. A: Using an Azure Policy that defines the allowed regions is the most efficient way to enforce this requirement, as it can automatically prevent deployments to unapproved regions using an Allowed Locations rule, ensuring consistent compliance. Manually checking each new deployment is labor intensive and prone to human error. A resource lock cannot restrict new deployments because locks only prevent changes or deletions of existing resources. Creating an Azure Monitor alert is reactive, not preventative, as it notifies administrators only after a noncompliant resource is deployed.

Index

A

access control, 211
    (see also Azure RBAC; RBAC)
    APIM, 134
    Azure Bastion, 154
    Azure Storage, 177
    management groups, 100
    management infrastructure, 101, 105
    resource groups, 99
    subscriptions, 71-72, 99
accessibility
    AVD, 118
    Azure Storage, 178
    as benefit of cloud services, 18
    cloud computing versus on-premises infrastructure, 6
    public cloud, 53
    SaaS, 36
accounts
    Azure Storage, 174, 180, 183-185
    creating, 74-77
    defined, 71
    overview of, 70-74
    relationship with subscriptions, 72
ACI (Azure Container Instances), 126-128, 132
AD (Azure Active Directory) (see Microsoft Entra ID)
Advisor (see Azure Advisor)
agility
    as benefit of Azure, 69
    hybrid clouds, 56
    multi-cloud model, 58
    public cloud, 53
AI (artificial intelligence)
    Azure AI Services, 24
    Azure Machine Learning, 67, 70
    Azure's leadership in, 68
    governance, 24
    Microsoft AI Cloud Partner Program, 226
    Microsoft Foundry, 70
    partnership with OpenAI, 68
AI-900 (Microsoft Azure AI Fundamentals) exam, xx
AKS (Azure Kubernetes Service), 123-126
    advantages of, 125
    compared to other compute services, 132
    defined, 7
    flexibility, 69
    food container analogy, 124
    functionality of, 124
    horizontal scaling, 17
    key features of, 124
    limitations of, 126
    nodes, 124
    pods, 124
    release of, 67
    use cases, 125, 131
Amazon Web Services (AWS), 3, 52
APIM (Azure API Management), 134
APIs (application programming interfaces)
    APIM, 134
    Azure App Service, 120
    Azure Application Gateway, 159
    Azure Functions, 123
    management in the cloud, 27
App Services (see Azure App Service)
Application Gateway, Azure, 157-159, 162
Application Insights (see Azure Monitor)

Arc (see Azure Arc)
ARM (Azure Resource Manager), 269-270
    best practices, 274
    compared to other IaC tools, 272
    defined, 257, 269
    key benefits of, 269
    RBAC, 214
    resource deployment templates, 26
    templates, 269
auditing
    Azure Key Vault, 215
    Azure Policy, 245-246
    governance, 24
    logging tools, 25
    Microsoft Purview, 243-244
    Service Trust Portal, 252
    unused resources, 239
authentication, 202, 204-207
    (see also MFA)
    comparison of methods, 207
    defined, 204
    Microsoft Entra ID, 202
    passwordless, 206-207
    SSO, 205
Automation, Azure, 13
availability
    availability sets, 108, 115-117
    availability zones, 86-89
    Azure Bastion, 153
    Azure DNS, 165
    Azure Firewall, 152
    Azure Load Balancer, 156-157
    Azure Storage, 176
    Azure VMs, 111
    Azure VMSSs, 114
    Azure VMware Solution, 60
    Azure VPN Gateway, 163
    as benefit of cloud services, 12-14
    performance predictability, 20
    public cloud, 53
    regional, 85
    sovereign regions, 94
AVD (Azure Virtual Desktop), 108, 117-118
AWS (Amazon Web Services), 3, 52
AZ-900 (Microsoft Azure Fundamentals) exam
    additional foundational certifications, xx
    blueprint alignment, 287
    final checklist, 287
    reasons for taking, xviii
    as stepping-stone to advanced certifications, xix
    structure and duration of, xix
    target audience, xviii
    topics covered in, xviii
AzCopy, 189, 192
Azure, 65-79
    accounts
        creating, 74-77
        defined, 71
        overview of, 71-72
    architectural components of, 83-94, 286
        availability zones, 86-89
        physical infrastructure, 83
        region pairs, 89-92
        regions, 84-86
        sovereign regions, 92-94
    availability sets, 115-117
    benefits of, 68-70
    history of, 66-68
    migrating to, 193-195
    offerings by cloud model, 59-61
    overview of services, 7
    product catalog, 79
    subscriptions
        management infrastructure, 99, 102-105
        overview of, 71-74
        types of, 72-74
        viewing details of, 78
Azure Active Directory (AD) (see Microsoft Entra ID)
Azure AD B2B and B2C (see Microsoft Entra External ID)
Azure Advisor, 231, 278-279
    compared to other monitoring tools, 283
    cost and performance optimization, 235
    fitness coach analogy, 278
    functionality of, 278
    performance predictability, 20
Azure AI Services, 24
Azure API Management (APIM), 134
Azure App Service, 119-121, 133-137
    advantages of, 120
    Azure Logic Apps, 135
    compared to other compute services, 132
    defined, 7
    functionality of, 119
    key features of, 119
    limitations of, 121

PaaS, 35
party room rental analogy, 119
release of, 67
shared responsibility model, 43
use cases, 39, 120, 131
Azure Application Gateway, 157-159, 162
Azure Arc
    defined, 257
    flexibility, 69
    functionality of, 60, 273-274
    hybrid clouds, 55, 68, 70
    key features of, 60
    managing hybrid and multi-cloud environments, 273-274
    market introduction, 67
    multi-cloud model, 57
    use case, 274
Azure Arc-enabled Kubernetes, 60
Azure Automation, 13
Azure Backup
    Azure Storage, 178
    functionality of, 14, 112
    integrating Azure VMware Solution with, 59
Azure Bastion, 153-154
Azure Blob Storage
    compared to other storage services, 181
    defined, 5, 7
    endpoint format, 181
    functionality of, 180
Azure Blueprints, 102
Azure CDN (Content Delivery Network), 166-168
Azure CLI (command-line interface), 263-265
    best practices, 275
    compared to Azure portal, 264
    compared to Azure PowerShell, 266
    compared to other IaC tools, 272
    creating resource groups, 264
    functionality of, 27, 263
    platforms, 264
    reasons for using, 263
Azure Cloud Shell, 261-263
    best practices, 275
    defined, 257
    functionality of, 261
    key features of, 262
    reasons for using, 262
    running Azure CLI, 264
    running Azure PowerShell, 266

Azure Cognitive Services, 67
Azure Container Apps, 129-131
    advantages of, 130
    compared to other compute services, 132
    functionality of, 129
    key features of, 129
    limitations of, 131
    rented exercise stations analogy, 129
    use cases, 130, 132
Azure Container Instances (ACI), 126-128, 132
Azure Cost Management, 223-239
    Azure Advisor, 231
    Azure Migrate, 228-229
    Azure pricing calculator, 229-231
    Azure tags, 235-237
    factors affecting costs, 225-227
    steps for using, 234-235
    tips for saving money, 237-239
Azure Cost Management + Billing, 88, 231-235, 238
Azure Data Box, 194-195
Azure Data Lake Storage, 180-181
Azure Databricks, 70
Azure DevOps
    agility, 69
    PaaS, 35
    SaaS, 37
Azure DNS (Domain Name System), 165-166
    functionality of, 165
    nonregional nature of, 85
    phone directory analogy, 165
Azure Event Grid, 135
Azure ExpressRoute, 163
    best practices for using, 164
    functionality of, 142, 163
    hybrid clouds, 55
    key features of, 164
    use cases, 142, 165
    work commute analogy, 164
Azure File Sync, 191-192
Azure Files, 5, 180-181
Azure Firewall, 23, 112, 151-153
    best practices for, 152
    functionality of, 151
    key features of, 152
    security checkpoint analogy, 151
    use cases, 153
Azure for Nonprofits accounts, 226
Azure for Students accounts, 73

costs, 226
creating, 77
Azure for Students Starter accounts, 73
    costs, 226
    creating, 77
Azure Front Door, 160-161
    compared to other load-balancing services, 162
    failover, 19
    functionality of, 160
    global airline hub analogy, 160
Azure Functions
    advantages of, 123
    compared to other compute services, 132
    defined, 7
    flexibility, 69
    functionality of, 121
    key features of, 122
    limitations of, 123
    on-demand plumber analogy, 121
    PaaS, 35
    use cases, 122, 131
Azure Government accounts, 226
Azure Hybrid Benefit, 69, 238
Azure Integration Services, 133-137
    Azure API Management, 134-134
    Azure Event Grid, 135
    Azure Service Bus, 136
Azure IoT Central, 70
Azure IoT Hub, 70
Azure Key Vault, 215-217
    application access, 216
    functionality of, 215
    real-world scenario, 216
    reasons for using, 215
Azure Kubernetes Service (see AKS)
Azure Lighthouse, 57
Azure Load Balancer, 156-157
    compared to other load-balancing services, 162
    functionality of, 142, 156
    theme park analogy, 156
    use case, 142
Azure Local
    functionality of, 60
    key features of, 60
    private cloud, 54
Azure Log Analytics, 282-283
Azure Logic Apps, 13, 135

Azure Machine Learning, 67, 70
Azure Migrate
    Assessment feature, 228-229, 234
    Business Case feature, 228-229, 234
    compared to Azure Data Box, 195
    cost predictability, 21
    defined, 7
    overview, 193
Azure Monitor, 281-283
    alerts, 27, 282
    Application Insights, 282
    Azure Log Analytics, 282
    compared to other monitoring tools, 283
    defined, 7
    functionality of, 13, 25, 281
    smart home system analogy, 281
    VMs, 113
Azure NetApp Files, 59
Azure Network Watcher, 144, 168-169
Azure Policy, 245-248
    built-in policies, 247
    centralized policy enforcement, 25
    compared to resource locks, 250
    custom policies, 247
    effects, 248
    functionality of, 24, 245
    importance of, 246
    integration with Microsoft Purview, 245
    key components of, 246
    monitoring and remediation, 247
    streamlining governance and resource provisioning, 102
    use cases, 246, 253
Azure portal, 258-261
    advantages of, 259, 261
    best practices, 274
    common tasks, 260
    compared to Azure CLI, 264
    defined, 257-258
    functionality of, 27, 77
    key features of, 259
    learning resources, 78
    limitations of, 261
    quick access links, 78
    use cases, 259
Azure PowerShell, 265-266
    best practices, 275
    compared to Azure CLI, 266
    compared to other IaC tools, 272

creating resource groups, 265
environments, 266
functionality of, 27, 265
reasons for using, 266
Azure Queues, 5, 180-181
Azure RBAC (Role-Based Access Control), 101, 211-214
    applying, 214
    components of, 213
    functionality of, 211
    real-world scenarios, 213
    role-based, 154
    roles and role assignments, 213-214
    scopes, 213, 214
    use cases, 212
Azure Reservations, 21
Azure Reserved Instances, 238
Azure Resource Manager (see ARM)
Azure Service Bus, 136
Azure Service Health, 279, 283
Azure Site Recovery
    Azure Storage, 178
    functionality of, 14, 112
Azure Sphere, 70
Azure Sponsorship subscriptions, 226
Azure Spot VMs, 109, 239
Azure SQL Database
    defined, 7
    PaaS, 36
    scaling, 17
    shared responsibility model, 43, 46
Azure SQL Managed Instance, 60
Azure Stack, 55, 67
Azure Storage, 173-195
    accounts
        choosing, 184
        defined, 174
        globally unique namespaces, 180
        types of, 183-184
    compared to on-premises storage, 175-178
    file transfer options, 189-192
    filing cabinet analogy, 174
    migration options, 193-195
    redundancy options, 185-189
    release of, 67
    services, 180-182
    storage types, 174
    supported data types, 179
Azure Storage Explorer, 190-192

Azure Synapse Analytics, 67, 245
Azure Tables, 5, 180-181
Azure Traffic Manager, 159-160
    air traffic control analogy, 159
    compared to other load-balancing services, 162
    failover, 19
    functionality of, 159
    nonregional nature of, 85
Azure Virtual Desktop (AVD), 108, 117-118
Azure Virtual Machine Scale Sets (see Azure VMSSs)
Azure VMs (Virtual Machines), 109-118
    advantages of, 111
    apartment rental analogy, 109
    auto-shutdown, 238
    benefits of, 34
    compared to other compute services, 132
    defined, 7
    deployment
        availability sets, 115-117
        AVD, 117-118
        Azure VMSSs, 113-115
    functionality of, 108, 109
    key features of, 110
    limitations of, 111
    resources required for, 111-113
    shared responsibility model, 42
    use cases, 38, 110, 131
Azure VMSSs (Virtual Machine Scale Sets)
    advantages of, 114
    compared to other compute services, 132
    functionality of, 108
    horizontal scaling, 16-17
    key features of, 113
    limitations of, 115
    use cases, 114, 131
    VM deployment, 113-115
Azure VMware Solution, 59
Azure VNet (Virtual Network)
    best practices for, 144
    creating, 144-148
    defined, 112, 143
    functionality of, 142
    hallways and doorways analogy, 141
    key features of, 143
    subnets, 141, 143
    use cases, 142, 144
    virtual network peering, 148-149

Azure VPN Gateway, 162-163
    functionality of, 142, 162
    hybrid clouds, 55
    tunnel analogy, 162
    use case, 142
Azure Well-Architected Framework, 18

B

B2B (business-to-business), 208
B2C (business-to-consumer), 208
Backup (see Azure Backup)
backup policies, 178
BCDR (business continuity and disaster recovery), 14
BGP (Border Gateway Protocol), 163
Bicep
    advantages of, 271
    best practices, 274
    compared to other IaC tools, 272
    defined, 270
    key features of, 270
    limitations of, 271
    resource deployment templates, 26
blob storage, 5
    (see also Azure Blob Storage)
    accounts for, 183-184
    defined, 5
Blueprints, Azure, 102
Border Gateway Protocol (BGP), 163
business continuity and disaster recovery (BCDR), 14
business-to-business (B2B), 208
business-to-consumer (B2C), 208

C

caching
    Azure CDN, 167
    Azure Front Door, 161
CDNs (content delivery networks)
    Azure CDN, 166-168
    resilience, 12
ChatGPT, 68
China regions, 93
CI/CD (continuous integration and deployment)
    AKS, 125
    Azure App Service, 120
    running Azure CLI, 264
    running Azure PowerShell, 266

CLI (see Azure CLI)
cloud computing, 3-8, 285
    (see also cloud models; cloud services)
    Azure services, 7
    cloud service models, 6
    compared to on-premises infrastructure, 5-6
    compute power, 4
    costs of, 8
    defined, 3
    storage capabilities, 4
cloud models, 51-61, 285
    Azure offerings for, 59-61
    comparison of, 58
    defined, 51
    hybrid clouds, 55-56
    multi-cloud model, 56-58
    overview of, 6
    private clouds, 53-55
    public cloud, 51-53
cloud security posture management (CSPM), 218
cloud service providers (CSPs), 3, 52
cloud services
    benefits of, 11-28, 285
        governance, 23-26
        high availability, 12-14
        manageability, 26-28
        predictability, 20-21
        reliability, 18-20
        scalability, 14-18
        security, 21-24
    types of, 31-39, 285
        choosing, 38-39
        IaaS, 33-34, 42, 108-118
        overview of, 31-32
        PaaS, 34-36, 119-131
        responsibilities tied to, 42
        SaaS, 36-38
Cloud Shell (see Azure Cloud Shell)
Cloud Solution Provider (CSP) subscriptions, 226
cloud workload protection platform (CWPP), 218
Cognitive Services, Azure, 67
command-line interface (see Azure CLI)
compliance (see governance and compliance)
compression, 167
compute power, 4

compute services, 107-137, 286
    Azure App Service, 133-137
    Azure Integration Services, 133, 137
    choosing, 131-133
    IaaS, 108-118
    PaaS, 119-131
consumption-based model (see pay-as-you-go model)
Container Apps, Azure, 129-131
containers and container services, 67
    (see also ACI; AKS; Azure Container Apps)
    Azure VNet, 144
    introduction of support for, 67
    PaaS, 123-131
content delivery networks (see Azure CDN; CDNs)
continuous integration and deployment (see CI/CD)
Cost Management (see Azure Cost Management)
Cost Management + Billing, Azure, 88, 231-235, 238
Cost Management, Microsoft, 25
costs, 223-239, 286
    ACI, 128
    AKS, 126
    alerts, 233
    availability sets, 116
    availability zones, 88
    AVD, 117-118
    Azure Advisor, 231, 279
    Azure App Service, 121
    Azure Cost Management + Billing, 231-234
    Azure Functions, 123
    Azure Migrate, 228-229
    Azure Policy, 247
    Azure pricing calculator, 21, 88, 229-231, 235
    Azure Storage, 175, 185, 225
    Azure VMs, 111, 225
    Azure VMSSs, 114-115
    budgets for spending limits, 233
    cloud computing, 6, 8
    consumption, 225
    factors influencing, 225-227
    governance, 25
    hybrid clouds, 56
    IaaS, 33
    management infrastructure, 101, 105

    multi-cloud model, 57
    PaaS, 35
    pay-as-you-go model, 8, 18
    predictability of, 21
    private clouds, 54
    public cloud, 52
    region pairs, 92
    regions, 226
    resource type and size, 225
    SaaS, 37
    savings, as benefit of Azure, 68
    shift from CapEx to OpEx, 68, 224
    sovereign regions, 94
    tags, 235-237
    tips for saving money, 237-239
    usage patterns, 225
CPUs, 4, 15
CSP (Cloud Solution Provider) subscriptions, 226
CSPM (cloud security posture management), 218
CSPs (cloud service providers), 3, 52
CWPP (cloud workload protection platform), 218

D

Data Box, Azure, 194-195
Data Lake Storage, Azure, 180-181
data residency
    region pairs, 91-92
    regions, 85
data sovereignty, 56
database replication, 157
Databricks, Azure, 70
datacenters
    expansion of, 67
    overview of, 83
DDoS (distributed denial-of-service) protection, 23
Defender for Cloud (see Microsoft Defender for Cloud)
defense-in-depth security model, 200-202
    Azure Key Vault, 216
    compared to Zero Trust, 200
    layers of, 201
deployment, 257
    (see also resource deployment and management)
    ACI, 127

AKS, 125
Azure App Service, 120
Azure CLI, 264
Azure Container Apps, 130
Azure VMs, 113-118
blocking noncompliant deployments, 245
cloud computing versus on-premises infrastructure, 6
management of the cloud, 26
SaaS, 37
dev/test subscriptions, 104
DevOps (see Azure DevOps)
disaster recovery
  availability sets, 116
  Azure Storage, 176
  Azure Traffic Manager, 160
  Azure VMs, 110
  Azure VPN Gateway, 163
  as benefit of cloud services, 14
  cloud computing versus on-premises infrastructure, 6
  hybrid clouds, 56
  region pairs, 89-91, 92
distributed denial-of-service (DDoS) protection, 23
DNS (see Azure DNS)
DNSSEC (DNS Security Extensions), 166
Docker, 124
domain controllers, 204
Domain Name System (see Azure DNS)
DP-900 (Microsoft Azure Data Fundamentals) exam, xx
Dynamics 365
  SaaS, 37
  shared responsibility model, 44

E

EA (Enterprise Agreement) subscriptions, 73, 104, 226
elasticity
  Azure Storage, 176
  as benefit of Azure, 68
  as benefit of cloud services, 15
  PaaS, 35
encryption, 246
  Azure Storage, 177
  as benefit of cloud services, 22
endpoints
  Azure Storage, 181
  public and private, 154-155
Enterprise Agreement (EA) subscriptions, 73, 104, 226
Entra Conditional Access, Microsoft, 209-211
Entra Connect Sync, Microsoft, 203
Entra Domain Services, Microsoft, 203-204
Entra External ID, Microsoft, 207-209
Entra ID (see Microsoft Entra ID)
Event Grid, Azure (see Azure Event Grid)
ExpressRoute (see Azure ExpressRoute)
external identities, 207
  (see also Microsoft Entra External ID)

F

Fabric, Microsoft, 70
failover
  automated, 13
  Azure ExpressRoute, 164
  defined, 12
fault domains, 115
FedRAMP (Federal Risk and Authorization Management Program), 252
FIDO2 (Fast IDentity Online) security keys, 206
File Sync, Azure, 191-192
files
  defined, 5
  transferring, 189-192
Files, Azure, 5, 180-181
Firewall (see Azure Firewall)
flexibility
  ACI, 127-128
  Azure Container Apps, 129
  Azure Functions, 122
  Azure VMs, 110
  as benefit of Azure, 68
  cloud computing versus on-premises infrastructure, 6
  hybrid clouds, 56
  IaaS, 33
  management infrastructure, 101
  multi-cloud model, 57
Foundry Tools, 7
free trial subscriptions, 72, 104, 226
Front Door (see Azure Front Door)
Functions (see Azure Functions)

G

GCP (Google Cloud Platform), 3, 52

GDPR (General Data Protection Regulation), 70, 253
   defined, 23
   Microsoft Purview, 244
   Service Trust Portal, 253
general-purpose v2 (GPv2) storage accounts, 183, 185
geo-redundant storage (GRS), 186, 188
geo-zone-redundant storage (GZRS), 187-188
GitHub, 69
global presence
   as benefit of Azure, 70
   as benefit of cloud services, 18
   public cloud, 53
Google Cloud Platform (GCP), 3, 52
governance and compliance, 241-254, 286
   AKS, 125
   Azure App Service, 120
   Azure Bastion, 154
   Azure ExpressRoute, 165
   Azure Firewall, 153
   Azure Policy, 245-248
   Azure Storage, 177
   Azure VMs, 113
   Azure VMware Solution, 60
   as benefit of Azure, 70
   as benefit of cloud services, 23-26
   management infrastructure, 101, 105
   Microsoft Purview, 241-245
   multi-cloud model, 57
   PaaS, 35
   policy enforcement, 24
   private clouds, 54
   region pairs, 91, 92
   regions, 85
   reporting, 25
   resource locks, 248-251
   SaaS, 37
   Service Trust Portal, 251-253
   sovereign regions, 93
   using tools together, 253-254
GPv2 (general-purpose v2) storage accounts, 183, 185
GRS (geo-redundant storage), 186, 188
GZRS (geo-zone-redundant storage), 187-188

H

HashiCorp Terraform, 271

high availability (see availability; availability sets)
HIPAA (Health Insurance Portability and Accountability Act), 23, 70, 244, 253
horizontal scaling (scale out/in)
   compared to vertical scaling, 16-17
   defined, 4, 16
Hybrid Benefit, Azure, 69, 238
hybrid clouds, 55-56
   advantages of, 56
   AKS, 125
   APIM, 134
   Azure Arc, 68, 273-274
   Azure VPN Gateway, 163
   as benefit of Azure, 70
   compared to other cloud models, 58
   defined, 55
hybrid connectivity, 162-165
   Azure ExpressRoute, 163-165
   Azure VPN Gateway, 162-163

I

IaaS (infrastructure as a service), 33-34, 108-118
   Azure VMs, 109-118
      deployment, 113-118
      resources required for, 111-113
   compared to PaaS and SaaS, 31-32, 45
   defined, 7, 108
   key benefits of, 33
   responsibilities tied to, 42
   shared responsibility for, 42, 46, 48
   use cases, 34, 38
IaC (infrastructure as code), 267-273
   ARM, 269-270
   Bicep, 270
   comparison of tools, 272
   declarative approach, 268
   defined, 267
   governance and resource provisioning, 102
   imperative approach, 268
   importance of, 268
   Terraform, 271
IAM (identity and access management), 286
   authentication, 204-207
   Azure Key Vault, 215-217
   as benefit of cloud services, 22
   defense-in-depth model, 200-202
   Microsoft Defender for Cloud, 217-218

    Microsoft Entra Conditional Access, 209-211
    Microsoft Entra External ID, 207-209
    Microsoft Entra ID, 68, 202-204
    RBAC, 211-214
    Zero Trust model, 198-200
identity and access management (see IAM)
infrastructure, 97
    (see also management infrastructure)
    elastic, 15
    on-premises versus cloud computing, 5-6
    physical, 83
    provisioning through IaaS, 33
    redundant, 12
infrastructure as a service (see IaaS)
infrastructure as code (see IaC)
innovation
    as benefit of Azure, 69
    hybrid clouds, 56
    multi-cloud model, 58
    public cloud, 53
integration
    ACI, 128
    AKS, 125-126
    availability sets, 116
    AVD, 117
    Azure App Service, 120, 121
    Azure Arc, 60
    Azure Bastion, 153
    Azure CLI, 264
    Azure Cloud Shell, 263
    Azure Container Apps, 130-131
    Azure DNS, 166
    Azure Event Grid, 136
    Azure Functions, 122
    Azure portal, 260
    Azure Service Bus, 136
    Azure VMs, 110-111
    Azure VMSSs, 114
    Azure VMware Solution, 59
    as benefit of Azure, 70
    Microsoft Purview, 243, 245
    sovereign regions, 94
Integration Services, Azure, 133-137
International Organization for Standardization (ISO), 23, 70, 252
interoperability of Azure, 70
IoT (Internet of Things), 70
IoT Central, Azure, 70

IoT Hub, Azure, 70
IP addresses
    Azure VNet, 143-144
    private, 142
    public, 112, 142, 153-154
ISO (International Organization for Standardization), 23, 70, 252
isolation
    Azure VNet, 143
    private clouds, 55

K

Kerberos, 203
Key Vault (see Azure Key Vault)
KQL (Kusto Query Language), 282
Kubernetes, 123-126
    (see also AKS)
Kusto Query Language (KQL), 282

L

LDAP (Lightweight Directory Access Protocol), 203
lift-and-shift migrations
    Azure VMs, 110
    defined, 38
Lighthouse, Azure, 57
load balancing and load balancers, 156-162
    (see also Azure Load Balancer)
    AKS, 125
    availability sets, 115-116
    Azure App Service, 120
    Azure Application Gateway, 157-159
    Azure Front Door, 160-161
    Azure Traffic Manager, 159-160
    Azure VMSSs, 113
    comparison of services, 162
    internal, 157
    performance predictability, 20
    public, 157
    resilience, 12
Local (see Azure Local)
Log Analytics, Azure, 282-283
Logic Apps, Azure, 13, 135
LRS (locally redundant storage), 186, 188

M

machine learning, 70
    (see also AI; Azure Machine Learning)

Machine Learning, Azure, 67, 70
maintenance
    cloud computing versus on-premises infrastructure, 6
    public cloud, 53
    region pairs, 90
manageability
    as benefit of cloud services, 26-28
    management in the cloud, 27
    management of the cloud, 26
    PaaS, 35
    SaaS, 36
managed disks, 181
management groups, 100
    example of, 102-105
    functionality of, 24
    IT Department and Marketing, 104
    nesting, 100
    root, 103
management infrastructure, 97-105
    benefits of, 101
    best practices for planning, 102
    defined, 97
    hierarchical integration example, 102-105
    overview of, 97-100
    resource groups, 99
    resources, 98
    subscriptions, 99
    workings of, 104
MCA (Microsoft Customer Agreement), 73, 226
memory (see RAM; storage)
MFA (multifactor authentication)
    compared to other authentication methods, 207
    Microsoft Entra Conditional Access, 211
    Microsoft Entra ID, 22, 202
    overview of, 205
microservices
    ACI, 128
    AKS, 125
    Azure Container Apps, 130
    Azure VNet, 144
Microsoft 365
    integration, 70
    integration with AVD, 117
    integration with Microsoft Purview, 243-244
    SaaS, 37
    shared responsibility model, 44, 46
    use case, 39
Microsoft AI Cloud Partner Program, 226
Microsoft Authenticator app, 206
Microsoft Azure (see Azure)
Microsoft Azure AI Fundamentals (AI-900) exam, xx
Microsoft Azure Data Fundamentals (DP-900) exam, xx
Microsoft Azure Fundamentals exam (see AZ-900 exam)
Microsoft Cost Management, 25
Microsoft Customer Agreement (MCA), 73, 226
Microsoft Defender for Cloud, 60, 112, 217-218
    functionality of, 22
    integration with Microsoft Purview, 245
    Secure Score, 217
Microsoft Enterprise Agreement (EA) subscriptions, 73, 226
Microsoft Entra Conditional Access, 209-211
    functionality of, 209
    importance of, 211
    real-world example, 210
    signals, 210
    use cases, 211
Microsoft Entra Connect Sync, 203
Microsoft Entra Domain Services, 203-204
Microsoft Entra External ID, 207-209
    external users, 208
    functionality of, 207
    key benefits of, 208
    main features of, 208
    real-world scenario, 209
Microsoft Entra ID, 202-204
    defined, 7
    functionality of, 197, 202
    identity and access management, 22
    integrating Azure VMware Solution with, 59
    integration, 70
    key features of, 202
    market introduction, 67
    reasons for using, 202
Microsoft Entra PIM (Privileged Identity Management), 212
Microsoft Fabric, 70
Microsoft Foundry, 70
Microsoft Purview, 241-245
    functionality of, 242-243

integration with Microsoft 365, 243
integration with Microsoft data ecosystem, 245
key features of, 243
portal, 242
real-world example, 244
use cases, 244, 254
Microsoft Purview Compliance Manager, 25
Microsoft Security, Compliance, and Identity Fundamentals (SC-900) exam, xx
Microsoft Sentinel, 23, 60
Microsoft sponsorships, 74
Migrate (see Azure Migrate)
migrating to Azure, 193-195
Monitor (see Azure Monitor)
monitoring, 277-283, 286
   (see also Azure Monitor)
   AKS, 125
   APIM, 134
   Azure Advisor, 278-279
   Azure CDN, 167
   Azure ExpressRoute, 164
   Azure Network Watcher, 144, 168-169
   Azure Policy, 247
   Azure portal, 259
   Azure Service Health, 279
   Azure Traffic Manager, 159-160
   Azure VMs, 113
   Azure VPN Gateway, 163
   car dashboard analogy, 277
   governance, 24
   management infrastructure, 102
   management of the cloud, 26
   NSG flow logs, 151
multi-cloud model, 56-58
   advantages of, 57
   AKS, 125
   APIM, 134
   Azure Arc, 273-274
   compared to other cloud models, 58
   defined, 56
multi-tenancy, 5
multifactor authentication (see MFA)

N

naming conventions, 102
National Institute of Standards and Technology (NIST), 253
NetApp Files, Azure, 59

Network File System (NFS), 184
network interface cards (NICs), 150
network security groups (see NSGs)
Network Watcher (see Azure Network Watcher)
networking services, 139-169, 286
   (see also Azure Network Watcher)
   ACI, 127
   Azure CDN, 166-168
   Azure DNS, 165-166
   Azure VMs, 109, 112
   Azure VNet, 143-148
   defined, 141
   functionality of, 142
   hallways and doorways analogy, 141
   hybrid connectivity, 162-165
   importance of, 141
   load balancing, 156-162
   OSI model, 139-140
   security, 150-155
   use cases, 142
   virtual network peering, 148-149
NFS (Network File System), 184
NICs (network interface cards), 150
NIST (National Institute of Standards and Technology), 253
non-regional services, 85, 87
NSGs (network security groups), 150-151
   best practices for, 144, 151
   defined, 112, 150
   flow logs, 151, 169
   functionality of, 142
   key features, 150
   security checkpoint analogy, 150
   use cases, 142, 151
NTLM (NT LAN Manager), 203

O

on-premises active directory, 203
on-premises infrastructure, 5-6
on-premises storage, 175-178
OpenAI, 68
OSI (Open Systems Interconnection) model, 139-140

P

PaaS (platform as a service), 34-36, 119-131
   compared to IaaS and SaaS, 32, 45
   container services, 123-131

defined, 7, 119
key benefits of, 35
responsibilities tied to, 43
serverless computing, 121-123
shared responsibility for, 43, 46, 48
use cases, 35, 38
passwordless authentication
    compared to other authentication methods, 207
    primary options for, 206-207
pay-as-you-go model, 8
    Azure Storage, 175
    Azure VMs, 110
    consumption and usage patterns, 225
    cost savings, 68
    scalability, 18
    subscriptions, 73, 226
PDC (Professional Developers Conference), 66
performance
    Azure Advisor, 279
    Azure Monitor Application Insights, 283
    Azure Storage, 178
    as benefit of Azure, 69
    multi-cloud model, 57
    predictability of, 20
PHI (personal health information), 244
PII (personally identifiable information), 243-244
PIM (Privileged Identity Management), 212
platform as a service (see PaaS)
Policy (see Azure Policy)
PowerShell (see Azure PowerShell)
premium block blob storage accounts, 183, 185
premium file shares storage accounts, 184-185
premium page blobs storage accounts, 184-185
principle of least privilege, 25, 151, 199, 211, 216
private clouds, 53-55
    advantages of, 54
    compared to other cloud models, 58
    compared to traditional data centers, 53
private endpoints, 154-155
Privileged Identity Management (PIM), 212
product catalog, Azure, 79
Professional Developers Conference (PDC), 66
provisioning
    Azure VMs and overprovisioning, 111
    IaaS, 33
public cloud, 51-53
    advantages of, 52
    compared to other cloud models, 58
    defined, 51
    top providers, 52
public endpoints, 154-155
Purview Compliance Manager, Microsoft, 25

Q

Queues, Azure, 180-181

R

RA-GRS (read-access geo-redundant storage), 187-188
RA-GZRS (read-access geo-zone-redundant storage), 188
RAM (memory), 4, 15
RBAC (role-based access control), 211-214
    (see also Azure RBAC)
    applying, 214
    Azure Bastion, 154
    Azure Storage, 177
    components of, 213
    management groups, 100
    management infrastructure, 101
    principle of least privilege, 25
    real-world scenarios, 213
    role in governance, 24-25
    use cases, 212
RDP (Remote Desktop Protocol), 153
read-access geo-redundant storage (RA-GRS), 187-188
read-access geo-redundant storage (RA-GZRS), 188
redundancy
    availability zones, 87
    Azure Storage, 185-189
    as benefit of cloud services, 12
region pairs, 89-92
    advantages of, 90
    considerations for, 91
    defined, 89
    reciprocal pairing, 91
    shared responsibility model, 91
    use cases, 92
regions
    availability sets, 116
    availability zones, 86-89
    Azure Network Watcher, 169
    Azure Traffic Manager, 160

cost-effective deployment, 239
defined, 84
expansion of Azure datacenters, 67
influence on costs, 226
map of, 85
overview of, 84-86
pairing, 89-92
public cloud, 53
restricting locations, 246-247
sovereign, 92, 94
virtual network peering, 149
without availability zones, 88
reliability
   Azure Advisor, 279
   Azure Event Grid, 136
   as benefit of Azure, 69
   as benefit of cloud services, 18-20
   designing for, 19
   IaaS, 33
Remote Desktop Protocol (RDP), 153
Reservations, Azure, 21
Reserved Instances, Azure, 238
resiliency
   availability zones, 87
   public cloud, 53
resource deployment and management, 257-275, 286
   (see also deployment)
   Azure Arc, 273-274
   Azure CLI, 263-265
   Azure Cloud Shell, 261-263
   Azure portal, 258-261
   Azure PowerShell, 265-266
   best practices for, 274-275
   choosing between tools, 267
   IaC, 267-273
resource groups
   creating with Azure CLI, 264
   creating with Azure PowerShell, 265
   defined, 99
   deleting, 99
   environment structure and management, 235
   example of, 102-105
resource locks, 248-251
   application levels, 249
   applying, 250
   best practices for, 251
   compared to Azure Policy, 250

delete locks, 249-251
limitations of, 251
ReadOnly locks, 249-251
use cases, 249, 253
resource pooling, 5
retention policies, 178
role-based access control (see Azure RBAC; RBAC)

S

SaaS (software as a service), 36-38
   compared to IaaS and PaaS, 32, 45
   defined, 7
   key benefits of, 36
   responsibilities tied to, 44
   shared responsibility for, 44-46, 48
   use cases, 37-39
SC-900 (Microsoft Security, Compliance, and Identity Fundamentals) exam, xx
scaling
   ACI, 128
   AKS, 125-126
   autoscaling, 4, 20, 26, 113, 120, 130, 158, 176
   availability sets, 117
   AVD, 117-118
   Azure App Service, 120
   Azure Application Gateway, 158
   Azure Container Apps, 129-130
   Azure DNS, 165
   Azure Event Grid, 136
   Azure Functions, 123
   Azure Load Balancer, 156
   Azure Local, 61
   Azure Logic Apps, 135
   Azure Storage, 176
   Azure Traffic Manager, 159
   Azure VMs, 110-111
   Azure VMSSs, 113-114
   Azure VMware Solution, 59
   as benefit of Azure, 68
   as benefit of cloud services, 14-18
   cloud computing versus on-premises infrastructure, 6, 16
   global reach and accessibility, 18
   horizontal, 4, 16-17
   hybrid clouds, 56
   IaaS, 33
   management infrastructure, 101
   management of the cloud, 26

overview of, 4
PaaS, 35
pay-as-you-go model, 18
performance predictability, 20
public cloud, 52
region pairs, 92
SaaS, 37
subscriptions, 72
vertical, 4, 14-18
Secure Shell (SSH), 153
security, 22, 286
   (see also IAM)
   AKS, 125-126
   APIM, 134
   AVD, 117-118
   Azure Advisor, 279
   Azure App Service, 120
   Azure Application Gateway, 159
   Azure CDN, 167
   Azure DNS, 166
   Azure ExpressRoute, 165
   Azure Local, 61
   Azure Network Watcher, 168-169
   Azure Policy, 247
   Azure Storage, 177
   Azure VMs, 112
   Azure VMware Solution, 60
   as benefit of Azure, 70
   as benefit of cloud services, 21-24
   cloud computing versus on-premises infrastructure, 6
   defense-in-depth model, 200-202
   enterprise-level, 3, 53
   IaaS, 33
   management infrastructure, 101
   Microsoft Entra External ID, 208
   Microsoft Entra ID, 68
   Microsoft Purview, 242
   networking, 150-155
   PaaS, 35
   private clouds, 54
   public cloud, 53
   SaaS, 37
   shared responsibility model, 47
   sovereign regions, 93
   Zero Trust model, 198-200
semi-structured data
   defined, 179
   storage services, 180
Sentinel, Microsoft, 23, 60
Server Message Block (SMB), 184
serverless computing, 121-123
Service Bus, Azure, 136
Service Health, Azure, 279, 283
service level agreements (SLAs), 12-13, 69
service level objectives (SLOs), 19
Service Trust Portal, 251-253
   functionality of, 251
   key features of, 252
   use cases, 253-254
shared responsibility model, 41-48
   division of responsibilities, 45-46
   examples of responsibilities by service type, 46
   IaaS, 42
   overview of, 21
   PaaS, 43
   region pairs, 91
   responsibilities tied to cloud service types, 42
   SaaS, 44
single sign-on (SSO), 202, 205, 207
Site Recovery (see Azure Site Recovery)
SKUs, 163
SLAs (service level agreements), 12-13, 69
SLOs (service level objectives), 19
SMB (Server Message Block), 184
SNAT (Source Network Address Translation), 152
SOC 1 (System and Organization Controls 1), 70, 252
SOC 2 (System and Organization Controls 2), 23, 70, 252
SOC 3 (System and Organization Controls 3), 252
software as a service (see SaaS)
Source Network Address Translation (SNAT), 152
sovereign regions, 92-94
   considerations for, 94
   types of, 92
   use cases, 93
Sphere, Azure, 70
Spot VMs, Azure, 109, 239
SQL Azure, 67
SQL Database (see Azure SQL Database)
SQL Server, 46
SSH (Secure Shell), 153

SSL
    offloading, 161
    termination, 158
SSO (single sign-on), 202, 205, 207
Stack, Azure, 55, 67
storage, 173-195, 286
    (see also Azure Storage)
    ACI, 127
    Azure Cloud Shell, 262
    Azure VMs, 112
    capabilities, 4
    cost optimization, 238
    managed disks, 181
    storage tiers, 5
    types of, 5
Storage Explorer, Azure, 190-192
structured data, 179
subnets, 141-144
    (see also Azure VNet)
    associating NSGs with, 150
    best practices, 144
    defined, 143
    functionality of, 141-142
    use case, 142
subscriptions
    costs, 226-227
    defined, 71
    environment structure and management, 235
    examples of, 104
    management infrastructure, 99, 102-105
    overview of, 70-74
    relationship with accounts, 72
    types of, 72
    viewing details of, 78
sustainability, 68
Synapse Analytics, Azure, 67, 245
System and Organization Controls 1 (SOC 1), 70, 252
System and Organization Controls 2 (SOC 2), 23, 70, 252
System and Organization Controls 3 (SOC 3), 252

T

Tables, Azure, 180-181
tags, 235-237, 246-247, 275
    benefits of, 236
    defined, 236
    management of, 236
TCO (Total Cost of Ownership) Calculator, 228
Terraform, 271
threat detection and prevention, 22
TLS (Transport Layer Security), 22
Total Cost of Ownership (TCO) Calculator, 228
traffic control
    Azure Application Gateway, 157-159
    Azure Front Door, 160-161
    Azure Load Balancer, 156-157
    Azure Traffic Manager, 159-160
    comparison of services, 162
    DNS-based routing, 12
Traffic Manager (see Azure Traffic Manager)
Transport Layer Security (TLS), 22
21Vianet, 93, 94

U

UID (unique identifier) systems, 203
unstructured data
    defined, 179
    storage services, 180
updates and upgrades
    cloud computing versus on-premises infrastructure, 6
    SaaS, 36
    update domains, 115
URL-based routing, 158
US government regions, 93

V

VDI (virtual desktop infrastructure), 157
version control, 268, 275
vertical scaling (scale up/down)
    compared to horizontal scaling, 16-17
    defined, 4, 15
Virtual Desktop, Azure, 108, 117-118
Virtual Machine Scale Sets (see Azure VMSSs)
Virtual Machines (see Azure VMs)
virtual network peering, 148-149
virtual private networks (VPNs) (see Azure VPN Gateway)
virtualization, 5
Visual Studio (see VS)
VMSSs (see Azure VMSSs)
VMware Solution, Azure, 59
VNet (see Azure VNet)
VPN Gateway (see Azure VPN Gateway)

VPNs (virtual private networks) (see Azure VPN Gateway)
VS (Visual Studio)
    running Azure CLI, 264
    running Azure PowerShell, 266
    subscriptions, 226

W

WAF (web application firewall)
    Azure Application Gateway, 158
    Azure Front Door, 161
web apps
    Azure App Service, 119-120
    Azure Application Gateway, 159
    Azure Container Apps, 130
    Azure Load Balancer, 157

NSGs, 151
Windows Azure, 66-67
    (see also Azure)
Windows Hello for Business, 206

Z

Zero Trust security model, 198-200
    Azure Key Vault, 216
    compared to traditional security model, 199
    core principles of, 199
    importance of, 198
    real-world scenario, 199
zonal services, 87
zone-redundant services, 87
ZRS (zone-redundant storage), 186, 188

About the Author

Jack Lee is a Microsoft Most Valuable Professional (MVP) and an Azure Certified Solutions Architect with a passion for Azure, AI, software development, and DevOps innovations. He is an active Microsoft tech community contributor and has presented at various user groups and conferences, among them the Global Azure Bootcamp at Microsoft Canada.

An experienced mentor and judge at hackathons, Jack is also the president of a user group that focuses on Azure, AI, DevOps, and software development. He has authored numerous books published by Packt, notably *Azure for Architects*, *Azure for Decision Makers*, *Azure Integration Guide for Business*, and *Cloud Analytics with Microsoft Azure*. In addition, he has earned multiple certifications including Microsoft Azure Solutions Architect Expert, Microsoft Azure AI Engineer Associate, and Microsoft DevOps Engineer Expert. You can follow Jack on Twitter/X at @jlee_consulting.

Colophon

The animal on the cover of *Azure Fundamentals (AZ-900) Study Guide* is the plush-crested jay (*Cyanocorax chrysops*). Part of the Corvidae family, the plush-crusted jay can be found in various parts of central-southern South America including Brazil, Paraguay, Bolivia, and northern Argentina.

The plush-crusted jay gets its name from the rounded array of feathers (crest) on its head. Its medium-sized body is covered in blue feathers that start out lighter near the nape of its neck and gradually darken toward the rest of the body. One of its most striking features is its bright yellow eyes, which stand out even more against its dark blue body.

Plush-crested jays are highly intelligent and social birds, often seen traveling in noisy flocks through dense forests, woodlands, and savannas. They are well known for their distinctive vocalizations, which include a range of loud calls and whistles. They can also mimic the sounds of other birds—and even monkeys. Their strong social behavior extends to nesting, where two or three other jays—often older offspring—help build and guard the nest, as well as feed the hatchlings.

The cover illustration is by José Marzan Jr., based on an antique line engraving from Lydekker's *Royal Natural History*. The series design is by Edie Freedman, Ellie Volckhausen, and Karen Montgomery. The cover fonts are Gilroy Semibold and Guardian Sans. The text font is Adobe Minion Pro; the heading font is Adobe Myriad Condensed; and the code font is Dalton Maag's Ubuntu Mono.

O'REILLY®

Learn from experts.
Become one yourself.

60,000+ titles | Live events with experts | Role-based courses
Interactive learning | Certification preparation | Verifiable skills

Try the O'Reilly learning platform free for 10 days.

www.ingramcontent.com/pod-product-compliance
Lightning Source LLC
Chambersburg PA
CBHW080903170526
45158CB00008B/1973